New Essays on *Paradise Lost*

New Essays on
PARADISE LOST

edited by

THOMAS KRANIDAS

UNIVERSITY OF CALIFORNIA PRESS

BERKELEY, LOS ANGELES, AND LONDON 1971

University of California Press
Berkeley and Los Angeles, California
University of California Press, Ltd.
London, England

Designed by W. H. Snyder
Printed in the United States of America

Foreword

ARNOLD STEIN

The first enduring criticism of *Paradise Lost* was written by a poet, Andrew Marvell; for the succeeding two hundred and fifty years, poets continued to demonstrate their personal fascination with the poem. In the twentieth century, for the first time, the criticism of Milton has lacked the support and stimulation (however personal or specialized or temporary) of major poets. And for the first time the charge has been made by a poet—Ezra Pound, who was not unaware that he was creating shock waves —that Milton's ear was a limited one and, in the long poems, capable of little more than thumping sonorities. Other proponents of this view have had to establish most or all of their authority in prose. Though many of the best poets in the language once acknowledged Milton to be a great and sensitive master of auditory effects, things have changed, and the poets who count most in the twentieth century have been drawn neither to Milton's subjects nor to his art of expression. What has happened is clear and unmistakable; it is not to be contradicted by quoting the opinions of, say, Landor, or Hopkins, or Ransom, or Dylan Thomas.

How have these new conditions affected the scholars and critics who have continued to study, teach, and write about *Paradise Lost*? At one extreme the concessions have been moderate; at the other extreme they have been extensive. I shall undertake to argue, briefly, that both responses merit attention and assist each other.

As long as the academic strongholds resisting change dominated all formal literary study, they offered convenient positions against which the talented young could exercise their own ideas and methods. To be out of touch with contemporary concerns and with twentieth-century literature became a mark of professional isolation. Scholars who could learn only from the past and not at all from the present might still acquire valuable knowledge, but they would convince fewer and fewer pupils to follow exactly in their footsteps. For one thing, the techniques of scholarship itself did not stand still. The older models, along with the principles on which they were based, were directed toward questions that, though not yet fully answered, have lost their power to generate the right kind of satisfaction or promise. Newer branches of learning, differently oriented, have appeared and have made undeniable contributions. As the sciences and social sciences have advanced and changed, so have their concepts of themselves, their tasks, and their procedures. If a literary historian wants to assert that his inherited principles are immutable, he must now do so in spite of the known history of when and how his own ideas came into practice. He can no longer count, as once he could, on the support of the most searching modern historians.

And so to some extent literary scholarship has made adjustments. One hears less of recovering the poem as it really was in Milton's mind. There is evidently less motive now for scholars to insist that their critical response has been shaped only by Milton and by what he read, and that it is immune to the influence of the intervening centuries. Whatever the differences between scholarship and criticism, they both seem to accept the present assumption that they do not thrive in a timeless nowhere. The achievement of discipline, detachment, and insight, however simple the effect of a superior performance, is always complex, for the achievement is based on values, the history and relevance of which cannot be taken for granted. No scholar can be uninfluenced by his relations to the values he has acquired, and the quality of his consciousness may be hindrance or help, or both. The aims of detached objectivity are not abandoned when the scholar tries to take into account the insuppressible facts of his own experience. These can be disciplined, out in the open, as they lead to personal distortion, but to reject them as mere distraction is to close one of the chief sources of insight. Nor does one disown one's respected teachers by recognizing that their critical response was influenced by their own historical experience.

In my view, then, the scholarship characterized by moderate changes demonstrates a greater awareness of itself and of the conditions under which it operates. More scholars have learned how to make skillful use of the similarities and differences that link and separate Milton's times and our own. The best achievements are still based on the conviction that background studies illuminate, but that conviction is now made effective by more exacting standards of relevance and by more sensitive efforts to improve the two-way communication between the seventeenth and the twentieth centuries. This latter is, incidentally, an accomplishment of historical recovery not available to scholarship working under the influence of theories derived from nineteenth-century science. When the twentieth century consults its own concerns, it resembles, though with an awareness that has developed fine controls, the seventeenth century, which still took its own age as the principal measure for understanding the past. Or to come down to the basic matter of reporting research: no seventeenth-century schoolboy would have been unaware that his composition had to be directed toward a particular audience. The more difficult and unfamiliar his material, the greater the need to master that material, but also to understand and speak to the living interests of his audience. Even the invented audience of the most eccentric assignment would have to be imagined as listeners alive in an actual time.

Meanwhile, not a few of the academic strongholds have changed hands and subsequently failed to produce universal satisfaction. If the valid passion of the antiquarian is less admired than formerly, there seems, nevertheless, little disposition to discredit the kind of contribution he alone can make. Only the restraint of honest, capable interest seems intolerable. No one should expect the humane disciplines to be all sweetness and light. Students of literature, or of its history, cannot escape the competition of values and the competition of individual performance. Nor are the issues resolved by offering a loose analogy between the applied research of criticism (answering an immediate, nameable desire) and the "pure" research of scholarship (following its own kind of abstract intellectual passion). The special privilege of the humane disciplines consists in the essential right to choose the tasks they assign themselves. The judgments that these produce are, of course, granted no special privilege.

As for those critics and scholars whose approach has been deeply influenced by modern developments, it is they who have felt the most direct pressure to justify the poetic ways of Milton to modern men. While accepting, by and large, the literary values that, in other quarters, have encouraged indifference or outright rejection, they have helped clarify the irrelevance of some of the more impatient charges; far more important, they have seriously pursued questions never asked of the poem before. No judicious observer, I believe, can doubt that we have learned some ways to know the poem that would have been unimaginable during any period of time when its greatness went unchallenged.

Those who argue that Milton is to blame for injurious effects on the poetry of the last two centuries may feel pleased at his lack of direct influence now. Yet the reputation of *Paradise Lost* reminds us how the offices performed by great masterpieces of the past cannot be judged only by their particular contributions to contemporary literature. The most challenging achievements —and not only in monumental forms like the epic or tragedy which no age can produce on order—do not ask to be borrowed from, even less to be imitated or improved on. They remain there for us to question, both in their own terms and ours. Only brittle arrogance, or varieties of intellectual inertia, will prefer to avoid that dialogue, which would not be continuous if we ourselves were not capable of changing. Revolutions in taste do occur. Milton himself lived through such a period, and his work survived the eighteenth and nineteenth centuries, evoking judgments that have themselves become part of the record that challenges our attention. The most important questions we ask a masterpiece become a form of dialogue, which may draw upon the materials of our specialized debates but is limited neither to them nor to their characteristic methods. We can seldom trust the latest masters of the *Zeitgeist* to pronounce judgment on cultural lags. Only historical scholarship can tell us the specific ways in which the first edition of *Paradise Lost* was itself in and out of touch with the times. Any epic must be retrospective, assimilating a vast amount of the relevant past; but if it is to live, it cannot lack some essential power of anticipation as well.

One of the recognizable features of the authentic masterpiece is its capacity to renew itself, to endure the loss of some kinds of immediate relevance while still answering the most important questions men can ask, including new ones they are just learning how to frame. It is true that part of the vitality of *Paradise Lost* consists in its being old in a particular way, one that reflects Milton's own concept of the epic; but that way has become uniquely valuable through some unforeseeable turns of history, for *Paradise Lost* is now the one work in English where most of the beliefs, and the valid currency of established literary allusion, myth, and symbol, and most of the traditions of thought and feeling of the previous two thousand years are assimilated. In an age when ideas and styles flourish and exhaust themselves at a pace never achieved before, a poem that continues to be read year after year has acquired a kind of identity that cannot be comprehended in the terms of any one age—not in our terms alone, certainly, and not in those of Milton's own present and past either. The need to defend the humanities in the modern world is a pressing one, but no methods would seem more likely to invite the morbid pleasures of predictable failure than methods wholly indifferent to questions that stir living readers. Whatever values men can attribute to knowledge that looks only backward, they will not trust it with any of the more important affairs of wisdom.

I have been trying to isolate and describe some of the conditions affecting those who write on *Paradise Lost*. The essays in this book demonstrate much of the admirable range, skill, and illumination that talented scholars and critics now bring to the poem. The scholarship represented here is confidently aware of itself and of its own traditions, with no need to justify commitments and procedures by debate rather than by demonstration. There is no gleaning of dry stubble; where it is most successful, the remastery of old materials leads to fresh discoveries and to new questions. At least two or three of the essays answer by example those who publicly worry about the imminent exhaustion of scholarship. As for the critical studies, it is their proper business to raise new questions directly, and they do so benefiting from the traditions of both scholarship and criticism. Readers who have been attracted to a poem for three hundred years are no longer few, and a book like this helps assure the continuity of their fitness.

Preface

THOMAS KRANIDAS

This collection of new essays was originally planned to celebrate the tercentenary of the publication of *Paradise Lost* and in a modest way to complement the vigorous and subtle criticism which helped to reestablish Milton in the fifties. The thesis of the book remains twofold: first, that three hundred years after its publication, the great epic is being read widely and well; second, that those scholars and critics who reestablished *Paradise Lost* at the center of the English literary tradition liberated and revitalized rather than exhausted the possibilities of Milton studies.

Of course, it is not only the peculiar brilliance of the best Milton criticism of the past fifteen years that has restored the poem. Time, new poetry, and war and the varieties of human behavior have changed our understanding of phrases once so potent, phrases such as "the achievement of T. S. Eliot," or "Milton's beastly hebraism." It is, as Professor Stein suggests above, our self-consciousness about ourselves as historians that has taught us to see the anti-Miltonism of this century as an episode.

xii PREFACE

It was an interesting episode, one which tried to get back to clear and distinct ideas about poetry. Pure reverence for the classic was dispatched, and the benefit to criticism is apparent in the essays in this volume. The best modern criticism has borrowed the serious and questioning procedure of critics such as F. R. Leavis while rejecting the eschatological pose which such critics often assumed. Very little is taken on faith, but the need for a final disposition seems less urgent.

All of the writers printed here are in mid-career, all are Americans teaching in American universities, and, perhaps, all are vulnerable to that charge of too much gravity, too little ease, of overspecialization, of "ingenuity," which so often provides amusement to the reviewer. And yet, this kind of professionalism is not naïvely assumed nor does it, at its best, rest in virtuosity or mere accretion. All of these essays point toward large and expanded views of *Paradise Lost*; all testify to the fecundity of Milton's poem as a source for serious, imaginative, and relevant inquiry into the problems of being man.

The delays in the making of this volume are largely mine. I wish to thank each of the contributors for his promptness and courtesy in meeting the several deadlines. Arnold Stein gave me much good advice for which I am grateful. The Faculty Research Committee of the University of Delaware provided funds for the preparation of the manuscript and for the monumental paper work and correspondence that preceded. My wife Kathleen once again cheerfully helped with the final stages of the manuscript.

Stony Brook, New York
September 1968

Contributors

ARNOLD STEIN, Professor of English, University of Washington, Seattle, Washington.

STANLEY EUGENE FISH, Associate Professor of English, University of California, Berkeley, California.

JOHN T. SHAWCROSS, Professor of English, University of Wisconsin, Madison, Wisconsin.

HAROLD E. TOLIVER, Associate Professor of English, University of California, Irvine, California.

BARBARA KIEFER LEWALSKI, Professor of English, Brown University, Providence, Rhode Island.

ISABEL GAMBLE MACCAFFREY, Associate Professor of English, Bryn Mawr College, Bryn Mawr, Pennsylvania.

A. B. CHAMBERS, Associate Professor of English, University of Wisconsin, Madison, Wisconsin.

MICHAEL FIXLER, Professor of English, Tufts University, Medford, Massachusetts.

Editor: THOMAS KRANIDAS, Professor of English, State University of New York at Stony Brook, Stony Brook, L.I., New York.

Contents

1

Discovery as Form in
Paradise Lost

STANLEY EUGENE FISH

▼

I

Recently I have argued that the true center of *Paradise Lost*[1] is
the reader's consciousness of the poem's *personal* relevance,
and that the arc of the poem describes, in addition to the careers
of the characters, the education of its readers.[2] This education
proceeds in two stages: in the first, the reader is brought face to
face with the corruption within him, as he is made aware of the
confusion reigning in his scale of values and of the inadequacy
of his perceptions; in the second, he is invited to cooperate with
the poem's effort to effect his regeneration, invited, in Milton's
words, to purge his "intellectual ray" until it is once more "fit
and proportionable to Truth the object, and end of it, as the eye
to the thing visible."[3] These stages correspond to the stages of
Plato's dialectic, the inducing in the respondent of a "healthy

---

[1] A shorter version of this paper was read before the Milton section of
the Modern Language Association meeting, 1967.

[2] *Surprised by Sin: The Reader in Paradise Lost* (London and New
York, 1967).

[3] Milton, *Complete Prose Works,* Vol. I, ed. D. M. Wolfe (New Haven,
1953), p. 566.

perplexity" followed by the refinement of his inner eye to the point where it recognizes and embraces the Supreme Good;[4] and the poem's operation is analogous to that of the Mosaic Law which, we are told in *The Christian Doctrine*, calls forth "our natural depravity, that by this means it might . . . bring us to the righteousness of Christ."[5] In its potential effect, then, *Paradise Lost* may claim the status of what Bunyan calls a "work of grace" in the soul; for it gives the sinner "conviction of sin, especially of the defilement of his nature, and the sin of unbelief."[6]

This description of *Paradise Lost*, as a poem concerned with the self-education of its readers, if it is accepted, throws a new light on some old questions. Specifically, it dictates a reorientation of the debate concerning the structure or form of the poem; for if the meaning of the poem is to be located in the reader's experience of it, the form of the poem is the form of that experience; and the outer or physical form, so obtrusive, and, in one sense, so undeniably there, is, in another sense, incidental and even irrelevant. This is a deliberately provocative thesis, the defense of which will be the concern of the following pages; and I would like to begin by explaining more fully what is meant by the phrase "the form of the reader's experience."

The stages of this experience mark advances in the reader's understanding, in the refining of his vision rather than in the organization of material. In *Paradise Lost*, *things* are not being clarified or ordered; rather, *eyes* are being made capable of seeing things as they truly are already in the clarity of God's order. The process, and its relationship to a truth that is evident to those who have eyes to see it, is adumbrated in this passage from *Of Reformation*:

> The very essence of Truth is plainnesse, and brightnes; the darknes and crookednesse is our own. . . . If our *understanding* have a film of *ignorance* over it, or be blear with gazing on other false glisterings, what is that to Truth? If we will but purge with sovrain eyesalve that intellectual ray which *God* hath planted in us, then we would beleeve the Scriptures protesting their own plainnes.[7]

[4] See Robert Cushman, *Therapeia* (Chapel Hill, N.C., 1958), p. 89.
[5] *The Works of John Milton*, ed. F. A. Patterson *et al.* (New York, 1933), XVI, 131.
[6] *The Pilgrim's Progress*, ed. J. B. Wharey, rev. R. Sharrock (Oxford, 1960), pp. 82–83.
[7] Milton, *Complete Prose Works*, I, 566.

In Augustine's *On Christian Doctrine* the Scriptures themselves
are the instrument by which the understanding can be made pro-
portional to their plainness; and Augustine's description of what
happens to the attentive reader of God's word is not unlike my
description of the reader's experience in *Paradise Lost*:

> The student first will discover in the Scriptures that he has been
> enmeshed in the love of this world. . . . Then . . . that fear which
> arises from the thought of God's judgment . . . will force him
> to lament his own situation. . . . And by means of this affection
> of the spirit he will extract himself from all mortal joy in transi-
> tory things . . . and turn toward the love of eternal things . . . he
> purges his mind, which is rising up and protesting in the appetite
> for inferior things, of its contaminations.[8]

Augustine then describes five steps or stages leading to a sixth
where the aspirant "cleanses that eye through which God may
be seen, in so far as He can be seen by those who die to the world
as much as they are able." "From fear to wisdom," he concludes,
"the way extends through these steps."

To some extent Augustine's "steps" suggest a regular and predictable, that is, linear, progression to wisdom; but, of course,
the movement from one step to the next cannot be predicted or
charted since the operative factor is the "purging of the mind"
or "the cleansing of the eye"; and the extent to which the mind
is distracted by the appeal of transitory things, and, consequently, the period of time which must elapse before the eyes are made
clear, will vary with the individual, who dies to the world as
much as *he* is able. Nor will progress be regular (linear) within
the discrete stages enumerated by Augustine. In how many differing contexts must the eye be challenged to distinguish true
beauty from the "false glisterings" of "fair outsides" before it is
able to see what is and is not truly beautiful *immediately*? No
one answer will serve for all eyes. In Plato's dialectic, A. E. Taylor explains, the apprehension of Reality "comes as a sudden
'revelation' though it is not to be had without the long preliminary process of travail of thought."[9] Taylor's point is that the
relationship between the "travail of thought" and the "revelation"
is indeterminate, partly because the thing to be known cannot be

---

[8] *On Christian Doctrine*, trans. D. W. Robertson (New York, 1958),
pp. 39–40.
[9] *Plato: The Man and his Work* (Meridian Books, New York, 1957),
p. 231.

known by "discursive knowledge about it," and partly because, as Robert Cushman observes, the effort that must be expended "to disengage the mind from preoccupation with sensibles" will be in proportion to the strength of the "fetters" binding the individual mind to earthly perception.[10]

Consider the case of Samson, whose experience in Milton's verse drama parallels that of the reader in *Paradise Lost*. When Manoa quarrels with God's dispensing of justice—"methinks whom God hath chosen once / . . . He should not so o'erwhelm" (ll. 368–370)—Samson answers firmly "Appoint not heavenly disposition" (l. 373). But within a few lines he too begins to appoint heavenly disposition when he declares himself ineligible for service to God in his present condition—"To what can I be useful?"—for, in effect, he is putting limits on God's ability to use him. No straight line can describe Samson's spiritual journey. At times, as in this instance, he seems to make an advance toward understanding, only in the next minute to embrace in another guise the error he has just rejected. When clarity of vision does come to Samson, we can look back and see a series of starts (gestures) toward it—intimations, partial illuminations—but no chartable and visible progression. Let me here anticipate a later argument by pointing out that since the concern of the play is Samson's regeneration, Dalila, Harapha, the messenger, the Chorus, and Manoa are important, not for themselves, but for the opportunities they bring to Samson's laboring mind.

In *Paradise Lost*, the reader is repeatedly forced to acknowledge the unworthiness of values and ideals he had previously admired, yet, like Samson, he will often fall into the same admiration when the context changes slightly. To take as an example something I have treated at length elsewhere, in the early books: Satan's false heroism draws from the reader a response that is immediately challenged by the epic voice, who at the same time challenges the concept of heroism in which the response is rooted. Subsequently, Satan's apparent heroism is discredited by covert allusions to other heroes in other epics, by his ignoble accommodation to the "family" he meets at the gates of Hell, by his later discoveries squatting at the ear of Eve in the form of a toad, and, most tellingly, by his own self-revelations in the extended soliloquy that opens Book IV. At *some point* during this sequence

---

[10] Cushman, *op. cit.*, pp. 163, 166.

of actions, the reader becomes immune to the Satanic appeal because he has learned what it is, or to be more precise, what it is not. "Some point," however, will be a different point for each reader, depending on the extent to which he is committed to the false ideal Satan exemplifies. Nor will the progress of any reader —of whatever capacity—be regular, since the learning of an individual lesson is not a guarantee against falling into a generic error. The reader who in Book I is led to resist the sophistries of the Satanic line when they are offered directly, may not recognize them in Book II when they are put forward in the Grand Council, especially if he has surrendered too much of his attention to the thrust and parry of the debate, that is, to the strategy rather than to the morality of the scene. And this same reader, when he is presented with a true hero in the person of Abdiel, is likely to admire him for the wrong reasons. That is to say, his response to Abdiel's action at the close of Book V will be a response to the melodramatic aspect of the situation—a lone figure rising to assert himself against innumerable foes—and therefore a response not enough differentiated from that originally given to the now discredited Satan. In Book VI, during the War in Heaven, the reader is given the opportunity to distinguish Abdiel's heroism from the *incidental* circumstances of its exercise. So that, at *some point* in the course of his struggles with the interpretative problems raised by the battle, the reader discovers the naked essence of heroism itself. It is important to realize that the poem does not move to this revelation; it has been there from the first, plainly visible to the eye capable of seeing it. It is the reader who moves, or advances, until his cleansed eye can see what has always been there. At least the reader is given the *opportunity* to advance. He may not take it, and so remain a captive of his clouded vision. It follows, then, that between Books I and VI Satan does not change at all. His degradation is a critical myth. The reader's capacity to see him clearly changes, although that change is gradual and fitful, uneven, unchartable, to some extent invisible, not easily separated from parallel changes in the reader's capacity to see other things clearly—virtue, heroism, love, beauty. (I am thinking, for example, of the contrast between the good and bad poetry of Satan's and God's speeches. I leave you to apply the labels.)

If Satan has not moved or altered, the only alteration being the reader's, it follows that the episodes in which Satan appears are not important for any light they throw on *him*, or for the challenges they present to *him*, but for the function they serve as a whetstone to the reader's laboring mind. Moreover the action of the poem is taking place in that mind, not in the narrative, whose world is static. For, strictly speaking, the plot of *Paradise Lost*, in the sense of a linear movement toward a dramatic and moral climax—the Fall—does not exist; simply because the concept of free will, as Milton defines it, precludes the usual process of decision—the interplay between circumstance, motivation, and choice—which in other works fills up a plot. The decision of an absolutely free will cannot be determined by forces outside it, and, in a causal sense, such a decision has no antecedents. I would suggest that the point of the scenes in Paradise from Book IV to Book IX is their irrelevance, as determining factors, to the moment of crisis experienced by the characters; and the action taking place in these scenes is the reader's discovery or comprehension of that irrelevance. In the middle books, and especially at those points where Milton has been accused of "necessary faking"—the phrase is Tillyard's—the reader is presented with a series of "interpretative choices." On the surface, the account of Eve's infatuation with her reflected image, and the fact of her dream, and of Adam's admission to Raphael of his weakness, seem to deny the freedom of the unfallen will by circumscribing our first parents in what Watkins has termed a "network of circumstance." Yet in each instance Milton provides evidence that makes it possible for the reader to disengage these incidents from the Fall—I am thinking for example of Adam's statement, "Evil into the mind of God or Man / May come and go . . . and leave / No spot . . . behind"—and finally to see them as moving away from, rather than toward, that crisis. This is the poet's solution to the problem of building a poem around an event that has no antecedents. He gives us a plot without a middle —Adam and Eve fall spontaneously—but he allows for a *psychological* middle, a middle to the reading experience, by leaving it to us to discover that the narrative middle does not, indeed could not, exist.

II

Now, for the obvious question: if the poem does not move, but the reader moves, if there is no plot except for the plot of the reader's education, and if the true form of the poem is the form of the individual reader's experience rather than the visible form represented by the division into twelve books; if, in sum, the action is interior, taking place inside the reader's mind, what is the function of the exterior form? Why is it there? What do we say, for instance, about the intricate patterning of words and phrases continually being uncovered by modern criticism? There are several answers to this question. The divisions in the narrative, in the physical artifact called *Paradise Lost*, mark out areas within which the process of regeneration can go forward, while the instances of parallelism provide "stations" at which the progress of the process can be checked. When the reader comes across a word or a phrase that recalls him to an earlier point in the poem, he is not being asked to compare the contents of two scenes now juxtaposed in his mind, but to apply whatever insights he has gained in the *psychological* interim to the single content these two scenes share. That is to say, the meaning of the parallel is determined not by its existence but by the success the reader has had in purging his intellectual ray. Anyone, even a computer, can point out echoes. Only a reader who has learned, only a reader with a cleansed eye, can create their meaning. *He* does it, not the poem. Echoes and cross-references are not saying, "Look at this." They are saying, "Do you know what to make of this *now*?"[11] The important time in the poem is psychological time. In the time consumed while reading, the poem is not developing, the reader is (or he isn't). And any significance one can attach to the sequence of events is to be found not in their relationship to the narrative situation—whose temporal structure, as many have observed, is confused—but to the reader's situation. Milton in effect tells us this when God sends Raphael down to warn Adam in Book V. In this way, the epic voice explains, "God fulfills all justice." But God here fulfills more than justice if Adam is meant, because Adam is sufficient to his test without Raphael's warning. Justice is being done to the reader, who is being given the opportunity Adam does not need, although what Adam will do in Book IX created the imperfection

---

[11] Again we find an analogue in the dialectic of Plato, where apparent progressions and/or digressions unexpectedly return to the point of origin, and the hapless respondent is asked to reassess his original position in the light of the truth he has ascended to, or, as is the case in most of the dialogues, in the light of the truth Socrates has drawn out of him.

that makes it necessary for the reader to *now* have the opportunity. When at the end of Book VI the phrase "nine days they fell" returns us to the opening lines of Book I, our attention is not being called to what has happened to Satan since he was first expelled (of course nothing has happened to Satan), but to what has happened to ourselves. Satan is in the same place; we, one hopes, are not. Thus, this halfway point in *Paradise Lost* (in its outer form, that is) *is* there for a reason; it does mark the end of something, not, however, of something going on in the world of the characters (in that context we are right back where we started), but of something going on in the world of the reader. This, in fact, is the end of the poet's attempt to refine the reader's sense of what true heroism is. And later in Book IX the superficial nobility of Adam's gesture will pose once again the same question, "Do you understand now?" And in his response the reader will give his answer.

What I have said here with reference to the single problem of heroism applies to other problems and to other patternings. In Book III, God delivers a speech whose arguments, if they are understood, assure a correct reading of the crucial scene in Book IX. At irregular intervals, phrases from this "ur speech" are repeated (I am thinking especially of "sufficient to have stood, though free to fall"), and each repetition asks a silent question, "Do you understand *now*?" In the intervals between repetitions, the same question is posed indirectly by the events of the narrative. When Eve questions the perfection of her situation ("frail is our happiness if this be so"), she betrays a complete misunderstanding of the concepts God has been at pains to define, and thus her speech becomes a negative test of the reader. That is, the reader's ability to perceive the fallacies in her argument measures the extent to which he *now* understands God's logic. And once again we return to a point made earlier: since the misconceptions Eve entertains here cannot affect her performance at the moment of temptation ("the seat of temptation is in the will, not in the understanding"), her speech is more important for the reader's state of mind than for her own; in relationship to the Fall, her state of mind does not matter. It is the reader who has the most at stake in the scenes preceding the crisis; and the patterns, the repetitions, the time passing—they are all for him.

In addition to providing the reader with stations at which he may check his progress, and with cases or problems whose consideration is the vehicle of that progress, the poem's Aristotelian superstructure—beginning, middle, end—has a negative value as one form of a way of knowing Milton believes to be inferior or secondary. Plato makes a distinction between knowledge "by way of division," that is, knowledge whose end is the clarification of objects in the material world (*dianoia*), and knowledge by illumination, knowledge whose end is the recognition of a suprasensible reality (*episteme*); and this distinction corresponds to that made by Augustine and other theologians between *scientia* and *sapientia*. In one sphere, the mind, with the help of certain aids—deductive logic, enumeration, denotation—performs a refining operation on the data of experience; in the other, the mind itself is led to transcend the flux of experience and to reinterpret it in the light of the reality to which it has ascended. True knowledge, then, is not reached by following a chain of inferences or by accurately labeling *things* (although inference and labeling may have some part in the attainment of it), but is the possession of the mind that has been made congruent with it; true knowledge cannot be brought to the mind (it is not transmissible), the mind must be brought to it; to the point where there is no longer any need for the aid logical inference can offer. One must take care not to extend illegitimately the province of *scientia* and so fail to distinguish between that which can be seen and measured by the physical eye and that which reveals itself only to the inner eye of the aspiring soul. It is this danger to which Milton deliberately exposes his reader when he suggests in the opening lines that the purpose of his poem is to provide a verifiable answer to the question "What cause?"; in its position, this question holds out a promise that proves in the course of the poem to be false, the promise that if the reader follows Milton's argument, from its beginning to its middle to its end, he will find the answer and along with it a rational justification of God's ways, awaiting him, as it were, at the end of a syllogism. But this is not the case. The promise is given so that its falseness can be more forcefully exposed and so that the reader can learn not to rely on the way of knowing it assumes, but to rely instead on illumination and revelation. Just as the search for cause and for a rational justification is an attempt to confine God within the limits of formal reasoning, and is thus a temptation, so is the

temporal-spatial structure of the poem, by means of which that
search is supposedly to be conducted, a temptation, since the
reader may fall into the error of looking to *it* as a revealer of
meaning: that is, to the limited and distorting, though organized,
picture of reality it presents, rather than to the inner light developing within him. (The more the inner light develops, of
course, the less a temptation the outer formal structure will offer,
since the reader's need of it, or of anything else, will progressively
lessen.) The reader's situation parallels Adam's and Eve's, who
are also tempted to look to the organization of experience, and
to the meaning conferred on things by accidents of time and
space, for guidance, rather than to revelation. So that, in summary, what we can call the outer form of the poem—twelve
books, a regular plot line, the illusion of cause and effect—is
(1) unnecessary (finally) to correct perception, and (2) a temptation, since dependence on it is enslavement to it and to the
earthly (rational) perspective of which it is one manifestation.
In other words, part of the poem's lesson is the superfluousness
of the mold of experience—of space and time—to the perception
of what is true; and thus the epic's outer form, inasmuch as it
is the area within which the inner eye is purified, is the vehicle
of its own abandonment. Like the hierarchical structure of the
early Church as it is described in *The Reason of Church-government*, the outer form of the poem is a "scaffolding" which "so
soon as the building is finished" is but a "troublesome disfigure-
ment" that is to be cast aside.[12] And this casting aside is imitated
in the *conceptual* movement of *Paradise Lost* by the rejection of
the external trappings of a public heroism in favor of a better
heroism whose successes are not visible to the physical eye.

III

And what does the reader who has reached this point discover
at the end of his labors? The truth, of course, or Truth, as it
awaits those who have climbed the Platonic ladder: the Supreme
Good concerning which nothing can be predicated, since it is
the basis of all predication; "a principle that requires justification
and explanation by reference to nothing besides itself,"[13] because

[12] Milton, *Complete Prose Works*, I, 791.
[13] Cushman, *op. cit.*, p. 177. See *Symposium*, 211*b*.

it is the basis of justification and that in the light of which all else is to be explained; a good whose value cannot be measured because it is the measure (or norm) of value. In Milton's poem, the position occupied by Plato's Supreme Good is occupied by Christ, whose action in Book XII—taking place not there but everywhere, not at one point in time, but at all points—is the measure of all other actions and the embodiment of everything that is truly valuable.

I began this paper by suggesting that the physical form of *Paradise Lost* has only an oblique relationship to its true form, which I identified with the form of the reader's experience. That experience, however, does not lend itself to the kind of description one usually associates with the word "formal"; here are no readily discernible beginning, middle, and end, no clearly marked transitions, no moments of crisis at which issues are pre-eminently resolved; instead, the form, if it can be called that, follows the convolutions of the reader's education, now describing an advance, now a backsliding, at one moment pointing upward, at another, downward, at a third, in both directions at once. Still, there is a pattern into which the experiences of all successful readers fall (although there are as many variations within it as there are readers) and we are now in a position to trace out that pattern:

(1) During the poem, the reader is being forced by the verse to sharpen his moral and spiritual perceptions to the point where they are answerable to those essences of which he has hitherto had only an imperfect and partial knowledge. This refining process is desultory and wandering, concerned randomly with the entire range of moral abstractions.

(2) At regular intervals, the reader is asked to assess his progress, asked if he is able to recognize the true form of one of these abstractions.

(3) There are in the poem two places where the answerability of the reader's vision to the *unity* of the conceptions he has been considering singly is tested: first in Book IX when Adam violates all of the values with whose identification the poem has been concerned—significantly he sins in their name and this "misnaming" becomes the legacy he leaves his sons—and again in Book XII when Christ restores to these much abused terms their true, that is spiritual, meaning.

The experience of the entire poem, then, moves toward this moment when the arc of the narrative action and the end of the reader's education coincide. (It is no accident that Adam's understanding is made perfect at the point where Christ is brought before his eyes at the end of a process very much like the education of the reader.) Knowledge of Christ is the end of all the smaller investigations and searches that go on in the body of the poem, investigations of the nature of heroism, love, beauty, innocence, happiness. He is the measure of them all and His essence *informs* them all. He gives form to the universe and to everything in it, including the things in this poem, including the poem itself. In an ultimate sense, *He* is the poem's true form,[14] and His relationship to the temporal-spatial structure of the poem is a reflection of His relationship to the temporal-spatial structure of post-Edenic experience. He enters both structures at once to fulfill them and to supersede them as conveyors of meaning by making good on the promises they could not keep. The promise to justify God's ways to men, for instance, cannot, we discover, be fulfilled within the rational and linear framework of the physical *Paradise Lost*; but it *is* fulfilled when the reader, who has been led to an intuitive understanding of Christ's significance, understands, at that moment, how much the mercy of God exceeds the requirements of reason. (Mercy, the word taking flesh and sacrificing itself, is unreasonable.)

For the reader who has been so led, the poem no longer has any parts; rather, like the universe God sees from his prospect high, it constitutes a unity, infused at every point with a single stable meaning. This meaning is apprehended through what become its parts when one is limited to anything but an all-inclusive glance. As the reader moves (irregularly) toward this illuminative height, the divisions into books and episodes, and all other markers indicating subordination and emphasis, recede into the background and reveal themselves finally as artificial heighteners of what is self-evident to the purged eye.[15] The units of the poem

[14] William Madsen makes a similar point in a review of Frye's *The Return of Eden*: "If it is formal symmetry we are looking for in *Paradise Lost*, the nearest approach to it is provided by the image of Christ which radiates from the exact center of the poem" (*Criticism* [Fall, 1966], p. 393). See also C. A. Patrides, *Milton and the Christian Tradition* (Oxford, 1966), p. 260: "I am persuaded that the God-man in *Paradise Lost* . . . renders coherence to the entire epic."

[15] In this overview the argument concerning the poem's crisis is re-

are now interchangeable, one with another, receptacles all of
the good and merciful news Christ proclaims in Book XII. The
illusion of a multiplicity of parts, or even of a clash of values (i.e.,
love vs. obedience), is now seen to have been the creation of the
distorting perspective of local contexts, a perspective that no
longer delimits the horizons of the reader's vision. In short, the
reader who finally knows Christ will experience none of the difficulties associated with Milton's poem; although, paradoxically,
it is these difficulties (tests, trials, temptations) as they have been
encountered in those (illusory) parts which have led him to
that knowledge.[16]

This leads me naturally to the question some of my readers
will have been asking. If knowledge of Christ is sufficient to
all our needs, including the needs *Paradise Lost* speaks to,
what claim does the poem have on us beyond a successful first
reading? The answer is bound up in the inability of the fallen
mind to prolong the moment of vision to which dialectical self-
examination can occasionally bring it. Augustine's spiritual history is a case in point:

> And now came I to have a sight of those invisible things of thee,
> which are understood by those things which are made. But I
> was not able to fix mine eye long upon them: but my infirmity
> being beaten back again, I was turned to my wonted fancies;
> carrying along with me no more but a liking of those new
> thoughts in my memory, and an appetite, as it were, to the
> meat I had smelt.[17]

The perishability of the insight that awaits us at the end of *Paradise Lost* assures the poem's continuing relevance. We may have

---

solved, or, to be more precise, dismissed. Since every moment at which
there is the possibility of seeing or not seeing truly (that is, every moment) is a crisis—this statement applies also to Adam and Eve—the concept becomes meaningless. Some "crises" are merely (and accidentally)
made spectacular. See Jackson Cope's description of the poem as having
no "center from which one might measure the distances relating beginning,
middle, end, or 'crisis'" (*The Metaphoric Structure of Paradise Lost*
[Baltimore, 1962], p. 77). See also G. A. Wilkes, *The Thesis of Paradise
Lost* (Melbourne, 1961), p. 42: "The weight of Milton's conception is
not poised on one episode . . . its weight is distributed through the whole
structure."

[16] Wilkes argues that these local difficulties are finally "submerged" in
the wholeness of the "great argument." What he does not see is that they
do exist for the reader while he is *inside* the poem, and that they *lead* him
to comprehend the "great argument."

[17] Quoted by Louis Martz, *The Paradise Within* (New Haven, 1964),
p. 50.

succeeded to some degree in purging our intellectual ray, but the
"film of ignorance" is not so easily removed, and a "sovrain eye-
salve" may be needed again. And in that (certain) event, the
first reading holds out the promise of another success. In the
meantime, the abandoned outer form—which has been the vehicle for the apprehension of meaning, although meaning is not
imbedded *in* it—remains as an area within which the interior
journey can be renegotiated. With Adam, we exit from the poem
into experience; but we can return to it, as he returns to the
memory of Paradise, for strength and sustenance.

2

The Style and Genre of
Paradise Lost

JOHN T. SHAWCROSS

▼

The difficulties inherent in discussing style grow out of individual preferences, knowledge, and point of view. No definition is quite acceptable, for the components of style, its techniques, and its effects do not seem determinable as a formula to satisfy all tastes. Yet the codifications Aristotle and other rhetoricians devised have proved useful, and have accordingly been "applied" to classify the style of such works as *Paradise Lost*. This technique of definition continues to underlie recent investigations of both the style and the genre of the poem. Since literary style is discussed primarily through an author's language and uses of language, Milton's style has been termed "grand" and "sublime." Christopher Ricks, devoting a full book to the subject, states the basic concept that places the poem in these categories: "Decorum (in the sense both of epic tradition and of aptness to Milton's subject) demanded that he should elevate his style by deviating greatly from common usage."[1] Elevation of style and wide deviation from common usage have confirmed the grandness and sublimity of Milton's verse for generations of readers; but I must

[1] *Milton's Grand Style* (Oxford, 1963), p. 24.

15

demur not only because of the rather facile acceptance of this concept by so many students of *Paradise Lost* but because I am convinced that Milton's intentions and achievements are in opposition to the statement. Ricks implies a limitation upon Milton by "epic tradition" and by "aptness to subject." And, of course, he also begs the question of what that subject is.

The present paper has not been written to take anyone to task for not recognizing in the poem that which I do. Indeed others have in recent years offered readings that are closely akin to some of my thoughts, but incidentally and in different frameworks. Rather it is my hope to show that the poem's genre, though epic, is a modification of tradition not previously noted, while abiding by the "rules"; to illustrate that its generic classification depends upon point of view; to establish the style as complex in range; and to argue that the style is calculated to drive home Milton's "message." This last point fits the demands of decorum but in a different way from that advanced by critics in the past with a different view of the poem's subject, intention, and achievement. Because the principles postulated by Aristotle and others are useful, even from my perspective, though I believe a reexamination of them when in the hands of Milton will counter usual interpretations, and because this technique of definition continues to be employed in one form or another,[2] I choose to pursue my ideas of the style and genre of *Paradise Lost* within this framework. A summary of previous scholarship on style and genre seems hardly necessary: the views presented here owe inspiration to many other people and their ideas, but despite remarks that hint at conclusions I shall present, my thoughts have a heretical cast that does not color such remarks.

Milton's modification of tradition, while working within it, can be observed in such poems as *Lycidas*, the *Ode to John*

---

[2] For example, Dennis H. Burden's comments in *The Logical Epic: A Study of the Argument of Paradise Lost* (London, 1967): "Book IX had dramatized an issue of literary theory: the Christian and satanic modes of tragedy and epic had been juxtaposed and discriminated. The Fall, seen in the proper way, is a model Christian tragedy: God is providential, and poetical justice is established" (pp. 180–181) and "Given Milton's concern with Christ as hero, it would be surprising if he did not make his account of the Redemption contribute to the literary contention of his poem. He develops it so as to achieve a nice paradox about the tragic and the epic. Michael's account to Adam of the coming of the Messiah is in the epic mode . . . and Adam accordingly proceeds to see Christ's fight with Satan in traditional (and hence wrong) epic terms . . ." (p. 197).

Rouse, and the translations of Psalms 1–8. Therefore, to assume that *Paradise Lost* necessarily was conditioned by what is "standard" for epic tradition and what is "apt" for its alleged subject is not justified. A more logical expectation would be that Milton created his own decorum, for he boasts that the poem "pursues things unattempted yet in Prose or Rime." First, however, the tradition must be investigated, and the full subject examined. Of significance in determining the tradition of the poem are its mode and its effect; of significance in determining the subject in the sense that Ricks uses the word are its thesis, its theme, and its intention. Recently I have argued that the mode and the effect of *Paradise Lost* are comic rather than tragic.[3] My conclusion arises from what I see as Milton's thesis, "message," structural organization, and central vision. With an emphasis upon the good that comes out of the evil within the poem, including the Fall, and upon the victory of the Son over Satan in time past, present, and future (at Judgment), with its accompanying return to the Godhead, the poem cannot be considered tragic of effect but hopeful, inspirational, and glorious. There has been no wastage of good in the poem by driving out of evil. Only Satan and the fallen angels illustrate a wastage of good but by no means in the process of driving out evil, and the good that Man loses is not wasted. The stated subject is Man's disobedience, but the thesis is that eternal providence will justify to Man God's ways toward him, and the theme is God's love. God's love for Man best illustrates His providence and best justifies His ways. The intention of the poem is thus the didactic aim of inculcating virtue in Man by showing God's truth, justice, and mercy, leading to peace, and Satan's deceit, injustice, and hate, leading to war. Fundamentally the poem is concerned with the opposition of Eros and Thanatos, that is, the opposition of love and hate, life and death, creation and uncreation.[4] Thus if the "tradition" within which Milton

---

[3] "The Balanced Structure of *Paradise Lost*," *SP*, LXII (1965), 696–718, and "The Son in His Ascending: A Reading of *Paradise Lost*," *MLQ*, XXVII (1966). See also the discussion of Charles T. Samuels, "The Tragic Vision in *Paradise Lost*," *UKCR*, XXVII (1960), 65–78.

[4] The term is specially chosen: Satan's aims and abilities are not simply noncreational, meaning that he wills to counter God's creation, but uncreational, meaning that his physical acts return creation to chaos. See for a typical example Satan's boast to "reduce" the region that Chaos has lost by God's creation of the Universe "to her original darkness" (II, 981–984). The Freudian overtones of all this are most worthy of investigation.

wrote is different from what it has been considered and if the full subject is also different, then the decorum must likewise differ and the style demanded will need reexamination.[5] Whether this style is to be considered "grand" or "sublime," "elevated," and "deviating greatly from common usage" follows as a necessary concern.

Part of the tradition of the poem is its genre. The classification of *Paradise Lost* as an epic has led to a number of predications: it is in the "high" style, it has a hero of noble status or virtue, it is concerned with heroic achievement. Consideration of the first must wait for a few pages, but it is obvious to twentieth-century readers of Milton that the last two are the basis for the so-called Satanic interpretation of the poem and its alleged failure. This censure of Milton's artistry thus implied has been laid to rest for scholars (although not for the general reader), for Satan is not a hero to the poem and by the same reasoning neither is the Son, who throughout is a contrast to Satan. Should we therefore search out a hero in Adam (or Adam and Eve, that is, Mankind)? This view held by E. M. W. Tillyard (and others) is not borne out by Adam's action or character. He cannot be thought of as "epic hero" despite the likenesses of the poem to such as the *Aeneid* and despite Adam's likeness to Aeneas as a progenitor. The worriment over the hero which has gone on seems to me to be pointless: to me there is no hero in the poem although Adam and Eve constitute a protagonist as representatives of Mankind in the drama of life. This is that kind of protagonist one finds in a morality play, a central character about whom the action revolves. He is not truly a "doer," an exemplar of achievement; he is one who plays out a part against great life forces, an example of what life encompasses. The poem was first outlined as a morality drama, and thus seen, it offers the Son and his attributes of love and faith as antagonist against Satan and his attributes of hate and unbelief as opposing antagonist (his name means "Adversary"). I do not wish to overstress the morality relationship of the poem, although appropriately its major structural and imagistic pattern is balance through contrast; yet an awareness of this relationship moves us far from requiring a hero (in the usual sense) for the poem and thus from requiring the presence of certain traditional epic qualities.

[5] As Hallett Smith suggested (*HLQ*, XV [1952], 159–172), "His song may be adventurous then, because of its style and content" (p. 161).

Placing the poem in the epic tradition has also sent readers in search of heroic achievement within it; but Adam neither achieves nor shows heroic action, and Satan corrupts, whether other angels or man, and intends uncreation. In no way can this be construed as fighting bravely for a cause against incalculable odds ("hitherto the onely Argument / Heroic deem'd," IX, 28–29). It is positive Promethean action that is the heroic action of the poem: such action sacrifices self for the love of others. It is the action of the Son or of Man when he follows the Son's example that predicates high achievement.[6] But the Son is greater than Prometheus since he obeys the Father and shows faith. Full heroic action is magnanimous, in Aristotle's definition of the word.[7] Milton calls *Paradise Lost* a Heroic Poem in the forenote on the verse, and this he justifies in the proem to Book IX. He does not mention any "hero." This passage alone, it seems to me, should direct readers to the differences from "epic tradition" that Milton was developing. His task is to tell of distrust, disloyalty, revolt, and disobedience—a sad task. In balance are the trust, loyalty, acceptance, and obedience of the Son throughout the poem and the admonitions (like Raphael's, "first of all / Him whom to love is to obey, and keep / His great command," just before in Book VIII, lines 633–635) which loom with ironic persistence. Here is an argument not less, but more heroic than those of the Greek and Roman epics. The word "argument" means subject as Milton indicates in line 24, but it also retains the meaning "proof" in a persuasive discourse. Quintilian (V. 8–11) called an argument the plot of a play or the theme of a speech, but added that proof and credibility are not the result of reason only but of *signa* (i.e., "indications"). Book IX, with its recounting of the Fall and the immediate aftermath, gives best proof of how Satan works, how Man is deceived, and what disobedience can bring.

Both as subject and as proof, this "argument" ranges throughout the poem. Book IX with the fall of Eve to Satan's blandishments and Adam's fall through his love for Eve becomes the hinge of Man's action in life. With this climax Satan has seemingly

[6] Milton related the Son to Prometheus in his two-line poem on the inventor of gunpowder; but he made clear the superiority of the Son to his type.

[7] See the discussion of Merritt Y. Hughes, "The Christ of *Paradise Regained* and the Renaissance Heroic Tradition," *Ten Perspectives on Milton* (Yale University Press, 1965).

triumphed and Man must hew a path upward to God through repentance and faith, or through obedience and love. It is interesting to note that whereas Death is introduced in Book II in line 666, the number of the Great Beast of Revelation, Adam perversely falls (and completes the entry of death into the world) at line 999 in Book IX. On the other hand the climax of Book III indicates the Son's future victory on earth as Man; and in this way the "argument" of Book IX will be totally reversed. It is part of the "great argument" of the full poem, for the Son's action will furnish the means by which Man will be saved. Those who will have preceded the Son as Man will receive salvation through the harrowing of Hell; those who will come after will have learned the way to fly from woe. The climax of Book III is the hinge of Man's salvation. But it is the climax of Book VI that is the keystone of the poem.[8] With the rebellion and defeat of Satan and his cohorts, the need to create Man has arisen. Without the falsely "heroic" action of the War in Heaven, there would have been no Man, no Fall, no Redemption, and no poem with its "great argument."

Certainly Man's action in life, whether Adam and Eve's in Book IX or most of their progeny's as related in Books XI and XII, is not heroic. The only heroic achievement is such as Noah's: faith in God, and love, implying obedience to Him. It is the example of the Son. But this does not constitute the narrative; it is rather the intended result of the narrative. Quintilian (V. 12) explicitly tells us that in each argument there is something requiring no proof, by means of which we can prove something else. What justly gives heroic name to person or to poem, Milton implies, is striving valiantly for good against opposing forces, and when those forces are basic, the term "heroic" is most suitable. What he will now present in Book IX gives higher argument (proof) to yield that name "heroic" for his poem. Though Adam and Eve fall, we see paradoxically the heroic action by which Man may prove heroic. Milton is concerned only with the name for his poem, not for a person. The meaningfulness of the definition I am posing can be appreciated when we remember Dryden's remarks. He rejected *Paradise Lost* as a heroic poem in "Original and Progress of Satire" (Ker, II, 89) because "His design is the

---

[8] Cf. "The Balanced Structure of *Paradise Lost*," *SP*, LXII (1965), 696–718.

losing of our happiness; his event is not prosperous, like that of all other epic works . . . ." It is thus understandable that Dryden was the first to cast Satan as hero, for he centers on the Fall rather than on the greater happiness that now may ensue, according to Michael in Book XII.

On the basis of the preceding, we can define the genre of the poem by looking at the properties of the epic-heroic poem found therein. First, there are the poem's sweep and length, its catalogues and war, and its organization of events. These are the elements that have so frequently categorized the poem for readers, but they are only narrative and structural motifs whose differences from epic form or use (in *Paradise Lost*) are more significant than their superficial likenesses. These elements we may label the "plot," which, according to Aristotle, is the arrangement of the incidents. In *Paradise Lost* motifs are arranged in a contrasting form (for example, the creation of Pandaemonium in Book I and the creation of the Universe in Book VII) and in comparative (or repetitious) form (for example, the assault on Eve in Book IV and the actual Fall in Book IX). Contrast shows disorder (the world of Satan); comparison shows order (the world of God).

As I have tried to show in the articles cited in note 2, the structure works in two ways, one emphasizing contrast, disorder, and cause and effect, the other emphasizing comparison, order, and the way to God. Books I and II contrast with VII and VIII; III with IX; IV with X; and V and VI with XI and XII. For example, Satan's soliloquy in IV, his means of entry into Eden, and his routing by Gabriel contrast with Adam's soliloquy in X, the ease of entry of Sin and Death into the world, and Satan's reception by the devils; IV has paved the way for the disorder of X. But seen the other way, Books I and II compare with XI and XII; III with X; IV with IX; and V and VI with VII and VIII. For example, the Judgment of God the Father in III compares with the Judgment pronounced by the Son in X, for both are merciful; the stairs to Heaven which Satan sees shining forth between the Universe and Heaven compare with the repentance that ends X, for both lead by steps to God. This comparison suggests order in things and the ultimate order that these specific acts will bring. Both views are necessary to make one aware of Good by knowing Evil and because all of life is made up of such opposites. The Spirit of God may be a dove and the meek may inherit the Earth, but to defeat Satan one must be eagle-winged. A human being is the fusion of Man and Woman, and though he needs the power of the Father to achieve by great deeds, he also needs the compassion of the Mother to achieve by small.

The two-part poem of contrasting halves which is achieved by this first structuring principle shows cause (the devils' decision of revenge, the begetting of Sin and Death, the nature of Satan's evil, the problems of innocence, the pride and envy of Satan, the rebellion and defeat of a third of the angels) and effect (the creation of the Universe, the creation of Man and Woman, the Fall, lust, anger, the seasons, etc., repentance, the Judgment, Man's history, and the First Coming). The movement upward and downward of the second structuring principle creates a mountain hieroglyphic, the mythic (or magic) mountain of Truth and Virtue. To scale the mountain to reach the Plains of Heaven one need only follow the example of the Son (difficult though some may find this path) and conclude with Adam

> that to obey is best,
> And love with fear the onely God, to walk
> As in his presence, ever to observe
> His providence, and on him sole depend . . .
>   (XII, 561–564)

Through following the Son's example, one metaphorically takes on the Father's three-bolted thunder with which the Son defeated Satan in Book VI, lines 760–766.

The chronological disruption of narrative—the beginning *in medias res*—was a staple of the epic, but Milton's use of it illustrates the thesis of the poem and becomes analogous to a major narrative element and motif. We have a disordered poem out of which comes order once we take perspective of the whole. But it is not just the poem that is disordered; it is Man too who can be made an ordered person through Milton's leading him to acknowledge the poem's theme and its thesis. Those who will not be led are disordered eternally, in Milton's philosophy.[9]

[9] Compare the like conclusion of Stanley Fish in a most provocative article entitled, "The Harassed Reader in *Paradise Lost*," *Critical Quarterly*, VII (1965), 162–182: "Milton's method is to recreate in the mind of the reader (which is, finally, the poem's scene) the drama of the Fall, to make him fall exactly as Adam did, and with Adam's troubled clarity, that is to say, 'not deceived' " (p. 162).

Paradise Lost is itself a creation, a type of God's creation. All parts have importance in the full scheme; all parts look forward to the period after that creation has ceased to be: for God's creation, life after the Final Judgment; for Milton's creation, the life his readers are leading which will subtend their ultimate life after the Final Judgment. Of course the poem can remain dis-ordered for those who do not see its integrity, just as God's provi-dence and ways, Milton would have surely felt, will not be acceptable to those who see from Satan's perspective only.

The structural motifs derive from epic example, but they are used more hieroglyphically, more metaphorically, more exten-sively and fully than in previous epics. *Paradise Lost* is epical but far from traditional.

Secondly, further properties of the epic-heroic poem can be discerned through consideration of other dicta for the epic. To Aristotle (*Poetics*, XIII. 11–13) the epic should be embraced in one view; it should unify beginning, middle, and end. Only a perspective view, therefore, of the complete, received *Paradise Lost* will allow understanding of the poem as epic. The emphasis on one aspect of "plot" (the Fall) or the classification of certain sections as unnecessary (the vision of Books XI and XII) or the dismissal of other elements as poorly articulated (the War in Heaven) do not permit perspective.[10] When, however, we see it

[10] These readings have not been totally eschewed today, and they lead to grave strictures on Milton's artistry. For example, analyze the three statements that follow. 1) To affirm his question "If the Fall is the great moral and theological turning-point of the poem, is it likewise the narra-tive climax?" (p. 316), H. V. S. Ogden remarks: "The poem has now reached its great turning-point; the mortal sin has been completed [IX, 1000–1004]. The forward drive of the narrative no longer comes from our dread of a coming event but from our concern with the results of the Fall and from our desire for Adam's and Eve's reconciliation with God" (p. 321). I quote from *Milton: Modern Essays in Criticism*, ed. Arthur Barker (New York, 1965); original publication in *PQ*, XXXVI (1957), 1–19. 2) "And now suddenly, at the last moment, just when we might expect the final fall of the curtain, we are switched away to a panorama of scenes and events in which the previous actors do not figure at all, of which even Adam is only a spectator," and again, "This view [Prince's] may not, does not I think, remove the awkwardness in the placing of this long interlude or of our having to attend so belatedly to this crowded pageant of people and events outside the straight story" (B. A. Wright, *Milton's Paradise Lost* [London, 1962], pp. 191, 192). In the text im-mediately preceding that quoted, Professor Wright acknowledged that the matter of Books XI and XII is "essential to the argument" and approv-

whole, the poem becomes unified and possible of embracement in one view. The theme that I have urged before is the view that thus arises, not the theme of the Fall, not the elements of plot which are rather Quintilian's *signa*. Awareness of the preceding is necessary to progress to a discussion of two further epic qualities of this heroic poem.

First, epic affords greater scope for the inexplicable, Aristotle observed (*Poetics*, XXIV. 15), because we do not actually see the persons of the story. The differences between *Samson Agonistes*, for example, where we are presented with definite persons speaking in character and performing specific actions (static as this dramatic poem is), and the *Aeneid*, where the epic voice comments and leads and unifies, illustrate what Aristotle was noting. In *Samson* we are limited by the dramatis personae, although the chorus at times—but certainly not always—seems to present part of Milton's "message," and although close reading of the speeches of the main characters will lead us to understand the inexplicable that Milton is trying to enunciate. The epic allows the author to insert his view and to lead the reader to awareness of what is happening, what the characters are like, how what they say is to be interpreted, and how the work itself should be read. The difference in point of view perhaps can be realized in this way: contrast what *Lycidas* says to us when we read the poem (the first ten verse paragraphs) as the author's direct and contemporary musing, and when we read it as the re-

---

ingly quoted F. T. Prince's analysis ("On the Last Two Books of *Paradise Lost*," *Essays and Studies*, XI [1958], 38–52). Contrary to Wright's conclusion that "in the main there is no falling off in the poetic interest" (p. 193), Louis L. Martz in his introduction to *Milton: A Collection of Critical Essays* (Englewood Cliffs, N.J., 1966), p. 10, iterates an evaluation he had expressed elsewhere: "But something goes wrong, I believe, in these closing books: the poetry flags, the vision of redemption wanes, a harsh and bitter tone gradually replaces the buoyant voice of the bard who has guided us through most of the poem . . . . Milton seems somehow to have lost touch with the creative center of his design." 3) "Book VI requires much less explication than the five that have preceded it. It is largely straightforward narration, involving almost no philosophical or theological problems," according to Marjorie Hope Nicolson (*John Milton: A Reader's Guide to His Poetry* [New York, 1963], p. 255); and she adds, "This does not mean that there are not great passages in Book VI . . . . But the greatness of the passage [VI, 748–773] comes not from Milton's narrative art but from his poetic genius. For the most part, the battles in Heaven seem fought by glorified tin soldiers" (p. 257).

flective musing of the uncouth swain of the last stanza observed by some superior voice (though swain and superior voice both be Milton).

In this regard *Paradise Lost* falls between *Samson* and the *Aeneid*. The fact that it was first planned as a play surely was influential in creating this dramatic-epic classification. Allan H. Gilbert in *On the Composition of Paradise Lost* has shown evidence that earlier brief tragedies were incorporated into the final epic. If we minimize the narrator's position and stress the dramatic speeches of certain characters—of the fallen angels in Books I and II; of Satan, Eve, and Adam in Books IX and X— we read drama and tend to interpret the speeches as "truth" and the characters as "real" people. If we recognize the role of the narrator—and it is noteworthy that Anne Davidson Ferry's extensive discussion of *Milton's Epic Voice* has caused many critics of the poem to reread it with surprising results—and realize that the characters are presented "in character," we read epic and, through perspective, see the range of "truth" from disobedience to obedience, and the characters as representative of ways of thinking and exercisers of will.

As drama *Paradise Lost* allows us to go wrong in Milton's view (even if some may think we are broaching the intentional fallacy); as epic it allows us to choose right in Milton's view. The form of the heroic poem thus becomes the very embodiment of Milton's full message. This is another example of the break with tradition; it is neither drama nor epic in an unrelenting classic definition. As Roy Daniells has argued in *Milton, Mannerist and Baroque*, it is an example of the baroque by virtue, here, of its placement between the manneristic and the neoclassic (or late baroque), despite some tendency toward the latter. By casting his work in epic form, while deriving it from drama and retaining dramatic sections, Milton acquired greater scope for the inexplicable and obtained answerable style.

Second, what is convincing though impossible, Aristotle wrote concerning epic (*Poetics*, XXIV. 19), should be preferred to what is possible and unconvincing. The application to a heroic poem like *Paradise Lost* as opposed to a drama like Jack Gelber's *The Connection* (I do not say *all dramas*) is obvious. Of course God cannot be depicted and quoted, nor how angels eat or make love, but these achieve conviction for Milton's theme through anthropomorphism and accommodation or symbolic meaning. We are convinced that we ourselves are involved in the cosmic scene before us. Gelber's narcotic addicts are all too real—they even sit next to the audience during the play and approach them at intermission for money for a fix. Actuality is before and around the audience, but they are unconvinced that they may become addicts or that the "scene" is a basic philosophic problem. The drama has the defensible and most necessary effect of making us aware of a *real* problem, but it has reservations in scope and depth. Or we may look at *Samson* where the scope and depth of what Milton is saying arises from our interpretation of such phrases as "inward eyes." Proof that *Samson* remains "unconvincing" in the sense that Aristotle meant can be seen in the denial by a number of present-day critics that Samson is regenerated or that he is intended as a type of Christ. The difficulty for them lies in not being able to accept Samson as more than a folk hero of biblical writing, who is employed to delineate the conquering of self and despair in himself and only by vicarious projection in us. *Paradise Lost* employs epic elements by moving into the impossible, which in the full view convinces that Eternal Providence exists and that God's ways are justified. It presents that which is possible only symbolically, but those who see Adam and Eve and Satan as true people doing real things have not been convinced of Milton's epical achievement.

A final point classifying the poem as epic is that it is a kind of praise: a praise of God rather than of hero and nation. We can call it epideictic because the example of the Son is seen and alluded to in Books III, VI, XII (or one like him—Abdiel, V, or Noah, XI) and because evil is shown so unfavorably in Books II, V, VI, IX, X, XI (the admonitory epic seen through blame). But besides this, the poem is an apostrophe to God's greatness and love for Man, to the need and wisdom of obeying Him. Milton's admonishment is to join in the forces of life (Eros) and renounce the forces of death (Thanatos). Looked at thus, the epic is a full-scale argument leading to the Song of Moses and the Song of the Lamb, sung by those who have achieved victory over the beast and his image and his mark: "Great and marvelous *are* thy works, Lord God Almighty; just and true *are* thy ways, thou King of saints" (Rev. 15 : 3). Milton, in his divine inspiration, becomes the voice of the multitude, singing, "Alleluia: for the Lord God omnipotent reigneth" (Rev. 19 : 6). The angelic praise of God figures prominently, of course, in the poem itself: III, 344–415; VI, 742–745, 882–888; VII, 180–192, 557–632; X, 641–648. The last is drawn from Revelation 15 : 3. This structure of praise in terms of the earlier ten-book version is balanced and paralleled.

Thus labeling *Paradise Lost* as epic, but an epic with a difference, we can examine what sense of decorum Milton would employ. The prior discussion suggests that Milton's decorum should be based on classical definitions of epic decorum but that it should also be altered within that framework in the direction of its more heroic argument. "This great Argument" involves the bringing of dovelike creatures out of the vast abyss. Decorum cannot therefore be defined in the simpler terms of hero or "standard" heroic action; rather it calls for a seeming disorder out of which will arise order, a new form representing the action considered heroic, and a code that implies praise of God and his works.

Literary decorum is defined as the fitting of the various parts of a poem together, the sound agreeing with the sense, the style with the thought. "Propriety of style will be obtained," wrote Aristotle (*Rhetoric*, III.vii. 1–2), "by the expression of emotion and character, and by proportion to the subject matter. Style is proportionate to the subject matter when neither weighty matters are treated offhand nor trifling matters with dignity. . . ." Order, characterization, tone, vocabulary, style, and meter should all accord.

Classically, the epic (based on praise) should be in a high style and its subject matter should concern gods, heroes, members of the nobility, great men, great occasions, or noble abstractions. Comedy (based on blame) should be in a middle style and its subject matter should concern the middle class, the person of the poet, or middle-class occasions (such as birth, marriage, and death). High style in *Paradise Lost* adheres to the subject matter concerned with God and the Son; middle style adheres to the narratives concerned with Adam and Eve and their progeny, which includes Milton, the narrative voice. The scenes involving Satan pretend to the high style as Satan and his crew envision themselves noble and as they undertake their great action; but he is instead an *eiron*, a staple of a comic mode (satire), when viewed from Man's reality, and an *alazon*, also a staple of comic mode (romance), when viewed with God's omniscience.[11]

The speech of God the Father (III, 274–343) is illustrative of the high style of the epic. The Father's joy at the Son's offer to become Man to redeem Mankind pervades the passage: by this act heavenly love will overcome hellish hate; the Son will be more glorified thereby, and He will reign on God's throne as both God and Man. The joy of Judgment will peal forth when the sign of the Son appears in the sky: the world will dissolve in a great conflagration and from its ashes will spring a new Heaven and Earth for the Just, who will dwell with Joy and Love and Truth. Then the Son's scepter put by, all will have been reduced (led back) to God who will once again be All in All.

The language is most appropriate. Note the reduplication: for example, line 292, "Thir own both *righteous and* un*righteous* deeds"; line 301, "So easily *destroy'd*, and still *destroyes*"; line 316, "*Both God and Man*, Son *both* of *God and Man*"; line 337, "S*ee Golden d*ays, fruitful of *golden dee*ds"; lines 339–340, "*Then* thou thy *regal Scepter shalt* lay by, / For *regal Scepter then* no more *shall* need"; line 341, "*God* shall be *All* in *All*. But *all* ye *Gods*." Note the lack of resting places within the periods of this passage: there are grammatical pauses (such as lines 280, 286, 289, 294, etc.), but there is no resting, as such a transition word as "So" in line 294 or line 298 makes clear.

[11] Harold Toliver investigated this range of decorum in "Complicity of Voice in *Paradise Lost*," *MLQ*, XXV (1964), 153–170. He remarked, "Insofar as each level of Milton's hierarchy is distinct, it has its own mode of being and its own rhetoric," but the difference of his concern from mine is evident when he writes: "The difficulty of communicating among levels (in the language of man before and after the Fall, the language of angels, and so forth) is involved in the difficulty of knowing one's unequals . . . . Satan's evil is an undermining of the accuracy of language and a self-willed creation of new places and names . . . . [O]ne of Milton's aims in *Paradise Lost* is to discover a style that can recite in all the tongues the glory of a single word" (p. 154). See also Louis L. Martz, *The Paradise Within* (New Haven, 1964), pp. 183 ff.

John M. Steadman, in "Demetrius, Tasso, and Stylistic Variation in *Paradise Lost*," *ES*, XLVII (1966), 329–341, likewise indicates the varieties of styles which Milton used in his poem. Such variation reflects the emphasis that rhetoric and poetics placed on the subject matter as an index of character and meaning.

Note the specific words: "complacent," "transplanted," "ran-somd," "fruition," "Humiliation," "incarnate," "dread," "tribulations," "compass"; the accents: line 279, "Thée frōm m̄y bósom̄ añd right hand tō sáve"; line 320, "Thrónes, Príncedom̄s, Pówers, Domíñioñs Í rēdúce"; line 338, "Wīth Jóy añd Lóve trīúmphiñg, añd fáir Trúth"; and the sound: lines 313–314, "Therefore thy Humiliation shall exalt / With thee thy Manhood also to this Throne"; line 329, "Shall hast'n, such a peal shall rouse thir sleep." The diction is elevated as in "all Power / I give thee" (lines 317–318); "All knees to thee shall bow" (line 321); or "Then all thy Saints assembl'd" (line 330). The symbol of the sign of the Son (to figure so importantly in Milton's account of the Son's previous defeat of Satan at the beginning of time [VI, 776] and drawn from Matt. 24 : 30) and of the Phoenix along with allusions to Isaiah 65 : 17–25, II Peter 3 : 12–13, and I Corinthians 15 : 28 manifest the high style of the passage.

Adam's denunciation of Eve in Book X, lines 867–908, may not be typical of the human sections, but it does indicate the mean style to be found in the poem. The wallowing blame with which Adam assails Eve pervades the passage: she is called a serpent and likened to Satan; except for her, Adam now laments, he would have continued happy. "O why did God create this noveltie on Earth?" God (who now receives Adam's censure) should have filled the world with men as angels or have found some other way to achieve generation. (Adam has forgotten the omnipotence and omniscience of God.) To Adam, Woman (not Man like himself) will be the cause of infinite calamity to human life.

The language again is appropriate. Note such puns as calling Eve Serpent, her name supposedly being an aspirated form of *Heva*, "serpent"; or the line "To trust thee from my side" soon followed by reference to his rib "More to the part sinister from me drawn," the adjective meaning both from the "left" and "evil"; or the sexually graphic "straight conjunction with this Sex"; or the word "fell" referring to Satan, who is both "dangerous" and "fallen." Note the way duplication is made trivial and comic: "supernumerarie," "number," "innumerable"; "Serpent," "Serpentine"; "snare," line 873, and "Femal snares," line 897. Hyperbole, employed by comic poets for comic effect and yielding a "frigid" style, occurs throughout: "Out of my sight, thou Serpent," "proof against all assaults," "Crooked by nature, bent," "innumerable Disturbances," "infinite calamitie," "and houshold peace confound." There is a feeling of choppiness in the passage, for phrases are interrupted and the flow of thought tends toward an arid style: "nothing wants // but that thy shape // Like his // and colour . . . "; "Fool'd and beguil'd // by him thou // I by thee // To trust thee from my side // imagin'd wise // Constant, / mature / proof against all assaults // And understood . . . "; "By a farr worse // or if she love // withheld By Parents // or his . . . ." Symbols and allusions that are integral to God's passage do not appear; the sounds are more plosive and sibilant, and the words themselves are not generally unusual or unusually employed. The middle-class concern is especially emphasized by the domestic strife lamented in the final lines of the passage.

Any one of his "glorious" speeches will suffice to show the false high style of Satan, dissembler and buffoon. Look at Book I, lines 622–662. Satan recounts his high exploit against God in the past and looks forward to further heroism in the future. Heroic war ("open or understood") has shown the rebellious angels to be "matchless" (except against the Almighty) and "puissant"; they have "emptied Heav'n"; they have shown God that "who overcomes / By force, hath overcome but half his foe." They will now resolve by new war to "repossess thir native seat." We need not cite the high-sounding rhetoric and language, or ringing accents, for those who have advanced Satan as hero have done so frequently. Dissembling—and thus the irony underlying all that Satan says—is always evident. The fallen angels are not "matchless" against God or his presence in others. The power of mind that could presage that they would be repulsed by God is in everyone who admits God's omnipotence. The War in Heaven has removed only a third of the angels (as Death and Raphael both report in II, 692, and V, 710). None of the fallen angels should illogically believe that they will reascend. In this speech Satan implies that they have lost hope (l. 637) and that they must come to a resolution because "Peace is despair'd" (note the etymological pun), although in line 190 he had been hopeful and denied that resolution could come from despair. God's concealment of His strength wrought their fall, according to Satan. They had hoped to gain by force although now, defeated, Satan says, as if he always knew, that force overcomes only half one's foe (note, too, his implied denial of God's omniscience). A comic element is seen thus in his self-deception; Milton is really so unsubtle that Satan becomes a caricature of the pompous braggart.

This effect is underlined by the contrasts that the poet builds. When we hear Satan say that the Abyss cannot long cover celestial spirits under darkness, we remember shortly before the dovelike creature that sits on the vast Abyss and makes it pregnant. The falseness of Satan's images is impressed upon us by contrast, and calling the fallen angels "Sons of Heav'n"—true though it may be—sharply reminds us of their unfilial love; the Son's filial love later will undercut this epithet more patently.

But over all lies the hint of Satan's soliloquies that all this heroic, high-flown language is but trivia: for, Milton makes clear throughout the poem, God is omnipotent, omniscient, and omnipresent. The important text from Psalms 2, that the Lord will have the kings of the earth in derision, alluded to by Belial in Book II, line 191, hangs over these sections, and shows the self-aggrandized devils to be but the swarm of bees or pygmies they become about one hundred lines after this particular passage. They are giants only to themselves. Their pettiness is here seen in their "prying" (l. 655); their pride in their desired and heretical "self-raising" of themselves to Heaven; their envy appears everywhere. As vacuous orator, Satan becomes a buffoon; viewed from God's position, the fancifulness of Satan's speech is sheer romance and laughable besides. The rhetorical devices become obvious and "contrived": the opening apostrophes, the rhetorical questions (ll. 626–630, 631–634, 661), the deliberate repetitions ("Warr then, Warr"). These caricature when read fully. It is Milton's genius that has led so many astray, not Satan.

What then is the style? It is high, and it is middle, and it is falsely high but really low. Its style depends on how we read the poem, but if we read it with Milton's thesis and theme firmly in mind, we see that the middle style predominates, the high offset by the low, though that is superficially high. (The style is a part of the total dialectic of the poem: it represents thesis, antithesis, and synthesis as much as the contrasts of good and evil, and the like. The point, of course, is that Man partakes of both the thesis which is God and the antithesis which is Satan.) Yet we realize a striving upward and we have a feeling that as we accept the "message" we soar with Milton with no middle flight. As a heroic poem, *Paradise Lost* partakes of epical style, but it is not limited by what is epic style any more than its author is by other elements of epic tradition. Milton's style is appropriate to his subject, Man's disobedience, but it also shifts aptly as the subject matter and characters shift. Milton has kept "propriety of style" if we recognize the shifts in expression of emotion and character and subject matter. Triviality does enter—when it should; and dignity is maintained—when it should be. The more heroic argument, encompassing *all* the basics of life, requires the full gamut of styles. It is not limited and it is a product of modified tradition.

Nonetheless we can apply the terms "grand" and "sublime" to the whole rather than just to certain parts; but these terms will not mean quite what they summarized for the eighteenth century, under the influence of Longinus and John Dennis. Rather than a mere equation of "sublime" with "high" or "epic" style, we have the sublimity of being upraised when the full effect and message of the poem is allowed to work upon us. It does not derive merely from language used and literary devices employed; it arises largely from the joy that pervades the whole poem when we recognize God's presence and the paradise within, happier far. It uplifts us when we see what is above the false grandeur of Satan and the mean existence of mankind. And we have this concept impressed upon us by the dignity (or grand-ness) of God's creations and ultimate plan. Justification of God's ways lies in recognition of true Good, impossible before the Fall, and in recognition of the need for joint endeavor of Man and God to reach high goals.

The poem is sublime in its elevation of the spirit and its tremendous joy: the elevation of the spirit is achieved through the style that moves from low to mean to high, and the joy is achieved by realizing that what has befallen Man is not tragic but ultimately blissful, once the seat has been regained. Rhetori-cally the style is grand in part, but not all parts are stylistically grand. The total effect may reach grandness, but that is not the same thing as classifying Milton's style in one traditional cate-gory.

Milton's style is answerable to the Renaissance concept of epic, and it satisfies the expectations of decorum.[12] And though the impersonal and universal strain toward the individual and personal (see Arnold Stein's essay in *Answerable Style*, pp. 136–137), this is all carefully calculated to bring God's message down from high to the common man, thereby to raise man up. In fact it is the individual and personal in the poem that are raised and supported. Man's habitat is the middle ground; the poet *intends* to soar with no middle flight above the Aonian mount. That he was successful is evident from the three centuries of readers who have soared with the poet. But the total view of the style of the poem and thus its answerability is not that simple.

The narrator inspired by God's spirit well exhibits the point being made in the poem: God works through Man to reach Man; He purges and disperses the mists, and, as it were, with inward eyes illuminated, the poet's intended wing is in no way depressed. Man's normal style is mean, his audience receives the mean best; but the spirit moves upward and the goal is upward, and fit audience will be led upward with the poet as he moves into the high and ultimately answerable style. The fusion of genres and the fusion of styles created a "new" genre and a "new" style, and thereby was wrought the only possible answer to argument above heroic.

[12] See Arnold Stein's essay in *Answerable Style* (Minneapolis, 1953), p. 121.

3

The Splinter Coalition

HAROLD E. TOLIVER

▼

In his mature poems Milton tends to think of politics and temporal power as satanic substitutions for divine communion, and he isolates them in a large parenthesis of time that begins (for man) when Eve asks for the vote. I intend to bring together some of these substitutions in *Paradise Lost* and the ideal relationship between creatures and creator: one a splinter coalition of fallen allies, the other a celestial host; one cemented by political rhetoric, armed with gun powder and secrecy, sealed by satanic epic, justified by satanic rationalization,[1] governed by military virtues; and the other united by communal hymn and dance, set in motion by epiphany, possessed of an authentic epic grandeur, and commanded in ranks by a sense of hierarchical status. Both are defined by their responses to divine manifestation, the central reality of Milton's universe. But whereas epiphany draws the celestial host closer to the center and stimulates a decorum from each according to his knowledge —a decorum manifest in all the celestial arts and achievements—

---

[1] Cf. Dennis H. Burden, *The Logical Epic* (London: Routledge and Kegan Paul, 1967), pp. 59–64.

it drives the fallen host further into its own plots of self-glorification and its own style, founded on veiled suggestion, rhetorical power, and conspiracy. In effect, Milton assigns most of the achievements of statesmanship to Satan as the type of the temporal leader—the general, diplomat, spy, and expert parliamentarian. But from the standpoint of the poem's full view of history, that achievement is happily enclosed on one end by the open and readable order of Eden and on the other by a final restored community of saints and angels. Even for men within the parenthesis, divine manifestation renews itself and reaffirms ultimate truths that cannot be incorporated into temporal plans of action. For the Christian hero, no secular activity is definable without reference to these eschatological realities, which give it its true orientation.

The splinter condition extends beyond the factions that wage Milton's cosmic wars: it intrudes also into individual consciousness and Adam and Eve's idyllic marriage. But I wish to concentrate for the moment on the public rather than the domestic or lyric areas, using Satan's language as an entry into infernal politics. What kinds of nodes and synapses can Satan discover to fabricate an order where there is none—to constitute a kingdom and sustain it above the bottomless abyss? What does he adhere to? How does his rhetoric contrast with that of the original communion? Can we talk of something like a "categorical decorum" in which speakers respond to glory in appropriate styles? What happens to holy communion and participation in the divine will when the igniting breath of Satan explodes it and weak members are courted into rebellion? In keeping with the notion of man's fortunate fall and recovery of paradise, are there modes of language that good angels can reassert against satanic parody and absurdity? In other words, is some new synthesis (or church communion) forthcoming to top Satan's counterplot on this level as well as on the level of human regeneration? Though these are primarily stylistic questions, they touch upon meaning as it is embedded in imitative form. Ultimately we approach the question of the poem's genre, which is anchored in the original pastoralism of Heaven and Eden, descends into heroic and mock-heroic modes, and eventually produces a new paradisal ordonnance.

I

Satan's "high words" in Book I reveal a typical confusion of heavenly and infernal values as they substitute political style for genuine homage to truth, yet draw upon that homage at strategic moments for the satanic sense of an epic program welding a nation of heroes. The narrator tells us that words in the high manner bear semblance of worth but lack substance (I, 527); the bluster of "warlike sounds" issues from a metaphysical abyss that undermines all heroic positions however firm they seem. One of the paradoxes of that language is that it renders all apparent realities in a literal manner and yet is inaccurate and veiled, like faulty allegory, substituting shadowy motives for the self-sufficient reason of the Logos. Whereas Christ as the Word comes forward to put some aspect of divine substance into visibility, Satan, in parody, comes forward to project illusions. He is the concealed side of what to a Manichaean would be God's own dark nature but to Milton is a dialectical stage in the narrative clarification of God's full plan. Having no means of returning to enlightenment, the splinter state is forced to make enmity its sole means of glory and derive modes of action and style from the values of war, with timely reinforcement from the departments of infernal philosophy, art, and literature.

The ambiguity of Satan's stature is an archetypal image of the program that grows out of it, just as the staging of the divine image is consistent with its source or "typical" of it. (The principle of analogy and generic likeness holds for devils as well as for chains of positive being.)

> Dark'n'd so, yet shone
> Above them all th' Arch-Angel: but his face
> Deep scars of Thunder had intrencht, and care
> Sat on his faded cheek, but under Brows
> Of dauntless courage, and considerate Pride
> Waiting revenge: cruel his eye, but cast
> Signs of remorse and passion to behold
> The fellows of his crime, the followers rather
> (Far other once beheld in bliss) condemn'd
> For ever now to have thir lot in pain,
> Millions of Spirits for his fault amerc't

Of Heav'n, and from Eternal Splendors flung
For his revolt, yet faithful how they stood,
Thir Glory wither'd.   (I, 599–612)

The movement of such a passage is complex, and the reaction
of the narrator contributes to its intricacy; but we can distinguish a clear echo of Satan's typical manner in its excessive contrasts: its counterchecks to feeling and corrected "readings" of
the portrait, its syntactical stumbling, its war of light and dark.
The former grandeur of the angels is borrowed to grace a military cause. Satan's eye is cruel but compassionate; the host is
composed of "fellows," no "followers"; they are glorious yet
withered; and so forth through a clotted inventory whose terms
are in transition between one host and the other. Since Satan
bases the inducement to war "open or understood" on the vigor
of the host and on hope, he must dispose of these contradictions
(or seem to), and he invents the plot of restoration, the heroic
program (in keeping with the Italian idea of epic as a form that
returns an outcast prince to power) as a means of concealing a
loss of responsive power. Rather than the unfolding of divine
events from a creative intelligence, we have the manipulation of
a plot by "considerate" (cunning) pride awaiting its moment.
The all-seeing divine eye shrinks to an eye of cruelty casting
forth "signs" of remorse which may be genuine or staged but in
any case are merely "signs," part of a shadowy pageant. If one
managed to peel aside the veil, one would find only more veils
and more ambiguity. The genres of celestial praise and mystical dance are metamorphosed into political hoopla; in order
to centralize the worship of the alliance, Satan must somehow
seat himself as monarch-deity with a suitably flexible language
of persuasion and ritual. Committing themselves to that substitution, the host may postpone if not prevent their realization that
Hell is Heaven in disrupted collocation, matter lapsing into
chaos, truth twisted and eroded, and thus allow the divine ironic
plot time to work their ruin, as proof of its own efficacy and its
capacity to correct any reversal.

As Satan's somewhat tarnished glory indicates, we run into
insurmountable difficulties with any questions concerning his
rhetoric and heroic stature unless we recognize clearly that all
designs on the future and all rationalizations of the splinter

party are grounded in futility: the vacuum is absolute. Yet Satan's belief in the potential of war and aggression as a means of gaining autonomy has at least one justification: since knowledge corresponds to being and knowledge of the highest would create gods, God must himself remain partly hidden in his cloud. Satan's assertion that his adversary's apparent weakness tempted him to rebel is, from his point of view, at least plausible: they had no way of knowing, he reminds his lieutenants, whether or not Heaven had room for expansion until they tried, and it was logical to assume that, if anyone had a chance, warriors such as they did. This argument supplies more than a pretext. In considering the rebellion narratively, Milton is obliged to supply an initiating event without implying that it is a necessary part of the divine nature or purpose. It is logical of Satan to ask, if antagonism can be *born*, why not *perpetuated*? The possibility of a Fall appears to give the splinter state both enduring tenure and a chance for success. In this and in God's limited participation in war generally, Milton chooses to follow scriptural narrative and tradition. Though it may seem that a Whole cannot divide itself into segments and "participate" in partisan affairs, the scriptural Jehovah changes neither himself nor the temporal nature of historical events by taking part in them. He allows Job to be tormented, drowns nations, puts cities to fire and the sword, orders fathers to sacrifice sons, condemns, cures, blesses, offers covenants, and burns deserts. He "parses" himself (so to speak) into active verbs addressed to particular people, focusing his Everywhereness into a single voice giving specific commands. As a person joined to Platonist cosmology, he should control not merely the special concerns of a chosen people but all creation, including Satan's experiment. But confronted with the choice of making him incommunicable as a vague Intelligence standing above the creation or available as a partisan in this way, Milton chose the alternative compatible with a religious consciousness and an epic poem: he has God both allow politics and (apparently) respond to its products yet direct its apparent vagaries toward his own ultimate goals. Instead of precluding individuating action to begin with, he makes use of it after it happens, though this course requires him to withdraw from areas given over to the free wills of the creatures. Such a figure was Milton's best compromise between an ideal universe and the real world he had to justify. Let God be permissive, then, but still capable of making good evolve from evil, and let evil itself be nothing more initially than good perverted into a shadowy substance, barely able to project signs of its illusory substance.

However, the narrative decision to make God's power operative after rather than before the event makes him appear fallible to Satan (and later to Eve), and in the first war in Heaven Satan mistakes this divine partition as a promise that dialectic can become a principle of universal statehood. If Heaven's dance of free agents has countermovements, why not a single Counter Movement from a grand Adversary, to "match" God himself? The harmony of divisible but complementary creatures may then become a duplicate harmony. But because Satan and his lieutenants lack the power to create something from nothing or to centralize authority in epiphany, they must substitute war and parliamentary procedure for it and hatch a plot that will give them directives and mandates.

We can say this much in reasoning after the fact; but our real interest is the satanic mode. The first rule of language and conduct in such a partition is that one's negatives must be as absolute as the enemy's positives: war becomes eternal as well as pseudoheroic. As to the metaphysical assumptions behind the absolute negative, Satan argues that Christ's recent exaltation has already imposed new circumscription on them, hence new "terms" (terminations, definitions, boundaries), and as these are necessarily antagonistic to the old ones, the outcome must be still further subdivision. As possibilities for alliances mushroom, they create new possibilities in language for cementing bonds, and together with antagonism toward the enemy comes the conditional agreement among friends. In *A Rhetoric of Motives* Kenneth Burke supplies one of the stages missing in Satan's account of these motives:

> The notion of the Son as bringer of light seems in its essence to suggest that the division of the part from the whole is enlightening, a principle that might be stated dialectically thus: Partition provides terms; thereby it allows the parts to comment upon one another. But this "loving" relation allows also for the "fall" into terms antagonistic in their *partiality*, until dialectically resolved by reduction to "higher" terms.[2]

[2] Kenneth Burke, *A Grammar of Motives* and *A Rhetoric of Motives* (New York: World Publishing Co., 1962), p. 664.

No one who observed the proliferation of sects in the 1640's would be likely to be unaware of the principle of splintering by enlightenment, just as no one living in the twentieth century is likely to be unaware of the multiplicity of terminological systems. Though the previous creation of the angels was also a subdivision of God, Satan points out scornfully to Abdiel that no one bore witness to it, and this time they are not to be caught napping: rather than answering epiphany with song and intricate dance, they are prepared to meet suspicious moves with *their* kind of maneuvers.

Enlightenment, translated as suspicion, thus becomes the initiating event (if not the sole cause) of the rebellion, and it is this that gives language its antagonistic twist, as satanic enlightenment quickly translates into enlightened self-interest. Linguistically, as this international drama is born, the contrastive conjunction kinks the movement of the sentence, qualifying the divine coordination that formerly linked reverent creatures to their source. In a sense, then, Satan is the original "however, . . ." Oxymoron, antinomy, ambivalence, and paradox are owed largely to him—not to mention irony, wit, the pun, and cleverness generally. By cross-referencing two separate bins incongruously, Satan's puns in effect deplete God's stock as they bolster Satan's, siphoning power for the splinter state and parodying what they borrow. (I will offer examples in a moment.) Satan is not only the first industrialist, field marshal (antagonistic to other "divisions" and enamored of his own voice in disciplining his), and statesman-diplomat, but also the first metaphysical poet, the father of the conceit that yokes heterogeneous things by violence together. The nodal points of his language and his secret compacts depend on his capacity to slip back and forth between orders, weaving them together in the incongruous pun. His speech is liberally sprinkled also with the severances of sprung logic, uneven cadences, and the rabbitlike movements of sentences.

The motives of the fallen host are no clearer than the mystery of Satan's original motives finally, but after this initial severance from the Word, members of the splinter kingdom collaborate in spinning a web of rationalization around the political bond. The difficulty is that rebellion, which ought to free the host from limits and promote a free-speaking democracy, makes them a slave to their own partiality, hence to nationalized "absolutes" and the fabrications they demand. Since straightforward truth would destroy them (or "reabsorb them into the single Word," "dissolve the grammar of politics into divine communion"), they must turn to action of a particular joint, yet disjoined kind. They can then argue that they are at least *making progress*, that their obvious restrictions will dissolve as their kingdom exfoliates into an empire, perhaps even a paradisal empire.

But in so arguing, they are caught up in futurism ("If you sacrifice now you'll get it all back later, with a large bonus"), and it is this futurism that we plunge into blindly in Book I, supposing that satanic time is not parenthetical, merely indefinite, and perhaps supposing also that chance rules some corner of the universe if God is not responsible for Hell.[3] Going backward chronologically as we move forward in the epic, we come gradually to see the war machine and parliament more clearly, measuring them against the full communion that they seek to destroy and discovering that not chance but the mystery of free will is the real source of their operating room. At the point of their entry into the parenthesis, the two hosts make a telling confrontation of each other that clarifies both this issue and the two modes of language that each illustrates thereafter. It is here that the nature of true heroism is first established chronologically and the definitive contest between Christ and Satan in the desert is first predicted. (The first contest sets the splinter party in motion and segregates it from the communal grammar of the Word; the last contest ends its earthly dominance and allows men caught in the parenthesis to join themselves to Christ.)

Beelzebub is Satan's initial victim. His fall is predictive of Eve's and thus, by contrast, of Christ's correction of Eve in the second great temptation. Since it results from a mistranslation of Christ's manifestation, the victory in the desert must *retranslate*, repairing the ruin that Satan now introduces into the language. Though Beelzebub is not aware of it, the principle of antagonistic

---

[3] Several critics have commented on the theme of adventure and wandering, among them Stanley E. Fish in *Surprised by Sin,* Arnold Stein in *Answerable Style,* and Joseph Summers in *The Muse's Method.* Northrop Frye in *The Return of Eden* also comments perceptively on the translation of God's attributes into elements of the satanic condition and upon demonic parody in general (pp. 34–35).

rhetoric and the appropriation of glory to the self is already implicit in the arguments that Satan practices on him:

> Sleep'st thou, Companion dear, what sleep can close
> Thy eye-lids? and rememb'rest what Decree
> Of yesterday, so late hath past the lips
> Of Heav'n's Almighty? Thou to me thy thoughts
> Was wont, I mine to thee was wont to impart;
> Both waking we were one; how then can now
> Thy sleep dissent? new Laws thou see'st impos'd;
> New Laws from him who reigns, new minds may raise
> In us who serve, new Counsels, to debate
> What doubtful may ensue.   (V, 673–682)

In wooing satellites, Satan is particularly effective in the intimacy of the duet where he can twist a specific arm. Here he adopts love language (much like Eve's after she has learned to maneuver with the wisdom of the serpent) to political persuasion, proceeding from companionship and union in their double one (their angelic marriage) to new decrees, subdivisions, modes of counsel and debate, and hence to a congress to make future policy against "What doubtful may ensue." He builds upon tradition in such a way as to bring the past—and therefore some remnant of the original created order—into his own radical state. Since the two of them have always been one, as communing angels free to talk before God, to sleep to each other now would be to remain "parted" when they should "impart" their enlightenment. Peaceful sleep somehow becomes dissent before we realize how it happened, and those awake to each other become one in a new manner. They require a common plot, the two of them, and a means to feel out the secret intelligence of their potential allies. Those awake to each other in counsel ("imparted" to them and sealed off from the rest) may in fact become one, but the psychology of conspiracy obviously replaces communion. The oily personality that Satan brings to bear on Beelzebub is doubly effective because all he need ask for the moment is that his friend listen: then perhaps, should they jointly see fit, they can issue a proclamation and devise public "entertainment" suitable to the kind of host they have become. It is to this end that he invents friendship as opposed to angel love and makes dialogue and democratic procedure the *modus operandi* of the new government. Each creature tempted henceforth—Eve, Adam, and

Christ in *Paradise Regained*—will be urged to take an apparently self-initiated action that will in effect orbit him around Satan and commit him to a similar style of partition.

II

If the foundation of moral responsibility is to be clear, Milton must repress the impulse for "enlightened" subdivision without destroying free will. As Abdiel points out, Christ's subdivision actually brings the host nearer to the center of *mediation* and offers them new intensities of communion. Satan's mistake is to make mediation "interposition"—as Eve later considers Adam no longer her enlightener but the main obstacle in her upward transformation. (Woman, born from man's rib, is man's "partition" principle, as Christ and Satan are God's.)

But let us back up a moment and examine more closely the initial society from which Satan gathers his subjects. As we have seen, it is created by the spoken epiphanies and material incarnations of the Word, which in turn prompt answering modes of celebration in appropriate styles, or categories of decorum. Thus the Word translates infinitude into partitioned existence. We can sum up the exchange between them by saying that those who would know the Word must settle for *analogy* rather than direct *perception*, for *talk about* rather than *vision of*. Analogy allows each creature to communicate with Allness and yet maintain his proper station and the speech of bounded substantives and limited verbs. An accurate description of something is simultaneously an analogical description of something higher that does not destroy the literal object by overpowering it. This metaphoric principle is the traditional basis of all Christian education, both in rhetoric and in the other sciences and arts, and amounts to saying that segmentation paradoxically transcends itself. According to Pseudo-Areopagite's *De Caelesti Hierarchia*, for instance,

> every creature, visible or invisible, is a light brought into being by the Father of the lights. . . . For I perceive that it is good and beautiful; that it exists according to its proper rules and proportion [hence has its "decorum"]; that it differs in kind and species from other kinds and species; that it is defined by its number, by virtue of which it is "one" thing; that it does not transgress its order. . . . As I perceive such and similar things in this tone they become lights to me, that is to say, they enlighten me. . . . and

soon, under the guidance of reason, I am led through all things
to that cause of all things which endows them with place and
order, with number, and species and kind, with goodness and
beauty and essence.[4]

But the mind pursuing such *vestigia dei in natura* must be agile
because echoes of the creator come back to it not from a single
exalted pole "mystically" but from all the objects upon which the
mind works, from all other communicants. Linguistically speaking, all things are synecdoches for "God"; theologically speaking,
subjects; metaphysically speaking, contingent substances and de-
rivative intelligences.

It is inevitable, then, that moments of "inspiration" be con-
stitutional insights into analogy. Imitations of God become ungodly only when one "aspires" to "set himself in Glory above his
Peers," trusting to *equal* the "most High" (I, 38–40), collapsing
analogy into identity. Whereas true inspiration does not "trans-
gress . . . order," aspiration releases energy against "proper rules
and proportion."

The analogical way to bear witness provides a framework
for judging the satanic coalition and the language of predatory
sterility. Satan cannot breathe life, only "blow," into his creation, uniting his followers by the "wind" of oratory until they
breathe "united force with fixed thought" (I, 560). Pandemonium, the center of confusion, rises like an "exhalation" of
breath, at once a parody of the inspired awakening to life that
recurs throughout the poem and of the music that accompanies
authentic creation. It is a creation, but a "devilish" one:

> As in an Organ from one blast of wind
> To many a row of Pipes the sound-board breathes.
> Anon out of the earth a Fabric huge
> Rose like an Exhalation, with the sound
> Of Dulcet Symphonies and voices sweet,
> Built like a Temple.   (I, 708–713)

It resembles a temple as a caricature resembles a type. (The
Limbo of Fools will eventually be filled with those similarly
puffed with wind, "vainly" inspired.) Though the martial intensity of Pandemonium's rising has the impact of genuine feeling
seeking answerable form, we instinctively distrust the "voices

[4] Quoted from Erwin Panofsky's *Meaning in the Visual Arts* (New
York: Doubleday, 1955), pp. 127–128.

sweet" of Hell; the "blast of wind" suggests a concealed discrepancy between creative impulse and form.

Despite the founding of the splinter state and its public building on air, Satan is also paradoxically "imbruited" and gives his creations material form. In doing so, he splits the original monism of the creation into an incurable dualism: immaterial wind and matter separate explosively, creating simultaneously the "lie" and material for the war machine. Thus in Heaven his *cannon* become *speaking machines*, which, as Belial "gamesomely" says, send "terms of weight, / Of hard contents, and full of force urg'd home" (VI, 621–622). These issue as from an "oracle":

> thir mouths
> With hideous orifice gap't on us wide,
> Portending hollow truce.   (VI, 576–578)

They "mean," but they mean "hollowness"; they portend duplicity rather than, say, pledged consistency. (The open "O," the "hideous orifice," and the gaping suggest too much mouth and too little enlivening breath.) Satan's "inspiration," when it does come, is a touch of fire which explodes the matter it "touches" on, and thus from the beginning he goes to battle with an artillery of doubly charged words. He confidently answers Abdiel with an "ambiguous language" that foreshadows his plan to materialize "entertainment," punning on "behold," "address," "begirt," and "beseeching or besieging," which mean both "surround with adoring celebration" (good songs) and "encircle and destroy" (oratorical epic blasts):

> Then thou shalt behold
> Whether by supplication we intend
> Address, and to begirt th' Almighty Throne
> Beseeching or besieging.   (V, 866–869)

He later taunts God's army in standard heroic decorum with a renewed stock of puns:

> Heav'n witness thou anon, while we discharge
> Freely our part: yee who appointed stand
> Do as you have in charge, and briefly touch
> What we propound, and loud that all may hear.
> (VI, 564–567)

The language of the gunpowder plot is both a smoke screen to baffle the enemy and a morale builder for the rebel troops "in" on the code.

God allows Satan to think that war provides new terms of weight because one of the necessities of the creation as analogy is that he maintain his distance and let creatures discover their own levels. Hence though the tactics eventually recoil, for some moments Satan is allowed to savor the good angels' astonishment. He joyfully interprets their manner of worship as false idolatry: for the freedom that angels claim to have in discharging their duties to God (who witnesses them and is witnessed by them), he substitutes his own scathing attack, tumbling good angel over good angel in parody of heavenly song and dance:

> O Friends, why come not on these Victors proud?
> Erewhile they fierce were coming, and when wee,
> To entertain them fair with open Front
> And Breast, (What could we more?) propounded terms
> Of composition, straight they chang'd thir minds,
> Flew off, and into strange vagaries fell,
> As they would dance, yet for a dance they seem'd
> Somewhat extravagant and wild, perhaps
> For joy of offer'd peace.   (VI, 609–617)

It is obvious that Satan's entertainment establishes a new range of duplicity in salutation, epiphany, and annunciation, a duplicity that makes friendly encounters into epic trials and gives them the shock of chance. As the gathering of his forces after the first day's battle reveals, he also founds the strategy of brainwashing, for the truth of the matter, as Nisroch lets slip, is that despite their embarrassments, the good angels have fought impassively and unwounded, while the militant army has been split, shattered, pained, and routed (as the material result of its spiritual splintering). Nonetheless, to Satan suffering his angelic epistaxis without flinching—speaking "undismay'd" with look "compos'd" and expecting imminent victory as Secretaries of Defense do—they have scored a signal victory. They have proved themselves "imperishable" and stopped losing the war. But they require new weapons, and Satan must furnish them by a further material parody of the Word. The material that "heav'n's ray" causes to show forth as beauty "op'ning to the ambient light" (VI, 480 ff.), he industriously, with customary aspiration, makes into substance to destroy substance. Industry, science, free enterprise, munitions, and propaganda form the first of many alliances.

III

How does God plan to compensate for the indignities of those injured by Satan's new weapons? Do the good not require some compensatory grace?

That Satan's weapons will backfire is foreseeable in the very translation they make of angelic worship. With Christ's entry into battle, the epic style shifts from a parody of high pretense to apocalyptic symbolism. As the golden compass shapes the universe, drawing a circle around Chaos, so the chariot reestablishes order in Heaven by converting martial confusion back into "vision." (It later finishes constructing Hell as a scene consistent with Satan's sulphurous charge.) Primarily, it adds a new dimension to the awareness of those who bear witness to it. Rather than advancing behind a facade and exploding a secret weapon, Christ arrives blindingly obvious. He tells the elected angels to watch from their positions of moral and metaphysical standfastness ("Stand still in bright array . . . here stand," "stand only and behold," VI, 801, 810); and then by the clear language of lightning, he punishes the literal-mindedness of those untouched by less tangible signs—who hold mere words to be fraudulent:

> And from about him fierce Effusion roll'd
> Of smoke and bickering flame, and sparkles dire;
> Attended with ten thousand thousand Saints,
> He onward came, far off his coming shone.
> (VI, 765–768)

A thousand eyes see lightning, reveal truthful doom. The machine itself is "instinct with Spirit" (VI, 752). (Later in Milton's balancing of war by creation, these spirits living in the celestial equipage come forth spontaneously, touched by Christ's igniting force, VII, 201 ff.). Christ comes to the victors with "fair open Front / And breast" (what could he more!), propounding new terms that straight change good angels' minds. Except for this, all irony is set aside, and Milton awards the angels their serious recompense. Though evil remains forever astonishing, they can understand new glory; so seeing what is revealed, they fall not into strange vagaries but into a better dance "For joy of offer'd peace," wilder and more extravagant, to be sure, but only in terms of intenser ecstasy.

Technically, part of their closer union with God through the exaltation of Christ comes before the fall of Satan, as Christ's later announcement of his sacrifice on behalf of man rewards them with a sample of the same fortune that some men will have at the end of time. He makes mercy "first and last . . . brightest shine" (III, 134), which he could not have done without the Fall:

> Thus while God spake, ambrosial fragrance fill'd
> All Heav'n, and in the blessed Spirits elect
> Sense of new joy ineffable diffus'd:
> Beyond compare the Son of God was seen
> Most glorious, in him all his Father shone
> Substantially express'd, and in his face
> Divine compassion visibly appear'd,
> Love without end, and without measure Grace.
> (III, 135–142)

This heightened revelation constitutes a new covenant or dispensation for all creatures.

But this is not an easy point for Milton to demonstrate in purely descriptive terms, and here the dramatic method of contrasts by which the splinter state is defined despite its "bottomlessness" is used in reverse. If the state of good defines and intensifies evil, the evils of the public state in turn reinforce our sense of good. Sequentially, the cosmos, like man's portion of it, moves from pastoral (Heaven untested), to parody (the absurd-heroic in Satan's and Eve's rebellions), to a higher synthesis (heroic pastoral in Paradise Restored). But tactically the poem offers its contrasts as cross-referenced counterpoint at structurally appropriate moments.

When Satan promotes himself for the perilous journey to Eden, for instance, Milton expects us eventually to connect his maneuver and his followers' response to it with Christ's promise to descend to man and the responsive anthems of the elect. The cross-reference helps us with both our problems, the slippery rhetoric of politics and the compensatory grandeur of the faithful angels:

> intermit no watch
> Against a wakeful Foe, while I abroad
> Through all the Coasts of dark destruction seek
> Deliverance for us all: this enterprise
> None shall partake with me. Thus saying rose
> The Monarch, and prevented all reply,

> Prudent, lest from his resolution rais'd
> Others among the chief might offer now
> (Certain to be refus'd) what erst they fear'd;
> And so refus'd might in opinion stand
> His Rivals, winning cheap the high repute
> Which he through hazard huge must earn. But they
> Dreaded not more th' adventure than his voice
> Forbidding; and at once with him they rose;
> Thir rising all at once was as the sound
> Of Thunder heard remote. Towards him they bend
> With awful reverence prone; and as God
> Extol him equal to the highest in Heav'n:
> Nor fail'd they to express how much they prais'd,
> That for the general safety he despis'd
> His own.   (II, 462–482)

Whereas Christ's manifestation makes possible new levels of love from "numbers without number," Satan's proposal releases a new clamor, because each of his followers would win repute as a patriot at the expense of the others—if he could manage it solely by parliamentary means. As in Hobbes's condition of man, the condition of the angels "is the condition or war of everyone against everyone," and as in Hobbesian political theory, Satan's answer is totalitarianism: his self-exaltation cannot *be responded to* since it raises no analogical glory and establishes no heroic paradigm. It arouses only a kind of dreadful misresponse, the host's applause being the concerted act of those "leveled" by their common chill: "*Nor failed they* to express . . . ." Since Satan has preempted further discussion, they can do nothing but cheer and try to make it look convincing. Milton has ironic words of praise for their "unity" and Satan's inimitable style: "Thus they thir doubtful consultations dark / Ended rejoicing in their *matchless* Chief."

Actually, all positions disintegrate under the relentless pressure of Hell's metaphysical bottomlessness. The speakers find each of their general principles giving way beneath them. The defining contrasts are again the kingdom of well-founded blessedness and the new kingdom available to repentant Protestants. Whereas Hell provokes frantic and continual change, Adam and his seed will find a true heroic program; and whereas Satan's kingdom of war relies increasingly on hate, concealed behind a semblance of unselfish leadership and devotion of the followers, Christ's scepter will be laid aside as the kingdom of saints dispenses with law and relics upon the bond of love made manifest.

The quickness of Satan's shifts in platform also contrasts to the certain, unerrant foreshadowings of destiny which bind the good angels to the program of the "church." Beginning with the proposition that they need not consider Heaven lost, Satan bases his "fortunate fall" on the several inconsistent versions of restoration:

> From this descent
> Celestial Virtues rising, will appear
> More glorious and more dread than from no fall
> And trust themselves to fear no second fate:
> Mee though just right and the fixt Laws of Heav'n
> Did first create your Leader, next, free choice,
> With what besides, in Counsel or in Fight,
> Hath been achiev'd of merit, yet this loss
> Thus far at least recover'd, hath much more
> Establisht in a safe unenvied Throne
> Yielded with full consent. The happier state
> In Heav'n, which follows dignity, might draw
> Envy from each inferior; but who here
> Will envy whom the highest place exposes
> Foremost to stand against the Thunderer's aim
> Your bulwark, and condemns to greatest share
> Of endless pain? where there is then no good
> For which to strive, no strife can grow up there
> From Faction.   (II, 14–32)

The difficulty is that to claim justice from the fixed law of Heaven is to raid ordinances they have already abandoned, which installed Christ as mediary. Sensing the implications of this argument, Satan reconstitutes the government as an elective monarchy: he has been nominated by full consent, has he not? Then sensing that any power established by election can be transferred by election, he argues that his throne is safe because unenvied: it has been a bad job from the beginning, no one would want it now, and with the prospect of being struck by lightning, the future looks equally grim. Momentarily for purposes of that argument, their prospect is assumed to be endless pain and they are allowed "no good / For which to strive," though strive they must.

Satan obviously cannot have it both ways: either he rules unenvied forever in Hell or puts his tenure in jeopardy among those who might want the job under better circumstances. The former

alternative leaves them without a plot and the latter with an
endlessly splintering kingdom. The dilemma from the standpoint
of governmental covenant is the same as that of the original rebellion: if all angels are equal, Satan has no inherited right to his
position; and if hierarchy prevails, he should not have rebelled.
That he rules by daring and intimidation in a military state is
lost in the rapid shuffle of political theories. But because the last
of his positions—that he protects them from endless pain by
drawing off much of the thunder and lightning that might land
on them—again leaves them with no principle of unity, and because they cannot define "God" accurately without giving up,
Satan returns to the notion that they are owed certain rights and
must now reclaim them:

> we now return
> To claim our just inheritance of old,
> Surer to prosper than prosperity
> Could have assur'd us.   (II, 37–40)

Though the last part is mere rhetoric, we are otherwise back
in direct contrast to the language of Heaven, with its solid state,
its traditions, its eternal decrees, where words demarcate un-
breakable boundaries. To those who live in the state of irony,
such statements are continually under siege by truth: Hell is an
extended conceit, a running comparison of nothingness to Everything, and those who would keep from collapsing need great
acrobatic skill.

IV

We pass now from the Ministry of War and Propaganda, Department of Interior, and Parliament to the State Department and
its foreign policy, which involves us in the problem of place,
home ground, and the satanic journey to Eden, where Satan nego-
tiates across his national boundaries. Adam's native perspective
is from a given place, and his poetry responds to the given terrain
and creatures of Eden: he looks up to God and appropriately
raises his voice in invocation, and he looks outward and hymns
what he sees as an analogy to God. Everything that he needs to
know is obvious to him or can be explained by Raphael. Satan,
however, must transport himself if he is to see, and speak in
guarded whispers at critical moments. Ignorance puts him in

motion: since foreign policy depends on intelligence reports, he becomes an uprooted spy defying chains and limits and exposing the limits of his vision. The difference between good and bad news—gospel and war intelligence—is clear when we think of the other angel messengers to earth, Raphael, Michael, and Gabriel. Even without the assistance of the poem's other messengers, however, we realize that Satan is a badly informed ambassador. Promising wisdom and aspiring to great ends himself, he begins as a quick-witted sleuth:

> Knowledge forbidd'n?
> Suspicious, reasonless. Why should thir Lord
> Envy them that?
>
> .   .   .   .
>
> Hence I will excite thir minds
> With more desire to know, and to reject
> Envious commands, invented with design
> To keep them low whom Knowledge might exalt
> Equal with Gods; aspiring to be such
> They taste and die: what likelier can ensue?
> But first with narrow search I must walk round
> This Garden, and no corner leave unspi'd.
>   (IV, 515–517, 522–529)

While maintaining that God's envy keeps others low, the best that Satan can do with his own curiosity is make a "narrow search" around the garden, to pry into this and that. His misinterpretation of Christ's enlightenment has spread into a misreading of the Word as incarnated in Eden's sacramental nature and into a suspicious discovery of "designs" and plots. Yet he perceptively realizes that the ignorance of Adam and Eve is a foundation on which to build a state of ruin. The processes of canny reason bring the sentence up short and the mind pivots looking for further enemy signs. The soliloquy proceeds with the rubbing of hands and wary glances as evidence of envy appears everywhere. The word "knowledge" and the scope of prophecy shrink; enlightenment once given freely as one's right is now sought with labor under bushes.

The central episodes of this counterconspiracy are Satan's sly approach to Eve and Eve's to the apple. With Eve a similar intellectual shrinkage sets in immediately, which adds pathos to her ratification of Satan's intelligence. She accepts his notion that

God's order is a vast plot, as divine wisdom becomes a secret and her assigned place a prison. Though her language incorporates a new range of insinuation and deviousness, she loses the analogical reflections of glory in the bounded, material things around her. She wants to rule them and must destroy their integrity to accommodate her romantic aspiration, meanwhile hoping that she herself can maneuver unobserved:

> Experience, next to thee I owe,
> Best guide; not following thee, I had remain'd
> In ignorance, thou op'n'st Wisdom's way,
> And giv'st access, though secret she retire.
> And I perhaps am secret; Heav'n is high,
> High and remote to see from thence distinct
> Each thing on Earth, and other care perhaps
> May have diverted from continued watch
> Our great Forbidder, safe with all his Spies
> About him.   (IX, 807–816)

Thus for the fallen Adam and Eve, too, what was curiosity becomes secret intelligence, wielded against an adversary safe among his spies (true messengers of wisdom they seemed before); and later even in looking at each other they will suddenly see themselves as forbidden objects. Parts will become "private" and need to be covered. Eve's glimpse of godhead thus quickly degenerates into the coy peeping of flirtation, and she approaches Adam with the glib tongue we remember from Satan's handling of Beelzebub. Telling of and seeing things "invisible to mortal sight" henceforth has a lower range of insinuations, with a native quickness of discernment and many syntactical flickers of suspicion. Their discovery of satanic ambiguity is in part, then, a discovery of incongruity between high designs and the lowest measures of bedroom politics. It will not be corrected until the second angel messenger accommodates his "news" to human intelligence and educates them in the ways of knowledge, wrested from the confusions of good and evil mixed, and in the communion of divine and human nature granted by the new covenant.

Whereas the Word creates, covenants maintain. As one would expect, the covenants of the celestial and infernal kingdoms are as different as their means of bearing witness. In Heaven a covenant is *enlightenment* translated as *law*, and the law, of course, directly concerns enlightenment—how much of it and what kind a given creature is permitted. A covenant is a categorical imperative whose original form is the "let there be" of the Logos with its completion in citations of forms fixed in their estates. Its application to individuals results in their being fixed in the orders and logical ranks prescribed for them in successive days of creation (*logical* priority taking the form of *chronological* priority, as Kenneth Burke points out). The covenant is summed up in one's title, as "Adam" means "man, the creature of clay," patriarch of a race. Each creature receives his being for all duration unless he himself revokes his title and seeks something higher.

In contrast, Satan's covenants derive from expediency and the necessities of continuous negotiation among partisans. The pressure of time weighs against them, both in the forming and in the breaking. For as he invents illusion and the bottomlessness of place, Satan predictably invents time in the sense of the erosion and shifting of bonds. Hurried expediency in meeting ever-recurring crises of state characterizes the tactics of his military government. Satan and his followers are continually shoring up weakened dignity, inventing new plots to meet ever-surprising turns of affairs:

> Thrones, Dominations, Princedoms, Virtues, Powers,
> If these magnific Titles yet remain
> Not merely titular, since by Decree
> Another now hath to himself ingross't
> All Power, and us eclipst under the name
> Of King anointed, for whom all this haste
> Of midnight march, and hurried meeting here,
> This only to consult how we may best
> With what may be devis'd of honors new
> Receive him coming to receive from us
> Knee-tribute yet unpaid
>
> . . . .
>
> Orders and Degrees
> Jar not with liberty, but well consist.
> Who can in reason then or right assume
> Monarchy over such as live by right
> His equals, if in power and splendor less,
> In freedom equal? or can introduce
> Law and Edict on us, who without law
> Err not? much less for this to be our Lord,
> And look for adoration to th' abuse
> Of those Imperial Titles which assert
> Our being ordain'd to govern, not to serve?
>   (V, 772–782, 792–802)

Satan finds Christ a king merely in name, and hence devises new honors for the new phenomenon, an empty "title." Yet, if all of them were equal or their titles equally in question as he makes Christ's, none would be "ordain'd to govern": whatever their positions, they would not be "Imperial" except by the same power that makes Christ monarch. In point of fact, titles seem imminently in danger to Satan, because he does not really believe in covenants and interprets them as unnecessary restrictions in both knowledge and power.

Satan's view of covenants bears directly upon Adam and Eve, whose covenant is pronounced clearly upon Adam's creation as its sustaining law. "Be fruitful, multiply, and fill the Earth, / Subdue it, and throughout Dominion hold" (VII, 531–532), and of course, beware "the interdicted tree." This decree provides a program of idyllic action which allows them to imitate God's creativity and power in propagating a kingdom (though "subdue" may seem too strong a word for what they are to do since there is no resistance). As we realize in observing Satan's view of covenants, their prohibition, though inexplicable with regard to this particular tree of Eden, is a sign of the total decrees by which bounds are given to all things. If all atoms of the universe were raised to infinite power, they would be "equalized" into chaos. Power is meaningful only as a relative term incompatible with unresisted free will: *decree* is inherent in *degree*, the opposite of con-fusion (fusion of equal substances) and of consubstantiality. (Milton uses both "confusion" and "equality," along with "perplexity," "astonishment," and "amazement" as opposites to the standfast group.) To disobey edicts is indeed to "die" by destroying the bounds of one's being. The tree is a "provoking object," as Milton calls it in *Christian Doctrine*, not in the sense that it is attractive and desirable (though Satan's description of it to Eve makes it seem so) but in the sense that it sets an apparently arbitrary limit to free will in Eden. Before the Fall, it is a *mysterious* provocation, however, resembling the invisible provocation that tempts Satan to probe God's unimaginable power; and as long as it remains mysterious it does not provoke either wit or punitive guilt, merely a celebration of the mystery itself and a tactful probing of the line one is not permitted to cross.

The sanctification of the ranks and degrees in covenants partially explains the erosion of Satan's being after the rebellion and his need to reconstitute his kingdom continuously, yet his incapacity to sustain a contractual agreement: even if he wanted to hold to his bond, the uncertainty of his own status would make his signature a forgery. In crossing the line, his own being is lost; it is drawn into the dissolving quantities of the state of flux. As his diplomatic handling of Chaos and Old Night and the temptation of Eve illustrate, his method of foreign courtship is based on misinformation and cloudy intent: he cannot foresee all contingencies as God can in granting a new covenant to Adam. Yet the temptations of *Paradise Lost* and the new covenants that arise from them do sometimes spring from a legitimate sensing of other orders with which one wants a connection. Eve senses the hierarchy above her as Satan senses Christ's station and as Sin senses the possibility of a better place for herself in Eden. The rumor of God's binding oath to man and its confirmation in Heaven not only sets Satan on his exploratory journey but eventually, when verified, sends Adam on the wayfaring path to regeneration. Though Satan proves incapable of making them permanent, the covenants that he proposes are therefore basically imitations of the Messiah's verbal confirmations. To travel among the various orders is to make encounters in pursuit of the Word's variants, to subscribe to new bonds, and to make oneself known in turn. In making covenants as in all other things—warfare, spying, speechmaking—Satan has the contagiousness of the creative impulse.

But he can only *affect* "equality with God, / In imitation of that Mount whereon / Messiah was declar'd in sight of Heav'n" (V, 764–765); he must settle for counterfeit contracts to hold the *disjecta membra* of his alliance together and is reminded at every turn of his own betrayal. While other creatures can forget their missions and live casually within the bounds established for them, Satan, God-obsessed, confronts his limits at every turn: every aspect of the created order that he encounters provokes knowledge of his antagonism. Seeking to have an impact on the original creation and be the active mover of all plots, he receives all blows himself, passively unable to ward them off. Having fathered paradox and surprise, he must abide by them and be the butt of all jokes. Meanwhile his capacity to maintain his alliance in Hell is also undermined. Whatever the source of his instinct for splintering, his final position is clearly predicted in Book X as he appears before the host without a cohesive rhetoric to unite them and the good news of his triumph turns to ashes in the saying. The fate of the diplomat (a professional liar abroad but supposedly honored at home) is to hiss and be answered in kind by his wordless choir, which wins unanimity only in its joylessness.

4

The Theme of *Paradise Lost,* Book III

ISABEL G. MACCAFFREY

▼

Readers of *Paradise Lost* have been aware almost from the poem's first appearance that the individual books of the epic are coherent substructures within an intricately articulated whole. There are, in fact, many structural units of varying size to be discerned within this whole, each exhibiting its own order, yet all reflecting from different angles Milton's central controlling imagination. Book III offers an enlightening instance of his skill in unfolding his themes so that all aspects of the great argument shall be successively given due weight, without at any point allowing us to lose sight of the main design. In the overall structure, the third book marks a major narrative transition. Within the cosmography of *Paradise Lost*, it is also a transition from one area to another since, through Book VI, narrative structure and spatial plan are virtually identified. This shift in perspective coincides with a concentration of thematic focus upon a particular aspect of Milton's enormous subject. The poem treats the ways of God to men; Book III deals specifically with divine epistemology, the ways whereby men can know, or come to know, God.

The shift of focus is first intimated when Milton arrests his poem's narrative momentum. Satan's voyage is interrupted at the point when he glimpses "this pendant World" at the close of Book II; it is resumed about the middle of Book III when, catching a "gleame / Of dawning light," he turns heavenward. The gleam emanates from that Holy Light whose illumination Satan will never again experience directly, but which the poet, a virtuous though fallen human being, has "revisited" in the first half of the book. The theme of "approaching heaven" is therefore called to our attention at the moment when the poem's temporal forward movement is interrupted, to be transposed into another mode of discourse. Throughout *Paradise Lost*, and most notably here, Milton counterpoints and periodically suspends the linear momentum by removing us from the flux of time and allowing us to share a divine or angelic point of view.

The speeches of the divine personages—the famous Dialogue in Heaven—occur during the suspension of action in the first half of Book III, and they inevitably provide the main axis for the book. The nature of their function has not, perhaps, been fully understood. There is involved here a theoretical problem concerning the way in which "ideas," more or less nakedly presented, function in poetry. The mere purveying of information is usually the least important role of such conceptual passages. An early instance is the speech of Theseus at the end of *The Knight's Tale*; its purpose is not primarily to convey stoic doctrine, but to provide for Chaucer's audience a "pagan" perspective, allowing them to place the action they have witnessed in a larger Christian context which the poet does not refer to directly. And so it is with the utterances of Father and Son in *Paradise Lost*. The doctrine conveyed was familiar to all of Milton's readers, and a great part of what God recites is to be dramatized in the action later on, or at least reiterated in the angels' discourses. What should engage our attention, then, is less the "content" of these passages than the fact that they enter into the poem's composition at all, and enter it *here*. This essay concerns their oblique expressiveness as part of that tacit statement that makes up the total meaning of *Paradise Lost*. This meaning derives from familiar literary elements: rhetoric, point of view, imagery and allusion, and dramatic interaction of personages—including one who is often ignored, the poet as narrator.

One of the narrator's primary functions, throughout the poem,

is to make possible narrative modulations like that at the opening of Book III. Up to this point, both narrator and audience
have participated in the temporal patterns expressed through the
fallen angels and the subplot of Satan's voyage. As the first sinful
creatures, they can exist only in the time-bound, future-haunted
mode of being that is our own constant condition. Dissociating
himself after two books from this point of view, the bard moves
into another universe of discourse, the timeless realm of Light.
The opening of the invocation which he now utters defines this
Light's being "before the Sun" (the Sun's presence at the end
of Book III will figure the redescent into time); the last part
removes the speaker from temporal pressures and limitations, as
befits his present situation.

> Thus with the Year
> Seasons return, but not to mee returns
> Day, or the sweet approach of Ev'n or Morn,
> Or sight of vernal bloom, or Summers Rose.
>   (III, 40–43)[1]

The passage is poignantly personal, but in the poem's large
scheme it is preparing us for a movement away from seasonal
cycles and "Natures works" to the cause of seasons and nature,
the still center of the universe where "mortal sight" is helpless.

Several features of this invocation deserve scrutiny if we are
considering the part played by Book III in Milton's justification
of God's ways to men. As Anne Ferry has shown,[2] the narrative
voice in *Paradise Lost* speaks sometimes as Everyman, trying to
fathom the mysteries of his predicament, and sometimes as the
bard, gifted with special privileges and power of "sight." The
narrator's "obscure sojourn" imitates the path of the human
soul, from the depths of fallen nature to recognition of the true
Son, the "sovran vital Lamp." With the *but* of line 22, we begin
to hear the voice of the bard whose blindness, shutting him out
from the book of Nature's works, enables him with extraordinary
concentration to fix his inner gaze on those spiritual verities that,
in St. Augustine's phrase, can be seen only by the eyes of the

---

[1] I have used the text of Helen Darbishire in the Oxford English Texts
series for Milton's poems: *The Poetical Works of John Milton*, 2 vols.
(Oxford, 1952–1955). Citations of the prose are from *The Student's
Milton*, ed. F. A. Patterson (2d ed.; New York, 1933), abbreviated *SM*.

[2] *Milton's Epic Voice: The Narrator in Paradise Lost* (Cambridge,
Mass., 1963). The terms I use to describe the two voices are not Mrs.
Ferry's.

mind, "pure from every taint of the body." Milton alludes to two
kinds of "vision" in his prologue: ordinary sight, which approaches God through the creatures, and the mind's sight which,
irradiated "through all her powers" by Celestial Light, can approach "unapproached Light," the truths of God, in a manner
analogous to physical sight. Augustine writes thus of the inner
and outer eyes:

> Reason . . . promises to let you see God with your mind as the
> sun is seen with the eye. The mind has, as it were, eyes of its
> own, analogous to the soul's senses. . . . And it is God himself
> who illumines all. I, Reason, am in minds as the power of look-
> ing is in the eyes.[3]

The question raised in the invocation concerns the powers of this
second sight—precisely what "things invisible" it will be permitted to "see," and how far it can penetrate.

It is not an accident that Milton in the next verse-paragraph
imagines the world as seen by God; bending down his eye, the
Father "surveys" the extended universe, and the poet's inner eye
follows his in imagination, for twenty lines reproducing the objects of divine survey at the moment of (human) time which
the poem's temporal plot has achieved. There is a static, visually
conveyed tableau: "About him all the Sanctities of Heaven," "on
his right" the Son, "on Earth . . . / Our two first Parents"; then
"Hell and the Gulf between, and *Satan* there." With this panorama, the poet has demonstrated that his prayer for the power to
render "things invisible" in the mode of imagination has not
been in vain. But with line 77, there is a movement away from
God's "physical" vision, which the poet's fiction allows him to
share, to a special timeless foreseeing which is beyond the power
of visualization.

> Him God beholding from his prospect high,
> Wherein past, present, future he beholds,
> Thus to his onely Son foreseeing spake.   (III, 77–79)

---

[3] *Soliloquies*, I.vi.12, in *Augustine: Earlier Writings*, trans. J. H. S.
Burleigh (Philadelphia, 1953), p. 30. See also the passage from *De
Trinitate*, vii: "Thus, in that realm of eternal truth from which all things
temporal were made, we behold with our mind's eye the pattern upon
which our being is ordered, and which rules all . . . in ourselves or in
the outer world. Thence we conceive a truthful knowledge of things,
which we have within us as a kind of *word*, begotten by an inward
speech." *Augustine: Later Works*, trans. John Burnaby (Philadelphia,
1955), p. 65.

Moving from sight to foresight, the poetry enters upon a new rhetoric. What follows is curious, when we consider that up to now Milton's lines have been saturated with references to vision, sight, eyes, underlined by the poet's definition of his genre in lines 51 through 55 as that visionary poetry that Blake was later to commend. Yet in the following section we, the audience, *see* almost nothing; God "sees," but our mode of apprehension shifts from seeing to hearing, and we are aware primarily of a voice speaking from its unapproachable sanctuary.[4]

Not only is God the Father invisible to us, but what he sees, once it has moved beyond the range of created space, is also inaccessible to the powers even of visionary poetry. The potent vision that Milton must now translate for us is the gaze of Providence, described by Boethius and many others: "ille omnia suo cernit aeterno."

> Quae sint, quae fuerint veniantque
> Uno mentis cernit in ictu;
> Quem, quia respicit omnia solus,
> Verum possis dicere solem.[5]

"The true Sun," fountain of light, beholds all time in one eternal instant; beholds, not only events in our "future," as human prophets have sometimes done, but their significance and total design as conceived by himself in "the infinite spaces of that which is past and to come."[6]

The Dialogue in Heaven, which has been the source of so many conflicting judgments by students of Milton, was contrived to communicate a distinction between divine and human understanding, and it must be read as a tacit statement concerning man's distance from God and the bewildering difficulty that attends our efforts to know him. The divinely illuminated bard can render imaginatively in poetry, through a kind of transcendent "memory," the vast spaces of God's creation and the primeval events played out in them; they are to be the substance of the poet's narrative as he approaches the Garden, the angelic visitants, the War in Heaven. This power of imagining was recog-

---

[4] See Jackson I. Cope, *The Metaphoric Structure of Paradise Lost* (Baltimore, 1962), p. 167.

[5] *Consolation of Philosophy,* Bk. V, met. ii, trans. "I. T.," rev. H. F. Stewart, in *Boethius* (Loeb Classical Library, London, 1953), p. 372.

[6] *Ibid.,* Bk. V, prosa vi, pp. 403–405.

nized in traditional epistemology; St. Augustine, for example, had allowed for a kind of "seeing" which he called *spiritual,* "by which we think of corporeal things that are absent."

> We think of heaven and earth and the visible things in them even when we are in the dark. In this case we see nothing with the eyes of the body but in the soul behold corporeal images: whether true images, representing the bodies that we have seen and still hold in memory, or fictitious images, fashioned by the power of thought.[7]

It is a special version of this power for which Milton prays in his invocation; he desires the Muse to "plant eyes" in the soul which will be able to "see" the great events of mankind's past history *as if* they had been "seen and still [held] in memory"—with the validity, that is, of Augustine's "true images," and not those "fictitious images" merely "fashioned" by the individual poet. Such powers were granted to the bards and (with reference to future time) to the prophets mentioned in lines 35 and 36, and Milton aspires to be numbered among them.

He does not aspire beyond that, however. Augustine had held that the truths of God are *invisible;* where they, and not the external events of history are concerned, analogies with physical sight are analogies merely. And Milton insists that the things now to be spoken of in *Paradise Lost* are invisible even to immortal sight: "brightest Seraphim / Approach not, but with both wings veil their eyes" (III, 381–382). The approach to God—not only the actual throne of glory, but the mysteries of his providential design—must be indirect. This bard cannot present

---

[7] "Ipsum quippe coelum et terram, et ea quae in eis videre possumus, etiam in tenebris constituti cogitamus; ubi nihil videntes oculis corporis, animo tamen corporales imagines intuemur, seu veras, sicut ipsa corpora videmus, et memoria retinemus; seu fictas, sicut cogitatio formare potuerit" (*De Genesi ad Litteram Libri XII,* XII.vi.15, in J.-P. Migne, *Patrologiae Cursus Completus* . . . , Series Latina, 221 vols. [Paris, 1844–1889], XXXIV, col. 458, hereafter abbreviated as Migne.) The translation in the text is that of J. H. Taylor, printed in *The Essential Augustine,* ed. Vernon J. Bourke (Mentor ed.; New York, 1964), p. 94. I do not attach special weight to Augustine's formulation, knowing Milton's scornful attitude toward even the patron saint of Protestantism. His debt to the Fathers was, of course, more considerable than he acknowledged. For other references to the "kinds of sight" and a discussion of the invocation, see A. B. Chambers, "Wisdom at One Entrance Quite Shut Out: *Paradise Lost,* III, 1–55," *PQ,* XLII (1963), 114–119; reprinted in *Milton: Modern Essays in Criticism,* ed. A. E. Barker (New York, 1965).

immediately in poetry the divine transcendence of time, the power that "sees" temporal patterns as spatial. The interlude from line 77 of Book III to the end of the celestial colloquy (line 343) thus acknowledges the failure of the poet's visionary powers and defines the boundary at which that failure occurs. It is followed by the angels' song, appropriately enough, as Augustine suggests in explaining the feebleness of human capacity in praising even the creatures.

> Now if in considering these creatures of God human language is so at a loss, what is it to do in regard to the Creator? When words fail, can aught but triumphant music remain? *I have gone round and have offered in His tabernacle a sacrifice of jubilation.*[8]

The "sacrifice of jubilation" is offered by the heavenly hosts, recorded by the bard whose own words have failed.

Yet Milton is committed to justifying the ways of God *to men,* and at least one meaning of the phrase implies, "in terms that men can comprehend." If a direct approach through visibly rendered images transcends the power even of the Heavenly Muse, some other means must be found to compass the providential mysteries and the drama of salvation. This means was available to the poet—and to men in general—in consequence of the divine condescension, centrally manifest in the taking on of flesh, which accommodates the godhead to human capacities. The peculiar channel of this condescension is, of course, the record of its revelation in history (i.e., Scripture), the second of the great books from which we derive knowledge of God.

> Man's knowledge of divine things is threefold. The first is when man, by the natural light of reason, rises through creatures to the knowledge of God. The second is when the divine truth which surpasses human intelligence comes down to us by way of revelation, yet not as shown to him that he may see it, but as expressed in words so that he may hear it. The third is when the human mind is raised to the perfect intuition of things revealed.[9]

The first of these modes of approach to God involves the "book of the creatures," from which the bard of *Paradise Lost* is cut

[8] *In Psalmos Enarrationes,* xxvi, Sermon 2, in *On the Psalms,* trans. S. Hebgin and F. Corrigan, 2 vols. (London, 1960), I, 273.
[9] Thomas Aquinas, *Summa Contra Gentiles,* IV.1. Literally translated by the English Dominican Fathers, 4 vols. (London, 1929), IV, 3.

off by his blindness, but which remains accessible to his characters: to Adam and Eve, to Uriel, and even to Satan, though he repudiates it. The second mode, requiring a countermovement down the scale from Heaven to earth, is imitated in the celestial dialogue. The third possibility, mystical vision, is excluded by Milton from his poem. The reasons for this have something to do with Milton's theological position and its effect on the imagining of *Paradise Lost,* especially its genre. The *Divine Comedy* is a dream vision, a genre that allowed for the dramatizing of mystical experience; as several critics have suggested, Aquinas' "perfect intuition" is reproduced by Dante in the *Paradiso* as the pilgrim's fictively immediate experience.[10] Milton's poem, generically very different, dramatizes an action whose crises occurred in the past or will occur in the future; the poem's fictional "present" is the time span in which the bard undertakes the recounting of these events, and neither the epic genre nor the poet's Protestant bias admits the possibility of a fictive present of dream-vision in which final things are rendered as if they were literally present to the dreamer.

God's "survey of the divine plan of salvation" derives, as Northrop Frye has said, from the encyclopedic Puritan sermon of the seventeenth century; the four hundred lines spoken by the Father in Book III "constitute a sermon of this type preached by God himself."[11] The fact that the mysteries are thus presented mediately, not immediately, verbally, not iconographically has several implications relevant to the theme of Book III—man's knowledge of the divine—and Milton's definition of his narrator's role and powers within the poem, which restates this major theme from a somewhat different point of view. Returning to Augustine's distinction between the imagination's corporeal "seeing" and the mind's eye, we recall that the former is appropriate only for reanimating the images of memory or invention. The latter can apprehend "love itself," the ultimate mystery.

> But love can neither be seen in its own essence with the eyes of the body nor be thought of in the spirit by means of an image

---

[10] See Vincent F. Hopper, *Medieval Number Symbolism* (New York, 1938), p. 157 n.; C. S. Singleton, *Dante Studies II: Journey to Beatrice* (Cambridge, Mass., 1958), pp. 23 ff.

[11] *The Return of Eden: Five Essays on Milton's Epics* (Toronto, 1965), p. 10.

like a body; but only in the mind, that is, in the intellect, can it be known and perceived.[12]

The chief means of acquiring this intellectual knowledge, for man, is through reading God's Word. The divine "sermon" of Book III acknowledges this, and the new rhetoric begun in line 77 is Milton's device for expressing the *nature* of our understanding of providential truth. God *speaks* to his creatures—the angels and the overhearing narrator—"descending" to provide that truth which the study of creation alone cannot supply.

Milton's well-known remarks in the *Christian Doctrine* on our conception of God may be usefully recalled here:

> We ought to entertain such a conception of him, as he, in condescending to accommodate himself to our capacities, has shown that he desires we should conceive. For it is on this very account that he has lowered himself to our level, lest in our flights above the reach of human understanding, and beyond the written word of Scripture, we should be tempted to indulge in vague cogitations and subtleties.[13]

The passage will recall to every reader of *Paradise Lost* the conversation in Book VIII between Raphael and Adam, the latter acquiescing in the angel's statement that "Heav'n is for thee too high / To know what passes there" (VIII, 172–173). There is, I believe, a relationship between the theme of Adam's obedience—at first perfect, then fatally wanting—and the narrator's conception of his material in Book III. One of the functions of the poem's fictive speaker is to enact the paradigm of virtuous behavior accessible to fallen man. This process can be seen in the poet's prayer in Book VII to be returned to his "Native Element" before his steed flies too high. It culminates in the prologue to Book IX where the poet's allusion to his Celestial Patroness is related to his choice of the new heroism of patience as his subject. His own patience (humility is its other name) is demonstrated in the acknowledgment that his poetic powers depend entirely upon her nightly visitations. The inspiration of the poem is carefully placed within divine dispensation; earlier, it was linked, at once presumptuously and humbly, with the Heavenly Muse who had visited Moses. Moses, Milton tells us in the *Christian*

---

[12] "Dilectio autem nec per substantiam suam potest oculis corporis cerni, nec per imaginem corporis similem spiritu cogitari, sed sola mente, id est intellectu, cognosci et percipi" (*De Genesi,* XII.xi.22, in Migne, XXXIV, col. 462).

[13] I.ii, in *SM,* p. 923.

Doctrine, is "in a certain sense . . . a type of Christ" as Mediator.[14] The author of the Pentateuch and the incarnate Word of God, typologically identified, are prototypes for the "patient" Christian poet, also favored by Urania. No wonder, then, that Milton depicted his persona as a bard obedient to the Word in all senses of the term; this obedience would include the belief that God must not be depicted in any fictive manner devised by merely human power, but must enter a Christian poem (if he enters it at all) in terms sanctioned by himself, the terms of Scripture.[15]

The special kind of humility that is expressed through complete submission to Scripture is, of course, particularly associated with Protestantism, and is specifically claimed by Milton at the beginning of the *Christian Doctrine.* It is discoverable in Protestant exegesis of Scripture, for example in the commentary on Revelation by the Swiss theologian, Augustin Marlorat. Here he speaks of the six wings of the angels (associating with Revelation 4 : 8 the passage from Isaiah 6 quoted by Milton in Book III, lines 381–382).

> The two wings wherewith they couered their faces, bewray right well, that not euen the Angelles are able to abide the brightnesse of God, and that they are so dazeled at the sight of God, as we be at the beholding of the sunne when he shyneth out. Now if the Angelles be not able to endure the maiestie of God: what a rashnesse is it of man, to goe about to rush so far forth? We may learne therefore, that we ought not to search for any more of God, than is meete and expedient: yet did not the Angels so hyde their faces, but they had some sight of God: for they flew not at all aduentures. So also must wee looke vpon God, howbeeit no more than the abilitie of our nature will beare. His maiestie shall be euident inough vnto vs, so long as we bee in this worlde, if we set it before vs to looke vpon in the glasse of the Gospell.[16]

"The glasse of the Gospell," a verbal, mediate way of approaching God, is the one adopted by Milton in the first part of Book

[14] I.xv, in *SM,* p. 1009.

[15] On Scriptural echoes in the Dialogue, see M. Y. Hughes, "The Filiations of Milton's Celestial Dialogue," in *Ten Perspectives on Milton* (New Haven, 1965), pp. 104–135.

[16] *A Catholike exposition vpon the Reuelation of Sainct Iohn* (London, 1574), p. 75. The commentary is of some interest for English literary history as having been translated by Arthur Golding. It is, in fact, a kind of anthology of commentary, compiled by Marlorat.

III. The genre is the sermon, which traditionally expounded Scripture. The matter is doctrine, the rationale of God's providential plan, as distinct from the events that compose its actual unfolding in history.

A similar kind of distinction between event (accessible to the visionary "eye") and doctrine (comprehended aurally) may be observed in the last two books of *Paradise Lost.* As critics have observed, Book XII is less completely realized, in terms of sensory detail, than its companion, Book XI. Addison noted in 1712 that "the exhibiting part of the history of mankind in vision, and part in narrative, is as if an history-painter should put in colors one half of his subject, and write down the remaining part of it." In spite of his negative judgment, Addison accurately discerned the reason for the change: "the difficulty which the poet would have found to have shadowed out so mixed and complicated a story in visible objects."[17] The story in Book XII is "mixed and complicated" in a particular sense made plain by Milton when he distinguished the two units of narrative into two separate books in 1674. The Arguments added then underline the distinction: in Book XI, Michael "sets before him in vision what shall happen till the Flood" while in Book XII, the Angel "comes by degrees to explain" such doctrines as Christ's "incarnation, death, resurrection, and ascension: the state of the Church till his second coming." In the first instance, Michael is called by Adam "true op'ner of mine eyes" (XI, 598); in the second, "Enlightner of my darkness" (XII, 271). Adam adds, "now first I finde / Mine eyes true op'ning" (XII, 273–274); this metaphorical eye-opening is *literaliter* the opening of the understanding to knowledge of God's mercy, "favour unmerited."

The situation of Adam in these final books is parallel to that of the poet in Book III; his visionary powers miraculously purged, Adam in Book XI wakes with his "mental sight" empowered to view things invisible in corporeal images: "To nobler sights / *Michael* from *Adams* eyes the Filme remov'd" (XI, 412–413). What follows is a series of masquelike spectacles, concluding with the great vision of the Deluge. Even these visions, however,

---

[17] *Spectator* #369, *Criticisms on Paradise Lost,* ed. A. S. Cook (New York, 1926), p. 148. For further remarks on Books XI and XII, compatible with mine, see H. R. MacCallum, "Milton and Sacred History," *Essays . . . Presented to A. S. P. Woodhouse* (Toronto, 1964), pp. 166–167.

must be "explained" by Michael before Adam comprehends their
meaning; the rhetorical pattern of exclamation, question, and
reply by the angel (e.g., XI, 500–529) enacts for us the dialectical mode in which our knowledge of God's ways must now be
mastered, and defines once more the limits of fallen human understanding. Finally, even the temporarily inspired visionary
power fails:

> I perceave
> Thy mortal sight to faile; objects divine
> Must needs impaire and wearie human sense.
> (XII, 8–10)

The voice of Michael takes over the narrative, as God's voice
strikes in to explicate the providential scheme in Book III. Voice
supplants vision, for much the same reason in each instance.
Michael is the "Seer blest" whose eye can pierce mysteries, as,
on a grander scale, God bends down his eye upon human history.
(The angel has been, Milton says in Book XI, line 115, specially
"enlightened" for his mission.) But what each *sees* can be given
to *us* (participating in the experience of the blind bard and of
Adam) only through our ears, the avenue of concepts, the path
to understanding.

The notion that certain kinds of truth may be audible but invisible long antedates Milton's intimation of it in *Paradise Lost*;
it is as old as the voice out of the whirlwind answering Job. In the
Catholic tradition, it is quaintly expressed in Lydgate's version
of *The Pilgrimage of the Life of Man*, where the Pilgrim is urged
by Grace Dieu to place his eyes in his ears in order to apprehend
the mystery of the Mass.

> And for to knowe the trouthe a-noon,
> And a trewe doom to make,
> A man muste the Eyen take,
> And to the Erys hem translate, . . .
> And ther, whan they be set aryht,
> They shal be cleryd so off syht
> To deme trouthe, and no-thyng erre,
> Bryht as any sonne or sterre.[18]

[18] *The Pilgrimage of the Life of Man,* Englisht by John Lydgate, ed.
F. J. Furnivall, Part I (London, 1899), 11. 6554–6562. (E.E.T.S., Ex.
Ser., LXXVII). In the *Anticlaudianus* of Alain de Lille, Theology chooses
Hearing, the second of five horses representing the senses, to draw the
chariot for the ascent to the Throne of God. *The "Anticlaudian" of Alain
de Lille,* trans. William H. Cornog (Philadelphia, 1935), p. 109.

The belief that the ear, as the least sensuous of the senses, is best fitted to receive the revelations of the supernatural was obviously congenial to Puritanism, and Thomas Greene has recently related Milton's religious position to his stress upon the "inner ear":

> His religion of the eye . . . did not really diminish the greater importance he laid upon the inner ear. This latter emphasis becomes immediately apparent if we think of the real purpose of Raphael's descent: to expound the truth. In this respect Milton's celestial messenger represents a unique departure from the convention. For he is despatched neither to prod nor to encourage nor to punish but to explain, almost indeed to lecture.[19]

Raphael's "lecture" is more amply illustrated than Michael's in Book XII, but Greene's point reiterates the importance of doctrinal matter and its discursive presentation in *Paradise Lost*. The stress placed by Protestants upon the expounding of the Word of God has been often noted; a favorite text was Romans 10 : 17, "So then faith cometh by hearing, and hearing by the word of God." This verse is used by Marlorat to illuminate Revelation 1 : 3 ("Blessed is he that readeth and heareth the words . . .").

> Notwithstanding forasmuch as it is not given to all menne to reade holie writ: there is expresse mention made of hearing, whiche ingendreth faith by the effectuall working of the holie Ghoste, in mens heartes.[20]

So in *Paradise Lost*, the Holy Spirit is invoked to "instruct" the bard, working as his habit is within "th' upright heart and pure" (I, 17–19). And in Book III, man is urged by God to *listen* to the voice of Conscience as a means of attaining "light."

> Whom if they will hear,
> Light after light well used they shall attain.
> (ll. 195–196)

So, finally, God's timeless vision is transposed to rhetoric that can outdistance the dazzled sight and touch the understanding.

---

[19] *The Descent from Heaven* (New Haven, 1963), p. 405.

[20] *Catholike exposition,* p. 6v. For a classical formulation, see Aristotle, *De Sensu et Sensibili,* 437a: "For developing intelligence, . . . hearing takes the precedence . . . . For rational discourse is a cause of instruction in virtue of its being audible, which it is, not directly but indirectly." The passage is quoted by Arnold Stein, *Answerable Style* (Minneapolis, 1953), p. 153, making a related point.

In Milton's choice of his mode for the Dialogue in Heaven, there is thus both doctrinal and aesthetic appropriateness. God is manifest in Book III as the Father and his expressive Word in colloquy.

> Son who art alone
> My word, my wisdom, and effectual might,
> All hast thou spoken as my thoughts are, all
> As my eternal purpose has decreed.   (ll. 169–172)

We are to read the speeches of the Son as his Father's spoken thoughts, his Word in a literal sense that is also a spiritual sense. The meanings of Book III emerge in the shape of an argument, an interior debate, and their aesthetic character is governed by their argumentative form. In the Cambridge manuscript, Milton had included, among his notes for a drama, a debate of Mercy and Justice; the debate materialized, transposed to an epic strain, in *Paradise Lost*, Book III.[21] The angels sing of "the strife / Of Mercy and Justice in thy face discern'd" (ll. 406–407). This is not to say that the debate is "dramatic" in any ordinary sense; the mode is dialectical, exposing for us in a form appropriate to "discourse of reason" the knowledge that we need in order to grasp God's plan.[22]

Three features of the material, therefore, dictate the verse in the first part of Book III. It is to convey *doctrine*, and therefore to be "heard" by our inner ears, not "seen" in imagination; here it resembles Book XII. It is a *debate*, stylized to be sure, but recognizably dialectical; we may think of *Paradise Regain'd*, Milton's most complex exercise in this manner. Finally, it is to convey God's foresight, his "simultaneous" vision; for this aspect of the subject, there is no analogue in Milton's poetry, or indeed in most other poetry, and the verse of Book III is to that extent a unique improvisation. The rhetoric can be described as a kind of skeletal or paradigmatic idiom, its language stripped of sensuous implication because designed to be spoken by a God who,

[21] For the background of this venerable literary motif, with appropriate comments on Milton, see Samuel C. Chew, *The Virtues Reconciled* (Toronto, 1947).

[22] Irene Samuel argues for the truly "dramatic" character of the colloquy in "The Dialogue in Heaven: A Reconsideration of *Paradise Lost*, III, 1–417," *PMLA*, LXXII (1957), 601–611, reprinted in Barker, *Modern Essays.* Jackson Cope calls it, "a rhetorical and nondramatic ritual," *Metaphoric Structure*, p. 173.

Milton wrote, "far transcends the powers of man's thoughts, much more of his perception."[23] We notice subliminally, I think, that something we have become used to in the style of *Paradise Lost* is missing; it is the weight of animistic implication, a dominant feature of Milton's "normal" style, which employs a language of persistent organic reference devised to render his sense of the vitality of Creation. The vitality of the Creator cannot be understood in the same way, however.

The rhetoric of the Dialogue has recently received pertinent comment by several critics, alert to the rhetorical stratagems available to Milton, so that the technical brilliance of his invention is more visible than it used to be.[24] The poet has fashioned a Platonic idiom, language moving through the range of its forms to suggest the universal scope of the ideas it designates. The Father's speeches are remarkable for their verbal acrobatics, a dance of words in which the life processes of a set of abstractions are manifest. This is especially noticeable in the first of his three long speeches (ll. 80–134), where the subjects are the Fall itself and its component concepts: freedom, necessity, and grace. *Free* is played upon in one set of lines:

> I made him just and right,
> Sufficient to have stood, though free to fall.
> Such I created all th' Ethereal Powers
> And Spirits, both them who stood & them who faild;
> Freely they stood who stood, and fell who fell.
> Not free, what proof could they have givn sincere
> Of true allegiance. . . .   (ll. 98–104)

Adjective, adverb, the negative of the adjective: in this sequence the range of man's possibilities is defined—*free, freely, not free.* The quality *freedom,* the noun, appears in line 109: "of freedom both despoild." The progress of Adam and Eve from act to condition is thus outlined.

A similar process can be observed in Milton's handling of the key word *fall:*[25] through future tense (l. 95), infinitive (l. 99), past tense (l. 102), the speaker sketches the various choices; at

---

[23] *Christian Doctrine,* I.ii, in *SM,* p. 923.

[24] See Stein, *Answerable Style,* pp. 127–130; Cope, *Metaphoric Structure,* chap. v *passim*; J. B. Broadbent, *Some Graver Subject: An Essay on Paradise Lost* (London, 1960), pp. 144–157.

[25] Noted by Cope, *Metaphoric Structure,* p. 174.

the end of the speech there is a kind of grammatical rhyme, binding together three successive lines:

> they themselves ordain'd thir fall.
> The first sort by thir own suggestion fell,
> Self-tempted, self-deprav'd: Man falls deceiv'd . . .
> (ll. 128–130)

Although, as Sir Thomas Browne observed, "in Eternity there is no distinction of tenses," Milton repeatedly uses linguistic accidence as a symbol of timelessness. Precisely because we do not ordinarily combine several tenses of the same verb in one sentence, their incorporation in one of the Father's periods conveys something of the strange inclusiveness of his vision. This effect is well summarized by J. B. Broadbent: "It represents the Father's speech as Logos, Alpha and Omega, I AM."[26]

There are a dozen linguistic sequences that reflect the artifice of eternity through rhetoric. God's third speech, dealing with the mystery of Incarnation, is full of verbal pairs that symbolize the paradoxes of redemption: *losing . . . lost* (1. 280), *thir nature . . . thy nature* (1. 282), *Man among men* (1. 283), *be restored . . . are restored* (ll. 288–289), *rise . . . rising . . . raise* (1. 296), *death . . . dying* (1. 299), *redeem . . . redeem* (ll. 299–300), *hate . . . hate* (ll. 298, 300), *destroyed . . . destroys* (1. 301).[27] Here one can observe both the progress through forms that records the accommodation of eternity to time, and an identity of terms reflecting Christ's service to mankind in the taking on of manhood. This aspect of God's "meaning" receives striking expression in the dramatic geometry of his question to the Hosts:

> He with his whole posteritie must die,
> Die hee or Justice must; unless for him
> Some other able, and as willing, pay
> The rigid satisfaction, death for death.
> Say Heav'nly Powers, where shall we find such love,
> Which of ye will be mortal to redeem
> Mans mortal crime, and just th' unjust to save,
> Dwels in all Heaven charitie so deare?
> (ll. 209–216)

[26] *Some Graver Subject*, p. 147. Broadbent's judgment of these speeches is negative, however.

[27] Cope calls the speech "an incredibly complex rhetorical knot," designed to convey "the paradox of the *felix culpa*," *Metaphoric Structure*, pp. 173–174.

"The rigid satisfaction" is linguistically reproduced in the chiasmus of the last four lines, where *mortal* echoes *mortal*; *just*, *unjust*; and in the framing lines *such love* is matched by *charitie so deare*.

These stylistic details will be familiar under traditional technical names to readers of Renaissance rhetoric books. Most of them fall into the group designated by Puttenham as "figures Sententious, otherwise called Rhetoricall." They are said to be especially useful to the orator, whichever of the three conventional ends he pursues, "to pleade, or to praise, or to advise." The orator addresses the ear, and through it, the understanding.

> For to say truely, what els is man but his minde? which, whosoever have skil to compasse, and make yeelding and flexible, what may not he commaund the body to perfourme? He therefore that hath vanquished the minde of man, hath made the greatest and most glorious conquest. But the minde is not assailable unlesse it be by sensible approaches, whereof the audible is of greatest force for instruction or discipline: the visible, for apprehension or exterior knowledges as the Philosopher saith. Therefore the well tuning of your words and clauses to the delight of the eare, maketh your information no lesse plausible to the minde than to the eare: no though you filled them with never so much sence and sententiousnes.[28]

Even the sententiousness of the Deity may properly be suggested by those rhetorical devices that gain access to the mind "for instruction or discipline." Many of his figures are based upon some version of *Traductio*, Puttenham's "Tranlacer," a figure exploiting in Latin the range of inflections, in English usually imitated by repeated words deriving from the same stem.

To these almost exclusively verbal figures may be added another development in God's third speech. The first two, severely doctrinal, deal respectively with the Fall (and its consequences), and with the abstract theory of salvation and grace, the second concluding with the great question, "Where shall we find such love?" which leads from theory to practice, from the "great idea" to history. The third speech is historical, though still doctrinal, relating the Incarnation and the Last Judgment, and bringing the wheel of time full circle. Its revolution is symbolized by an unfolding and explication of the image that introduces both the

[28] *The Arte of English Poesie,* ed. G. D. Willcock and Alice Walker (Cambridge, 1936), p. 197.

heavenly colloquy of Book III, and the poem itself. In the opening lines of *Paradise Lost*, it is a metaphor emerging from actuality: "the Fruit / Of that Forbidden Tree"; in Book III, in a yet
unfallen world, it is neither metaphorical nor literal, but both at
once; Adam and Eve are seen "Reaping immortal fruits of joy
and love" (l. 67).[29] When God unfolds the significance of his
Son's birth, "of virgin seed" (l. 284), he adds two phrases that
deepen the key image: man shall be restored in Christ "As from
a second root" (l. 288), "And live in thee transplanted" (l. 293).
Such transplanting will in turn make possible the return of the
Golden Age:

> gold'n days, fruitful of gold'n deeds,
> With Joy and Love triumphing, and fair Truth.
> (ll. 337–338)

So history is led to its conclusion, which is a new version of its
beginning, and the transformation of an image from metaphor
to literal event is completed through the fecundity of the ruined
stock's second root, which will produce the fruit to be hung on
another Tree. The utter conventionality of these locutions does
not detract from their effectiveness in this context. Milton is, of
course, drawing on the ancient identification of "Christ's Cross
and Adam's Tree" that pervades the iconography of the Middle
Ages. Marlorat quite predictably reminds us that "the fruite of
that tree is Christ himselfe, who is the Apple wherewith the
choosen faithfull are deyntely fed for euermore."[30] God's artistry
is manifest in the life history of such emblems, perceptible to man
enlightened by grace, but intelligible in their totality only to the
Divine Artificer.

With this speech, "the strife of Mercy and Justice" ends, and
"the multitude of Angels" (ll. 344–345) celebrate the revelation
of the immense design. The song makes a careful distinction between the Persons of God, thus defining the implications of what
we have just heard and preparing for the further exploration,
later in Book III, of the Son's role as Mediator.

[29] "God sees what he has made as simultaneously metaphoric and
literal in its reality," Cope, *Metaphoric Structure*, p. 168. See also Ferry,
Milton's Epic Voice, chap. iv, on Milton's imitation of the language of
Scripture, "in which concrete and abstract meanings are true and indi-
visible," p. 94.

[30] *Catholike exposition*, p. 35r.

> Begott'n Son, Divine Similitude,
> In whose conspicuous count'nance, without cloud
> Made visible, th' Almighty Father shines,
> Whom else no Creature can behold. (ll. 384–387)

The Son, the divine Word, permits the creature to approach his Creator; and this approach is Milton's subject in Book III.

The voice of the bard locates the angelic singers precisely at the song's conclusion; the song itself begins the majestic downward spiral by which Milton returns us to the *visible* action and the poem's "normal" mode, within the created world where the pilgrimage of poet, reader, and Satan unfolds.

> Thus they in Heav'n, above the starry Sphear,
> Thir happie hours in joy and hymning spent.
> Mean while upon the firm opacous Globe
> Of this round World, whose first convex divides
> The luminous inferior Orbs, enclos'd
> From *Chaos,* and th' inroad of Darkness old,
> *Satan* alighted walks. (ll. 416–422)

Between the two major episodes of Book III, the Dialogue and the visit to the Sun, Milton interposes the curious passage on the Limbo of Vanity. It is usually read as an epic "digression," an Ariostan diversion, or as Milton's indulgence of a petulant anti-Romanism. Though it may be all of these, it is also related to the book's main themes. Frye's recent analysis suggests this idea:

> The people who arrive in the Limbo of Vanities are of two kinds: they are the people who have tried to take the kingdom of heaven either by force or by fraud. The former are those who have committed suicide in order to reach heaven; the latter are hypocrites who have tried to disguise themselves.[31]

If we read Book III as centrally concerned with man's knowledge of God, we can see these misguided efforts "to take the kingdom of heaven" as a negative aspect of Milton's theme. Elsewhere, legitimate ways of achieving that kingdom are defined: an obedient hearkening to the Word of God, whether manifest in Scripture or in the promptings of Conscience; later, the study of Creation. Satan, of course, is the prime vessel of misconceived efforts to regain the Kingdom, and some of his particular misconceptions are about to be elucidated.

[31] *Return of Eden,* p. 73.

The structural function of this false "paradise," its place in the poem's action, is to provide an interlude where Book III's two planes of narrative can intersect. The geography of this place is carefully specified, and we are made aware of the resumption of the journey through space, which is also a temporal "progress." What follows is, however, a last echo of the supertemporal vision just achieved from God's high prospect. The repentant and the stony-hearted are early in the book foreseen as future types of mankind. Milton says of the latter:

> This my long sufferance and my day of Grace
> They who neglect and scorn, shall never taste;
> But heart be hard'nd, blind be blinded more,
> That they may stumble on, and deeper fall;
> And none but such from mercy I exclude.
>   (ll. 198–202)

Now, as their corrupter approaches, these outcasts are brought closer to us in space and time: first, in the simile, the unenlightened "roving *Tartar*" and "*Chineses*"; then the overreachers of history: the builders of Babel, the pagan "fools" Empedocles and Cleombrotus, and the idiot "Eremits and Friers" who symbolize the corruption of the new dispensation. The traditional threefold pattern of history—pagan, Jewish, Christian—is here condensed. This excursion into a future that is for us, the poem's hearers and spectators, the past, offers a diminished counterpart of God's omniscience and confirms the bard's powers (though limited) as a prophet. Ranging through time, the narrative comes finally to rest in the spatial "present" or foreground, signaled, as in Book I, by the present tense:

> . . . turnd thither-ward in haste
> His traveld steps; farr distant he descries . . .
>   (ll. 500–501)

In the latter half of Book III, the normal mode of vision of *Paradise Lost* is restored, and the visionary whose second sight is the medium of the audience's perception resumes his importance as narrator. Satan is the dramatic focus of the experiences to be recounted; but we are often reminded of the visionary "frame," most commonly by Milton's allusions. The stairs of Heaven are to be seen by us as they were "seen" by Jacob, his physical senses extinguished in sleep, his spiritual eyes opened to

visionary experience (ll. 510–515); he thus becomes an analogue
to the speaker of the invocation to Book III.

Milton's reference to Jacob's Dream deserves some attention.
Knowing his low opinion of biblical exegetes, who "persist in
darkening the most momentous truths of religion by intricate
metaphysical comments,"[32] we may hesitate to invoke them here.
But to a poet the long tradition of typological parallels between
the Old and New Testaments was irresistible, as scholars have
demonstrated.[33] Milton dignifies typology on one occasion by
placing it in the mouth of the angel Michael, who refers to Joshua
as a type of Christ (XII, 310 ff.). Jacob's Dream was ordinarily
read typologically as a statement of the God-man relationship,
centrally expressed in the Incarnation but continuously present
in the many channels of communication kept open between
Heaven and Earth. The emblem of the ladder readily "contains"
these meanings, and the angels "ascending and descending" can
easily be made to allude to the complementary movements of
man striving upward toward God and God reaching down to man.
Bede's discussion in his commentary on the Pentateuch may stand
as typical of the patristic tradition.

> Angeli autem ascendentes et descendentes praedicatores sancti
> sunt. Ascendunt utique, cum ad intelligandam illius eminen-
> tissimam divinitatem excedunt universam creaturam, ut illum
> inveniant, ut, *In principio erat Verbum.* . . . Descendunt autem,
> ut illum inveniant, ut, *Factum ex muliere, factum sub lege.* . . .
> Ipsum ergo scalam intelligimus, quia per ipsum ascenditur, ut
> excelsa intelligat; et ad ipsum descenditur, ut in membris illius
> parvulus nutriatur; et per ipsum solum se erigunt, ut illum sub-
> limiter exspectent, per ipsum se etiam humilient, ne illum hu-
> militer ac temporaliter enuntient.[34]

[32] *Christian Doctrine,* I.xxx, in *SM,* p. 1039.

[33] On Milton's knowledge of patristic and later traditions of biblical
exegesis, see Arnold Williams, "Milton and the Renaissance Commentaries on Genesis," *MP,* XXXVII (1939–40), 263–278; W. G. Madsen,
"Earth the Shadow of Heaven: Typological Symbolism in *Paradise Lost,*"
PMLA, LXXV (1960), 519–526, reprinted in Barker, *Modern Essays.*
C. A. Patrides, *Milton and the Christian Tradition* (Oxford, 1966), pp.
128–130, gives examples of Protestant typology in the seventeenth century, including interpretations of Jacob's Ladder as prefiguring "the dual
nature of the Christ," and "his reconciliation of heaven and earth." More
detailed instances can be found in an article by the same author: "Renaissance Interpretations of Jacob's Ladder," *Theologische Zeitschrift,* XVIII
(1962), 411–418.

[34] *In Pentateuchum Commentarii,* in Migne, XCI, col. 252–253.

Rabanus Maurus, following an almost identical passage, adds:

> Angelos vero ascendentes et descendentes cernere, est cives
> supernae patriae contemplari; vel quanto amore suo auctori
> super semeteipsos inhaereant, vel quanta compassione charitatis
> nostris infirmitatibus condescendant.[35]

And Calvin's *Commentaries* carry over the signification virtually
unchanged, though with a predictably stronger emphasis on the
sole efficacy of Christ as Mediator.

> It is Christ alone who joins heaven to earth. He alone is Media-
> tor, reaching from heaven to the earth. He it is through whom
> the fullness of all heavenly gifts flows down to us and through
> whom we on our part may ascend to God. . . . Therefore, if we
> say that the ladder is a symbol of Christ, the interpretation is not
> forced. For the metaphor of a ladder is most suited to a Medi-
> ator through whom the service of angels, righteousness and
> truth, and all the spirits of holy grace descend to us step by
> step. We, on our part, who are firmly fixed not only upon the
> earth but in the abyss of the curse, and are submerged in hell
> itself, through him climb up to God.[36]

If we can believe that Jacob's Ladder shadowed distantly, in Milton's imagination, the mediatory function of Christ, his allusion
takes on renewed pertinence in the context of Book III, where
one of the poet's tasks is to suggest how the unimaginable distance between Heaven and Earth can be bridged, so that man
may eventually regain his true home.

Two minor allusions assist Milton in refining this theme; both
occur in the section on the Sun, where he is moving away from
the absolutes of Heaven into the complexities and ambiguities
of history. One is historical, one mythological. Both refer to
efforts of the human mind to reach beyond itself through science
or "powerful Art" (l. 602). As Satan lands on the Sun, there is
the famous allusion to Galileo, framed in lines that remind us of
God's vision at the opening of Book III, when he saw "*Satan*
there / Coasting the wall of Heav'n" (ll. 70–71).

> There lands the Fiend, a spot like which perhaps
> Astronomer in the Suns lucent Orbe
> Through his glaz'd Optic Tube yet never saw.
> (ll. 588–590)

---

[35] *Commentariorum in Genesim Libri Quatuor,* in Migne, CVII, col.
592.
[36] Trans. J. Haroutunian and L. P. Smith (Philadelphia, 1958), p. 147.

God looking down, man looking up: their lines of vision converge on the small black figure whose journey unites them in
complex and paradoxical bonds. It is, of course, the poet, not the
astronomer, who "sees" Satan as a sunspot; in these lines, then,
Milton, reiterates the extraordinary quality of his—and his
poem's—vision. To observe Satan's landing is to see something
inaccessible to the mortal sight of any ordinary fallen seer, even
one aided by an "Optic Tube." The poet, aided by the Heavenly
Muse, can—*like* God, up to a point—"see and tell" of things beyond the limits of merely human vision.

A few lines later, Milton speaks of alchemy in the mythological
terms familiar to Renaissance readers. The myth of Proteus was
regularly read as referring to physical substance and its changes;
alchemists, "vexers" of matter, attempted to "call up unbound
. . . old *Proteus* from the Sea" (ll. 603–604).[37] Their philosophy,
like that of the fallen angels, is "vain," another misdirected effort
of imperfect creatures to fathom and control the mysteries of
Creation. The allusions together become, therefore, part of the
negative pattern of the narrative in Book III: that group of references that define frustrated and unacceptable struggles to win
Heaven. The Paradise of Fools is a major instance, and Satan's
own efforts draw, of course, the paradigm. Over against this pattern is another, with the Son as its focus, Uriel, Jacob, and St.
John as *exempla,* and the narrator as demonstrator in the action
of a valid relation to God.

The two chief antagonists converge metaphorically as Milton
follows Satan's voyage to earth, in the description of the Sun,
where the "literal" basis for the Son/Sun parallel is insisted upon.
The Sun, as Raphael later tells Adam, is the "Fountain" from
which "other Starrs . . . draw Light" (VII, 364–365); and one
writer has suggested that the Holy Light, "Fountain of Light,"
invoked in Book III is actually a name for the Son, who is called

---

[37] Bacon writes of the Proteus myth: "This Fable may seem to unfold
the secrets of Nature, and the properties of Matter. . . . Now whereas it is
feigned that *Proteus* was a Prophet, well skilled in three differences of
Times, it hath an excellent Agreement with the Nature of Matter: for it
is necessary that he that will know the Properties and Proceedings of
Matter should comprehend in his Understanding the sum of all things
which have been, which are, or which shall be, although no Knowledge
can extend so far as to singular and individual Beings." *The Essays . . .
with the Wisdom of the Ancients,* ed. S. W. Singer (London, 1857), pp.
291–293.

upon for illumination.[38] Whether or not we accept the entire argument, it seems likely that Milton was deliberately paralleling his physical light bearer and the vessel of the Father's effulgence:

> In whose conspicuous count'nance, without cloud
> Made visible, th' Almighty Father shines,
> Whom else no Creature can behold.   (ll. 385–387)

Satan, landed on the Sun, is able to *see* with absolute clarity:

> Undazl'd, farr and wide his eye commands,
> For sight no obstacle found here, nor shade,
> But all Sun-shine.   (ll. 614–616)

With the aid of this light, vision is unsealed and the beholder "undazzled," in contrast to the blinding dazzle that baffles his visual approach to the seat of Deity. He is able to see the world below him with perfect accuracy, as Satan beholds "objects distant farr." As the incarnate Son joins man to God, so the created Sun gathers and diffuses the light of Heaven for the use of man, and even of the Devil, who in Book IV will express his hatred for Son and Sun alike.

Milton, throughout the latter part of Book III, is following his common practice of using Satan's perceptions and reactions to refract our vision and fix it upon a concept of the behavior appropriate to other fallen creatures, those who are *not* damned. This entire phase of Satan's voyage, from the moment when, catching a gleam "of dawning light," he turns his steps heavenward, to the concluding movement when he leaves Uriel to descend upon "the coast of Earth," is designed by Milton as a mirror of our salvation. We have just seen Christ accepting the role of Mediator; Satan, gazing upon the Gate of Heaven, figures for us the "sad exclusion from the dores of Bliss" (525) that will be the fate of any who refuse to mount the stairs provided for our reascent to God.[39] Opposite them, there "op'nd from beneath . . .

---

[38] William B. Hunter, "The Meaning of 'Holy Light' in *Paradise Lost* III," *MLN*, LXXIV (1959), 589–592.

[39] Cf. James H. Sims, *The Bible in Milton's Epics* (Gainesville, Fla., 1962), pp. 227–228: "Satan's leap from the stair . . . is a disdainful act which precedes the full expression of his disdain . . . in the soliloquy of Book IV. He has rejected the Son as Messiah in Heaven, spurned him as Jacob's Ladder on the rim of the world, and is soon to express his hatred for the Son as the Sun of Righteousness." As Sims and others point out, interpretations of Jacob's Ladder derive ultimately from the saying of Jesus in John 1 : 51: "Hereafter ye shall see heaven open, and the angels of God ascending and descending upon the Son of man."

A passage down to th' Earth." The poet, describing it, is also
describing, typologically, the mercy of God which we have heard
dramatized in the heavenly colloquy. When Mercy enters history,
the passage to the Promised Land is made accessible to us. The
heavens opened for Jacob, and we hear of Lazarus and Elijah,
rapt to Heaven by special grace. This passage to earth is wider
even than that over the first *"Promised Land* to God so dear"
(1. 531). It can be entered upon by every man who will accept
the Mediator, but by none who (like Satan) reject him.

In the final segment of the voyage, Milton defines the role that
contemplation of the created world can play in our salvation.
The panorama spread before Satan as he stands on the lower
stair of Heaven's steps elicits from him a double response:

> Such wonder seis'd, though after Heaven seen,
> The Spirit maligne, but much more envy seis'd
> At sight of all this World beheld so Faire.
> (ll. 552–554)

Envy is, of course, Satan's principal emotion; the wonder, however, evoked before he can arrest it (as later it will be evoked by
the virtuous Eve), is the response appropriate to the creature approaching his Creator through his works. The point is made explicit in Uriel's words later, praising the "cherub" for his zealous
"desire . . . to know"

> The works of God, thereby to glorifie
> The great Work-Maister.   (ll. 695–696)

The fraudulent angel and the true angel confront each other at
the threshold of God's universe, one envious and destructive, the
other admiring and obedient. It is a scene full of significance for
the reader of *Paradise Lost.*

Thus the two ways of knowing God—through the outer eye,
ascending through the marvelous universe to the love of its Creator, and through the eye of the understanding, opened by the revealed truth of God's Word—have been imagined by Milton in
the narrative pattern and the rhetoric of Book III. At the same
time, he has deepened our understanding of his own role as a
poet making a poem on this extraordinary theme. The vision
of the speaker, both its scope and its limitations, is carefully
bounded. The book's first half gives us the limitations, the second
half the capacities, of the poetic insight invoked at the beginning.

Having veiled his sight and opened his imagination's ear to the heavenly dialogue and the angelic hosannas of the first movement, the narrator in the second part revels in regained vision: what Jacob and John *saw,* what Satan *sees,* are the objects of his undazzled contemplation.[40] Satan's "sudden view" of the universe (ll. 540 ff.) is rendered in language that insists upon sight, contrasting unmistakably with the intellectually conceived dogmas of God the Father. The scout's *eye* (l. 547), Satan's *sight* (l. 554), *beheld* (l. 554), *surveys* (l. 555), *views* (l. 561). Finally, the Sun "allur'd his eye" (l. 573); and Milton moves into the great focal emblem of Book III, the being that warms, enlightens, and transfigures the lower world, as Christ "lighteth every man that cometh into the world," transfiguring and redeeming Nature.

At the upper limit of vision there remains, however, a darkness and a mystery; at this margin of unapproachability, the ear of faith must open. Too intense a reliance on sight involves a closing of the ears to the Word, and results in a kind of spiritual blindness. Milton had imagined the Lady in his masque rebuking Comus:

> Thou hast nor Eare, nor Soul to apprehend
> The sublime notion, and high mystery
> That must be utter'd . . .   (*Comus,* 783–785)

The highest mysteries must gain access to the soul through God's utterance. In the last episode of Book III, Milton insists once more upon both the power and the weakness of the imagination's sight, employing again the pattern of statement/restatement on which he constructed *Paradise Lost.* Uriel is one of the "eyes of God" whose function traditionally is to mediate between Heaven and Earth; as "Regent of the Sun" he is furthermore "the sharpest sighted Spirit of all in Heav'n" (ll. 590–591). In the poem's plot he is Satan's unwitting accomplice; as a participant in the theme of Book III, he embodies that celestial vision for which the poet

---

[40] It is interesting that Milton should allude to the author of Revelation in Book III. His equation of the angel in Revelation 19 with Uriel reminds us that the Apocalypse was read as a record of "past" events perhaps more often than as a vision of the future. It is possible, too, that Milton is encouraging us to distinguish the saint's vision from the more modest claims he makes for his own access to God, in the invocation and throughout Book III.

prayed in the invocation. His eye ranges through the whole
world, described eloquently for Satan in the book's last lines; he
has been, too, the observer of the great event to be unfolded by
the poet to Adam in Book VII.

> I saw when at his Word the formless Mass,
> This Worlds material mould, came to a heap:
> Confusion heard his voice, and wilde uproar
> Stood rul'd, stood vast infinitude confin'd.
>   (ll. 708–711)

"I saw"—it is the visionary who speaks: Uriel, Jacob, John, the
blind illuminated bard.

What Uriel does *not* see is, however, just as significant.

> For neither Man nor Angel can discern
> Hypocrisie, the onely evil that walks
> Invisible, except to God alone.   (ll. 682–684)

The capacities of created beings—men or angels—are distinguished from the powers belonging "to God alone," and those
powers are in Book III consciously disclaimed by the poet.
Though both prophets and bards are acknowledged as models in
the invocation—Tiresias and Phineus, as well as Thamyris and
Homer—Milton reserves the prophetic power in *Paradise Lost*
almost exclusively for the Deity or his spokesman. The seer of
the *Odyssey* may claim foresight: "He saw the field of time, past
and to come"; and a century after Milton, Blake was urging his
reader to "Hear the voice of the bard! that present, past, future
sees." But the voice of this Christian bard speaks only of the past
with the firsthand authority that makes dramatically realized
poetry, claiming knowledge of the future by faith alone, by doctrine imparted to the soul's "ear." For a reaffirmation of the principle, we may turn to the poem's opening lines, where the Muse
is to "instruct" the speaker concerning the great primeval events
of Rebellion, War, and Creation. Illumination is to prepare him
for the highest task:

> What in mee is dark
> Illumin, what is low raise and support;
> That to the highth of this great Argument
> I may assert Eternal Providence.   (ll. 22–25)

The height of the great Argument, as it concerns Eternal Providence, has been reached in Book III. The providential design for

the future of mankind is asserted by the only Being who has a right to do so; it is dramatized, unlike the major *past* events of the poem, as a "great Argument" in a strict sense. Milton, in offering us argument within the fiction of *Paradise Lost,* is not merely—not even primarily—giving a bald and redundant reminder of doctrines to which his audience already subscribes; he is drawing his readers into the poem as fellow listeners and candidates for salvation, thereby delineating through the oblique means of poetry the proper relationship of the creature to his Creator.

5

Innocence and Experience in Milton's Eden

BARBARA KIEFER LEWALSKI

▼

The heavy freight of mythic and theological meanings conveyed by the situations, characters, and language of *Paradise Lost* gives the poem a profound suggestiveness which accounts in part for the warm admiration or strong dislike it evokes: readers are seldom simply indifferent. But this very suggestiveness often leads the reader to invest Milton's terms with his own meanings, without attending carefully enough to the poem's own definitions. Thus, Shelley saw Milton's Satan as a grand romantic rebel, Empson exactly equated Milton's God with the Divine Tyrant he abhorred in conventional Christian theology, C. S. Lewis assumed that Milton's conception of hierarchy must exactly accord with that of Aquinas. Milton's image of the Garden of Paradise and his presentation of the State of Innocence have proved especially susceptible to unconscious distortion—usually as a result of readers' too facile identification of them with the paradisiacal garden of archetypal myth or with the Eden of traditional theology.

According to Northrop Frye's archetypal analysis, *Paradise Lost* treats "the ultimate myth of the gate of origin," the primal pattern God established for man on earth, which is "not a city but a garden . . . not Utopian but Arcadian, not historical but pastoral, not a social construct but an individual state of mind."[1] In J. B. Broadbent's conventional mythic interpretation, the poem shows that "as they fall, Adam and Eve are humanized . . . that personality should coincide with sin is precisely the comment that the myth is trying to make: individuation is man's glory, and his peril."[2] C. S. Lewis, on the other hand, finds that Milton's Garden conforms to the orthodox Augustinian view of Eden,[3] and B. Rajan agrees, arguing that Milton omitted, or played down, or presented as mere literary decoration in *Paradise Lost* all those personal heresies and unusual beliefs he defended so cogently in his *Christian Doctrine*, because he realized that the successful Christian epic must be written in terms of the central Christian tradition.[4]

The poem of course invites multiple perspectives and survives temporary distortions. Milton's frequent comparisons of Eden to those other famous paradises of myth and legend—the grove of Enna, the gardens of the Hesperides and of Alcinoüs and of Adonis, the *hortus conclusus* of the Song of Solomon—lend support to the archetypal reading. And the poem's fully demonstrated indebtedness to hexameral, exegetical, and literary treatments of the first chapters of Genesis helps to justify the approach through traditional theology.[5] Nevertheless, the reader who expects to find the paradisiacal garden of archetypal myth or of traditional theology in *Paradise Lost* will encounter several surprises which are not minor and are not played down. Milton indeed highlights these novel aspects of the Edenic life, not, of course, to invite the perverse view of Adam and Eve as fallen before they fell (the poem terms them "innocent" and "yet sinless" moments before they eat the fruit); not to display his

[1] Frye, *The Return of Eden* (Toronto, 1965), pp. 113–114.
[2] Broadbent, *Some Graver Subject* (London, 1960), p. 192.
[3] Lewis, *A Preface to Paradise Lost* (London, 1960), p. 66.
[4] Rajan, *Paradise Lost and the Seventeenth Century Reader* (London, 1947).
[5] See F. E. Robbins, *The Hexaemeral Literature* (Chicago, 1912); Arnold Williams, *The Common Expositor* (Chapel Hill, N.C., 1948); Sister Mary Irma Corcoran, *Milton's Paradise with Reference to the Hexameral Background* (Washington, D.C., 1945); Watson Kirkconnell, *The Celestial Cycle* (Toronto, 1952).

acquaintance with strange and recondite lore; and not to serve as a forum for his own unusual theological views. Nor, though these effects are important and have been brilliantly analyzed in modern criticism, does Milton depart from the expected only to foreshadow the Fall, to establish dramatic causality for it, and to render the unfallen state more credible by presenting it from fallen man's perspective or with the fallen condition "potentially" present in it.[6] Rather, these Miltonic novelties are of the essence of the poem's vision, for they effect a redefinition of the State of Innocence which is a very far cry from the stable, serene completeness attributed to that state both in myth and in traditional theology. In *Paradise Lost* the Edenic life is radical growth and process,[7] a mode of life steadily increasing in complexity and challenge and difficulty but at the same time and by that very fact, in perfection.

Some of these changes, highly significant in themselves and in their symbolic suggestiveness for the entire poem, involve the physical character of the Garden. The Happy Garden in classical myth and the Earthly Paradise in Christian poetry and biblical exegesis share many qualities: both gardens are sensuous, pastoral, inaccessible; both have a perfect climate, perpetual springtime, a balmy west wind, sweet odors, cool waters; in both the flora grow in vast but ordered profusion, the trees bear golden fruit, and there are no noxious plants or savage animals. In both gardens man is in complete harmony with Nature, which supplies

[6] See for example, E. M. W. Tillyard, *Studies in Milton* (London, 1951), pp. 10–11; Isabel G. MacCaffrey, *Paradise Lost as "Myth"* (Cambridge, 1959), pp. 148–156; Arnold Stein, *Answerable Style* (Minneapolis: University of Minnesota Press, 1953), pp. 52–88; A. Bartlett Giamatti, *The Earthly Paradise and the Renaissance Epic* (Princeton, N.J., 1966), pp. 295–351.

[7] I am delighted to note that J. M. Evans' valuable study of the entire range of exegetical and literary treatments of the Genesis story, *Paradise Lost and the Genesis Tradition* (Oxford, 1968), which appeared while this volume was awaiting publication, also argues Milton's profoundly original conception of Edenic Innocence. (See chap. x, pp. 242–271.) The importance of growth in Eden is discussed in somewhat different terms in Joseph Summers, *The Muse's Method* (Cambridge, 1962), pp. 71–95; Irene Samuel, *Dante and Milton* (Ithica, N.Y., 1966), pp. 13, 146–162, 185–204; Arthur Barker, "Structural and Doctrinal Pattern in Milton's Later Poems," in *Essays in English Literature . . . Presented to A. S. P. Woodhouse,* ed. Millar MacLure and F. W. Watt (Toronto, 1964), pp. 183–194; Thomas Kranidas, "Adam and Eve in the Garden: A Study of *Paradise Lost,* Book V," *SEL* IV (1964), 71–83.

all his wants without any need for his labor.[8] In Genesis Adam
is charged to dress and keep the Garden, but Christian exegetes
do not understand this as imposing necessary labor; it is merely
a provision for pleasant exercise, or a deterrent to idleness, or
else—in Augustine's symbolic reading—a directive to man to
care for his own soul or a promise that God will work in man as
in a garden.[9] One essential difference between the mythic garden
and the Christian Eden concerns the aspect of time. Life in the
mythic garden state, though doomed ultimately to deterioration
or destruction, is felt as "timeless" and complete, consisting, as
Eliade points out, of repeated ritual gestures rather than of
change and development in historical time.[10] But this static timelessness is less a feature of the Christian paradise, primarily because man's tenure of Eden was seen to be extremely brief: most
exegetes allowed Adam and Eve only one day in the Garden,
some said a week or eight days, while a very few thought they
might have remained thirty-three or forty days.[11]

Milton's Eden has most of the expected beauties and delights
of the mythic garden and the Christian Eden, but there are important differences. As several readers have noted, the Garden in
Paradise Lost has a surprising tendency to excess and disorder,
to overprofuseness and languid softness—the "mazy error" of
the brooks, the "wanton" fertility of the vegetation, the "luxuri-

[8] See the excellent discussion of the Garden trope in Giamatti, *The
Earthly Paradise,* pp. 11–86.
[9] For typical statements see Corcoran, *Hexameral Background,* pp. 54–
56; Williams, *Common Expositor,* pp. 108–111; Augustine, *De Genesi ad
Litteram,* VIII, 8–10, in *Pat. Lat.,* XXXIV, 379–382; Aquinas, *Summa
Theologica,* Q. 102, A. 3, in *Basic Writings,* ed. Anton C. Pegis, 2 vols.
(New York, 1945), I, 949; Luther, *Commentary on Genesis,* trans. J.
Theodore Mueller, 2 vols. (Grand Rapids, Mich., 1958), I, 51; John
Salkeld, *A Treatise of Paradise* (London, 1617), pp. 144–145; The Bible
(Geneva version; London, 1608), notes to Genesis 2 : 15.
[10] Mircea Eliade, *Cosmos and History: The Myth of the Eternal Return,*
trans. Willard R. Trask (New York, 1959), pp. 88–92.
[11] See Williams, *Common Expositor,* p. 137; Grant McColley, *Paradise
Lost* (Chicago, 1940), pp. 158–160; Augustine, *De Genesi ad Litteram,*
IX.4, in *Pat. Lat.,* XXXIV, 395–396; Calvin, *Commentarie . . . upon . . .
Genesis,* trans. Thomas Tymme (London, 1578), p. 96. The short time
in Eden was usually inferred from some analogue in Christ's life (usually
the day of the crucifixion), and received strong support from the belief
that had Adam and Eve remained one night in Eden they would have had
sexual intercourse and so conceived a child not affected at conception by
original sin.

ant" vines, the "pendant shades" (IV, 239, 259–260).[12] This condition of the Garden makes Adam and Eve's labor not merely the expected ritual gesture, but a necessary and immense task. Yet another surprise is the indeterminate time Adam and Eve occupy Paradise. We know that Satan, expelled from the Garden by Gabriel, circled the earth seven nights before he reentered Paradise in a rising mist, and that the Fall occurred on the following day. But we do not know how long Adam and Eve resided in Eden before Satan's first view of them, for on that occasion Eve refers to some unspecified day in the recent past as the time of her creation—"That day I oft remember, when from sleep / I first awak't" (IV, 449–450).

These alterations in the usual portrayal of the Garden should be seen in terms of the subtle relationship the poem establishes between the nature of a place and the nature of the beings who dwell in it. In the beginning God created places suitable for the various orders of being; his creative act was immediate and instantaneous (VII, 176–178) but is realized as process, as a continuing creative activity which the inhabitants of each place imitate according to their measure, and in which they actively participate. The place God made for man, and made "fit" for him is, in the first instance, the earth: man himself is made of the earth's substance, of the dust of the ground, and he is charged to "subdue" all the earth and hold dominion over every living thing that moves upon it. The earth is a beautiful place of various landscape—"Hill, Dale, and shady Woods, and sunny Plains" (VIII, 262)—but parts of it are still chaos-like: for example, the mountain outside Eden is a "steep wilderness . . . / With thicket overgrown, grotesque and wild" (IV, 135–136). The place more particularly contrived for primal man is the Garden in Eden: newly created Adam was led to this Garden as his "Mansion," his "seat prepar'd" (VIII, 296, 299), and given the fruits of the Garden as his appointed sustenance. The Garden, like the entire earth, is a place of profuse growth and tremendous fecundity, and it too tends to wild, though not to the same degree. It con-

---

[12] See MacCaffrey, *Paradise Lost as "Myth"*, pp. 148–156; Stein, *Answerable Style*, pp. 57–72; Giamatti, *The Earthly Paradise*, pp. 299–313. Quotations from *Paradise Lost* in text and notes are from Merritt Y. Hughes, ed., *Milton: Complete Poems and Major Prose* (New York, 1957).

tains no savage wildernesses or grotesque thickets, but its groves
are "A Wilderness of sweets; for Nature here / Wanton'd as in
her prime . . . / Wild above Rule or Art, enormous bliss" (V,
294–297). The "nice art" of curious flower beds has no place
in the garden (IV, 241–243), but Art perfectly fused with Nature has: the Divine Cultivator has brought within the "narrow
room" of Eden "Nature's whole wealth," and has so heightened
Nature that the trees bear "Blossoms and fruits at once of golden
hue / . . . with gay enamell'd colors mixt" (IV, 207, 148–149).[13]
The place uniquely belonging to Adam and Eve, their bower
which other creatures dare not approach, is yet more artful: here
the "sovran Planter, when he fram'd / All things to man's delightful use . . . wrought / Mosaic" about the walls, by interweaving
"each odorous bushy shrub" with "each beauteous flow'r," and
he "Broider'd the ground" with violet, crocus, and hyacinth, a
"rich inlay / . . . more color'd than with stone / Of costliest
Emblem" (IV, 690–703).

As images of God, Adam and Eve are also gardeners, responsible for the world that was made for them by the "sovran
Planter," but which must be preserved, cultivated, sustained, and
raised to higher states of perfection by their own proper labor.
In the vision of the poem, this fundamental responsibility of man
for his world is not a postlapsarian condition but has obtained
from the beginning. As sharers in the continuing "creation" of
their world, Adam and Eve confront in their sphere the abiding
tension between order and chaos which is felt throughout the
poem's universe. As the materials of chaos are the substratum
of everything made, everything has a tendency to regress to the
chaotic state[14] unless continually acted upon by a creative force
akin to the divine creative power that first brought order out of
chaos. The highly cultivated Garden which yet tends to "wild"
manifests this tension and so defines the responsibility of Adam
and Eve as gardeners. Their labor is "pleasant" and unarduous,
but even in the idyll of Book IV Adam observes that they can
only barely cope on a day to day basis with the immense task of
maintaining the Garden in a condition of ordered beauty, and

[13] See Douglas Bush, *Paradise Lost in Our Time* (Ithaca, N.Y., 1945),
p. 95; Broadbent, *Some Graver Subject*, p. 184.
[14] See W. C. Curry, *Milton's Ontology, Cosmogony, and Physics* (Louis-
ville, Ky., 1957), pp. 65–73.

indeed that it is at times marred by overgrown paths and "unsightly" blossoms strewn about. Adam says:

> Tomorrow ere fresh Morning streak the East
> With first approach of light, we must be ris'n,
> And at our pleasant labor, to reform
> Yon flow'ry Arbors, yonder Alleys green,
> Our walk at noon, with branches overgrown,
> That mock our scant manuring, and require
> More hands than ours to lop thir wanton growth:
> Those Blossoms also, and those dropping Gums,
> That lie bestrown unsightly and unsmooth,
> Ask riddance, if we mean to tread with ease
>   (IV, 623–632).

Later, Eve makes the same point: the work is "Our pleasant task," but yet "what we by day / Lop overgrown, or prune, or prop, or bind, / One night or two with wanton growth derides / Tending to wild" (IX, 207–212). And lest we suppose Eve exaggerates here in order to find an excuse for gardening alone, the narrator testifies to the truth of her description: "much thir work outgrew / The hands' dispatch of two Gard'ning so wide" (IX, 202–203).

Adam and Eve seek to preserve the Garden from wildness and excess by pruning and cutting and by plucking the fruits, restrictive actions that at the same time stimulate greater fertility: as Adam observes, "Nature . . . by disburd'ning grows / More fruitful" (V, 318–320). They also direct the growth of the Garden, laboring "where any row / Of Fruit-trees overwoody reach'd too far / Thir pamper'd boughs, and needed hands to check / Fruitless imbraces" (V, 212–215). Eve especially supplies constant supportive care: "her fair tendance" causes the flowers to spring and "gladlier" grow, and she regards the Garden as her "Nursery" where "with tender hand" she bred up the flowers that are in some sense her images and her children, named them and reared them to the sun (VIII, 46–47, XI, 275–278). Moreover, Adam and Eve imitate the Divine Gardener in enhancing Eden's natural beauties by art. Eve further adorns the bower by decking her marriage bed and strewing the floor of the dining place with odorous flowers; the pair has rude gardening tools and drinking vessels; and Eve in preparing hospitality for Raphael produces delicacies and refinements of taste beyond what mere Nature provides: "for drink the Grape / She crushes, inoffensive must, and meaths / From many a berry, and from sweet kernels prest / She tempers dulcet creams" (V, 344–347). These terms then define man's work in the Garden, his share in the divine process of creating and maintaining the external world. This work, which Adam and Eve are to accomplish in due course, with due proportion, and without undue anxiety, is unlaborious, but it is absolutely necessary and it increases daily in complexity and challenge.

The poem's garden imagery identifies Adam and Eve not only as gardeners but also as part of the Garden: they too are "planted" by God, expected to grow and perfect themselves through cultivation, and to bear appropriate fruits. The first descriptions of Adam and Eve insist upon the analogy: Adam's "Hyacinthine Locks / Round from his parted forelock manly hung / Clust'ring"; Eve's dishevelled "golden tresses . . . in wanton ringlets wav'd / As the Vine curls her tendrils" (IV, 301–307). Satan makes the same analogy in referring to the rumor that God in some new world would "plant / A generation," and to Adam and Eve as "Imparadis't in one another's arms / The happier *Eden*" (I, 652–653, IV, 506–507). In the event, the fruit of that forbidden tree was death and all our woe, but Adam and Eve's first, and intended, harvest was very different—"in the happy Garden plac't, / Reaping immortal fruits of joy and love, / Uninterrupted joy, unrivall'd love" (III, 66–68). These harvest images make Adam and Eve gardeners also of their own paradise within, that is, responsible for perfecting their own natures. Sir Walter Raleigh had used much the same imagery to make much the same point about Adam and Eve:

> God gave unto man all kind of Seeds and Grafts of life (to wit) the vegetative life of Plants, the sensuall of Beasts, the rationall of Man, and the intellectuall of Angels; whereof which soever he took pleasure to plant and cultive, the same should futurely grow in him, and bring forth fruit, agreeable to his owne choice and plantation.[15]

Much of the work Adam and Eve perform in Eden is an image of the work they should accomplish in the paradise within. They "led the Vine / To wed her Elm; she spous'd about him twines / Her marriageable arms, and with her brings / Her dow'r th'

---

[15] Raleigh, *The History of the World* (London, 1614), p. 27.

adopted Clusters, to adorn / His barren leaves" (V, 215–219);
Eve has been identified as a "vine" with tendrils clustering about
Adam, and she is to solace his loneliness, bring him progeny,
cleave to him. The analogy is further urged as the flowerlike
Eve, who for Adam (and Satan) sums up in herself all the
beauties of the Garden, goes forth to work in the external garden
but is "mindless" of her prior responsibility toward the paradise within:

> Each Flow'r of slender stalk, whose head though gay
> Carnation, Purple, Azure, or speckt with Gold,
> Hung drooping unsustain'd, them she upstays
> Gently with Myrtle band, mindless the while
> Herself, though fairest unsupported Flow'r,
> From her best prop so far, and storm so nigh.
>   (IX, 428–433)

The point is again made when God directs Adam to "subdue"
the earth and hold dominion over every living thing, and immediately thereafter to "govern well thy appetite, lest sin / Surprise thee" (VII, 532–534, 546–547).

The implication of the analogy we have been tracing is that
Adam and Eve, like the Garden, have natures capable of a
prodigious growth of good things, but which require constant
pruning to remove excessive or unsightly growth, constant direction of overreaching tendencies, constant propping of possible
weaknesses, and also, one supposes, further cultivation through
art. The *Areopagitica* had described primal man's nature in very
similar terms—as comprised of passions and capacities for pleasure which are potentially dangerous but which are also the very
materials for growth in virtue if properly "tempered":

> Many there be that complain of divin Providence for suffering
> *Adam* to transgresse, foolish tongues! when God gave him
> reason, he gave him freedom to choose, for reason is but choos-
> ing; he had bin else a meer artificiall *Adam*, such an *Adam* as he
> is in the motions. We our selves esteem not of that obedience,
> or love, or gift, which is of force: God therefore left him free,
> set before him a provoking object, ever almost in his eyes;
> herein consisted his merit, herein the right of his reward, the
> praise of his abstinence. Wherefore did he creat passions within
> us, pleasures round about us, but that these rightly temper'd are
> the very ingredients of vertu?[16]

[16] *The Works of John Milton,* ed. F. A. Patterson *et al.,* 18 vols. (New
York, 1931–1938), IV, 319. Subsequent references to Milton's prose are
to this Columbia edition (*CE*).

In addition, the Garden's fertility provides an analogy for the projected growth of human society through human procreation —yet another way in which man participates in the divine creative process. Raphael quite explicitly compares Eve's destined fertility to that of the Garden: "Hail Mother of Mankind, whose fruitful Womb / Shall fill the World more numerous with thy Sons / Than with these various fruits the Trees of God / Have heap'd this Table" (V, 388–391). Adam and Eve constantly assume that humankind and the human world will grow in perfection as the solitary Garden becomes a flourishing, ordered society. Adam's divinely approved argument with his Creator about a mate urges the human need for progeny: "Man by number is to manifest / His single imperfection, and beget / Like of his like, his Image multipli'd / In unity defective" (VIII, 422–425). Adam and Eve also expect the control and enhancement of the Garden to become easier and more permanent when the flora of the Garden will have "More hands than ours to lop thir wanton growth," when "more hands / Aid us" (IV, 629; IX, 207–208). After the Garden has been irretrievably lost, Michael projects what would have been its ideal state, its closest resemblance to the heavenly paradigm—a fusion of garden and capital city from which Adam's sons would go forth to civilize all the earth (XI, 340–346).

The growth of human society begins with the creation of Eve, and Adam is, in a very real sense, her co-creator.[17] Though God knew that it was not good for man to be alone, he did not act until Adam himself realized and expressed to God his need for human companionship, a need prior to that of progeny: "Of fellowship I speak / Such as I seek, fit to participate / All rational delight . . . / Thou in thyself art perfet, and in thee / Is no deficience found; not so is Man, / But in degree, the cause of his desire / By conversation with his like to help, / Or solace his defects" (VIII, 389–391, 415–419). God promised Adam's mate "exactly to thy heart's desire," and he formed her out of Adam's substance, drawing her out of his side in an analogy of birth. She is then bone of Adam's bone, flesh of his flesh, "Part of my Soul . . . my other half," but she is also separate, "an individual solace dear." And she does perfect him and the Garden for him:

[17] Stein, *Answerable Style,* p. 81, suggests something of this shared creativity.

"Her looks . . . from that time infus'd / Sweetness into my heart, unfelt before, / And into all things from her Air inspir'd / The spirit of love and amorous delight" (VIII, 474–477). Yet this very movement toward completion introduces new problems, new tensions—"here passion first I felt" (VIII, 530)—which render human life more complex, more challenging, more difficult.

Another unusual feature of Milton's Eden, which also reflects the prelapsarian human condition, is its perilous exposure despite numerous safeguards. In keeping with both myth and biblical exegesis, the Garden's physical protections are formidable: the "steep wilderness" of "insuperable highth," the overgrown thickets that deny access, the walls of trees, the single, well-guarded gate. But Satan nevertheless "At one slight bound high overleap'd all bound / Of Hill or highest Wall" (IV, 181–182). Also, the Garden is protected by angelic guards who seem to be curiously ineffective. Uriel, the Regent of the Sun and the "sharpest-sighted Spirit of all in Heav'n" (III, 690–691) yet directs the disguised Satan to earth. The militant Gabriel guards the gate of Paradise and about him exercise the "Youth of Heaven" in heroic games, but they do not prevent Satan's first entry—or his second—into the Garden. The angelic guard do surprise and eject Satan in his toadlike posture, but not before he has induced Eve's dream. This perilous exposure of Eden in the midst of apparent security is the emblem of a moral reality which Milton sees as perpetual, and which he clearly defined in *Areopagitica*: physical or external protections cannot really safeguard man from the attractions of evil, so that his only true security is in watchfulness and constant growth in virtue and wisdom. For Adam and Eve the external paradise can be secure only so long as they cultivate and enhance the paradise within.

The garden analogy that we have been tracing suggests a great deal about the natures of Adam and Eve as the poem renders them, but there is more to be said on this score, and there are other significant departures from myth and traditional theology to be noted. In many mythic accounts the imagery associates the Paradisiacal Garden with the mother's womb or the female body, and man within the Garden is simple, childlike, ignorant of evil and complexity; like Blake's *Thel*, some versions or interpretations of these myths associate expulsion from the Garden with sexual awakening, with the painful progress toward adult knowledge and experience, with the development of personality and individuation.[18] On the other hand, according to Christian biblical exegesis and most poetic renderings of the Genesis story, Adam was created at full maturity (probably at thirty years of age). He was the "image and likeness of God," which is variously understood to refer to the powers of his intellect and spirit, or to the perfect control his reason exercised over appetites and senses and will, or to the dominion he enjoyed over all living things, or to his spiritual qualities of wisdom, righteousness, charity, virtue, integrity. Christ excepted, Adam was commonly thought to have surpassed all his sons, even Solomon, in gifts of intellect. His naming of the animals showed his perfect knowledge, infused or by immediate apprehension, of all natural things (including, many thought, astronomy); he had also knowledge of himself; and he had revealed, supernatural knowledge of the fall of the angels and perhaps of the Trinity and the Incarnation. It was generally agreed that he did not have knowledge of the future, or of the secrets of God or the angels, and many exegetes assumed certain other limitations in his knowledge to be overcome through experience and study.[19] But all assumed that he would gain such subsequent knowledge easily, without perturbation or chance of error: as Aquinas put it, "The rectitude of the first state was incompatible with any deception of the intellect."[20] In his passional nature, Adam was free from fear or sorrow or distress. He would have reproduced his kind through sexual intercourse delightful to the senses but wholly without

---

[18] See C. G. Jung, *The Archetypes and the Collective Unconscious*, trans. R. F. C. Hull (New York, 1959), pp. 34–35, 81–84, 96; Maud Bodkin, *Archetypal Patterns in Poetry* (New York, 1958), pp. 159–169; Northrop Frye, *Fearful Symmetry* (Princeton, N.J., 1947), pp. 42–43; Frye, *Anatomy of Criticism* (New York, 1966), pp. 151–153, 199–200, 220.

[19] Williams, *Common Expositor*, pp. 80–83; Corcoran, *Hexameral Background*, pp. 83–94; Augustine, *De Genesi ad Litteram*, III.20, VIII.16, in *Pat. Lat.*, XXXIV, 292–293, 386; Aquinas, *Summa Theologica*, Q. 93, A. 5, Q. 94, A. 1–4, in *Basic Writings*, I, 890–909; Luther, *Commentary on Genesis*, I, 24–35, 57; Calvin, *Commentarie . . . upon Genesis*, pp. 44–63; Calvin, *Institutes of the Christian Religion*, I, xv, ed. John T. McNeill, in "Library of Christian Classics" XX (Philadelphia, 1960), pp. 189–196; John Salkeld, *A Treatise of Paradise*, pp. 97–124, 185–197; John Weemse, *The Portraiture of the Image of God in Man* (London, 1636), pp. 61–91; Andrew Willet, *Hexapla in Genesin* (London, 1608), pp. 14–16, 31, 39.

[20] *Summa Theologica*, Q. 94, A. 4, in *Basic Writings*, I, 909.

concupiscence or passion, though it was almost universally believed that Adam was expelled from the Garden before such intercourse took place. And he would have avoided sin tranquilly, with no fear of falling and no "mental perturbation."[21] A

[21] The following statements suggest typical views:

Their avoidance of sin was tranquil. . . . They were agitated by no mental perturbations, and annoyed by no bodily discomforts. . . . The man, then, would have sown the seed, and the woman received it, as need required, the generative organs being moved by the will, not excited by lust. . . . In Paradise, then, man . . . had food that he might not hunger, drink that he might not thirst, the tree of life that old age might not waste him; there was in his body no corruption, nor seed of corruption, which could produce in him any unpleasant sensation. He feared no inward disease, no outward accident. Soundest health blessed his body, absolute tranquillity his soul. As in Paradise there was no excessive heat or cold, so its inhabitants were exempt from the vicissitudes of fear and desire. No sadness of any kind was there, nor any foolish joy; true gladness ceaselessly flowed from the presence of God. . . . The honest love of husband and wife made a sure harmony between them. Body and spirit worked harmoniously together. (Augustine, *City of God*, XIV.10, 24, 26, ed. Marcus Dods [New York, 1950], pp. 456–457, 472–475).

Adam had no passion with evil as its object, such as fear, sorrow, and the like; neither had he passions in respect of good not possessed, but to be possessed then, as burning concupiscence. . . . Our first parents did not come together in Paradise, for they were ejected from Paradise because of sin shortly after the creation of woman. . . . If man had not sinned, there would have been such intercourse, to which the distinction of sex is ordained . . . [but] nothing of this kind would have happened that was not regulated by reason, not because delight of sense would be less (rather indeed would sensible delight have been the greater in proportion to the greater purity of nature and the greater sensibility of the body. . . . Intensity of pleasure [is not excluded] from the state of innocence, but the ardor of lust and restlessness of the soul. (Aquinas, *Summa Theologica* Q 98. A 2, in *Basic Writings*, I, 931–932)

[In Adam] there was no leprosy of sin in either the intellect or the will, but man was altogether righteous both within and without. His intellect was absolutely uncorrupt; his memory was perfect, and his will was in every way upright; his conscience was wholly good, and there was no fear of death in him. To these perfections of the mind were added those of the body. . . . Adam would have known Eve only with quiet and peaceful love and with willing obedience to God, without any sinful lusts or passions. . . . He not only knew God and trusted in His goodness, but also led a perfectly holy life, knowing no fear of death or danger. . . . Our first parents . . . had a perfect knowledge of God, and, in addition, a perfect knowledge of the stars and the whole astronomy. (Luther, *Commentary on Genesis I*, 31–33)

See also Williams, *Common Expositor*, pp. 85–93; Corcoran, *Hexameral Background*, pp. 70–76, 105–120.

fixed hierarchy of being determined his social relationships: Adam was absolute ruler of the animals with whom he shared a corporal body but whom he wholly surpassed in intellect; he was civil governor of Eve whose nature was like but inferior to his own in intellectual powers; he was subordinate to the angels who are incorporeal pure spirits and whose intellect operates by the more excellent process of intuition rather than by discourse of reason as man's does.[22] Though not naturally immortal Adam had power not to die as long as he remained innocent, and finally he was to be translated to heaven where he would receive a spiritual body.[23]

In sharp contrast to all of this, in *Paradise Lost* Adam and Eve have sexual relations in Eden, accompanied not only with pleasure and delight but with a powerful sensuality which threatens to subject the reason and which causes the perturbations of passion.[24] There are other surprising passions as well—Eve's tendency to vanity and Adam's to uxoriousness—and other perturbations such as the distress and anxiety occasioned by Eve's dream. In the intellectual realm Adam's and Eve's accomplishments are impressive but limited: they do not know astronomy, they need to deepen and perfect their self-knowledge, and before Raphael's visit, very little supernatural knowledge has been revealed to them. But the true surprise here is that in all these categories of knowledge they are subject to mistake, misjudgment, and error. Finally, the monism of the poem's universe creates a fluid hierarchy according to which the differences among beings and especially among intelligent beings are differences of degree only, and for every order of being the expectation is that "body up to spirit work, in bounds / Proportion'd to each kind" (V, 478–479). By means of such departures from the expected, primal man's nature is shown to be complex and constantly developing, not simple and stable. Each new situation in Milton's

[22] Augustine, *City of God*, XII.22, p. 406; Aquinas, *Summa Theologica*, Q. 90–92, in *Basic Writings*, I, 868–881.

[23] Augustine, *De Genesi ad Litteram*, VI.23–24, in *Pat. Lat.*, XXXIV, 353–354; Raleigh, *History of the World*, p. 57.

[24] Some Hebrew commentary assumes sexual consummation in Eden, e.g. *Pentateuch with . . . Rashi's Commentary*, trans. M. Rosenbaum and A. M. Silbermann (London, 1946), p. 17, as do also some literary treatments of the Fall, notably Hugo Grotius, *Adamus Exul*, in Kirkconnell, *Celestial Cycle*, pp. 106–107, 176, 180; but there are no precedents for Adam's distressing passion.

Eden is an opportunity to grow in wisdom, virtue, and perfection, and normally Adam and Eve must take the initiative in interpreting what happens to them and in seeking new knowledge and experience. Normally, too, they respond to a new situation by one or two false starts or false guesses before they find or are led to the proper stance. But this human growth by trial and error, like the excessive growth of the Garden, is wholly without prejudice, so long as they prune and direct and reform what grows amiss. Despite constant foreshadowings of the Fall as each new situation reveals possibilities for wrong choices and wrong directions, Adam and Eve's life in Eden, until the fateful marital dispute, describes a pattern, not of declining innocence but of steady growth toward perfection through ever-increasing knowledge and experience. This process of growth is forwarded by all of the events that occur in Eden, and it is the very meaning of the State of Innocence, as the poem redefines it.

Adam begins this process of growth seconds after his creation. He first observes the heavens and instinctively stands upright. Then, perusing the planets, all the creatures of the earth, and himself, he finds he can speak and name whatever he sees, but as yet he does not understand the natures of the creatures or his own origin and purpose. By discourse of reason he works out the fact that he is not self-generated, and that he ought to discover and adore his Creator, so he asks the creatures (not yet knowing they are mute) who he is, and who his maker is. Adam declares to Raphael that he "call'd and stray'd" in wrong directions (VIII, 283), but God through the Son responded by leading him as in a dream to his Garden. The fruit stirs Adam's desire to pluck and eat, but the Garden in itself does not satisfy him; still searching for knowledge of self and God he would have begun "wand'ring" anew, he admits, had not his guide then revealed himself as "Author of all this thou seest," and defined Adam's role and duty in the Garden. Next God brings the creatures two by two before Adam in subjection, and "endues" him with knowledge of their natures, but Adam concludes from this experience that he can find neither happiness nor contentment in the Garden without a mate of his own kind. At this point God presents Adam with a formidable challenge, for he seems to order him to be content with the Garden as it is, and to find pastime with the beasts (VIII, 373–377). But Adam proceeds to work out by discourse of reason his difference from the beasts on the score of rationality, and his difference from God on the score of his finiteness, thereby proving that he requires a mate for conversation, help, and progeny. Adam is praised by God for his self-knowledge and given his heart's desire; he names her woman, knows her nature, prophesies the conditions of human marriage, woos her successfully, finds himself perfected by the "new sweetness" she infuses, but also troubled by the novel experience of passion—which provides a new challenge. His first few hours of life have brought a tremendous growth in Adam's knowledge and experience of God, of Nature, of Eve, and of himself, making him more complex, more subject to tension, but also more complete and perfect than at the moment of his creation.

Eve's creation story also displays an impressive advance in knowledge after some false starts: indeed she tells it to illustrate how she came to understand her right relationship to Adam and the true scale of human values. Though much less speculative than Adam, she too began life questioning "what I was, whence thither brought, and how" (IV, 452); she too began "wand'ring," and went "With unexperienc't thought" to the lake where, Narcissus-like, she was attracted to her own image and where, Narcissus-like, she would have remained "pin'd with vain desire" had not God guided her to her proper mate, whose image she is (IV, 457, 466). Her momentary turning back displays an impulse to vanity and self-centeredness grounded in an overvaluation of the beauty, softness, and mildness of the "smooth, wat'ry image," thus far the only human goods she understands. This time Adam saves her, instructing her forcefully and rationally about her origin and purpose, and pressing his rightful claim to her. Her experience of Adam's superlative qualities causes her to yield, and to conclude that "beauty is excell'd by manly grace / And wisdom, which alone is truly fair" (IV, 490–491).

Eve's query about astronomy is a response to the challenge of Nature, an effort to extend knowledge of Nature's ways by speculation. It arises quite naturally from Eve's mention of "glittering Star-light" in her lovely lyric celebrating her delight in all the beauties of the Garden, and her far greater delight in Adam (IV, 656). Her question to her rightful teacher, "wherefore all night long shine these, for whom / This glorious sight, when sleep hath shut all eyes" (IV, 657–658), assumes a Ptolemaic universe (an indifferent matter morally) and in itself is not culpable. But the question involves certain faulty assumptions—

that not only the earth but the entire cosmos was made for man, and that it was made somewhat inexpertly since the stars apparently shine when no one enjoys them—assumptions that, if uncorrected, could lead to overweening human pride. Adam lacks certain knowledge in astronomy and he too assumes a Ptolemaic universe, though he evidently continues speculating about these matters and is ready with more sophisticated queries for Raphael. But he can and does correct Eve's potentially dangerous assumptions by suggesting uses for starlight unrelated to themselves: to prepare enlightenment for nations yet unborn; to stave off the power of total darkness; to nourish and influence all the creatures of the earth; to give light to spiritual creatures who walk the earth while man sleeps. Adam hereby reestablishes the right moral context for speculations about nature.

The next challenge to Adam and Eve is Eve's dream which Satan "induces" in an effort to raise "discontented thoughts, . . . inordinate desires / . . . high conceits ingend'ring pride" (IV, 807–809), but Adam can accommodate even this event to the great Edenic good of growth and development. The dream itself seems a trial run for the Fall: a voice (Eve mistakes it for Adam's) flatters her that the stars at night wake only to behold her, and then leads her to the tree; a seeming angel eats the forbidden fruit and offers it to Eve as divine food that will elevate her to Godhead; a savory odor quickens her appetite; a sense of intoxication follows. But the whole event, the dream and the awakening, offers something more, a virtual experience of evil which reveals much about evil's true nature—its seeming attractiveness, its culmination in "offense and trouble," its aftermath of tears and remorse. Eve is alarmed by the dream and seeks help from Adam.[25] In this area also Adam lacks complete knowledge: he understands faculty psychology and can account for part of the dream as the product of Eve's fancy, in the absence of reason misjoining elements from their previous night's talk about the stars and the prohibition on the tree.[26] However, not knowing

[25] Irene Samuel (*Dante and Milton*, p. 13) notes that this incident gives Adam a clear opportunity to assume responsibility for Eve, to show himself her head.
[26] As Stein suggests (*Answerable Style*, pp. 87–88) the reader may also recognize as a component in the dream (though Adam does not) Eve's subconscious desire to have Adam praise her in the dream's excessive measure.

that Satan induced the dream, Adam cannot account for certain things in it—the evil that could not come from her "created pure," the "addition strange" to the materials that could be supplied by her mind (V, 100, 116). But again Adam works out the most important point: that one cannot do evil in a dream, that evil may "come and go" in the mind without blame, so long as it is not approved. And so he can cheer Eve with the reasonable hope that "what in sleep thou didst abhor to dream, / Waking thou never wilt consent to do" (V, 120–121). In the moral climate of Milton's Eden, Eve's virtual experience of evil no doubt creates new tensions within her, but by making her so much more aware of evil's true nature, it could greatly enhance her ability and her determination to shun the actual experience.

Raphael's visit presents Adam and Eve with a new social situation, and their civilized impulse to offer Raphael their best hospitality, coupled with their doubts as to whether or what he can eat, prompts Adam to ask about angelic food. Raphael's response explains the poem's metaphysics: the fact that all orders of being are interdependent since "whatever was created, needs / To be sustain'd and fed"; the additional fact that sustenance is always from below, "The grosser feeds the purer"; and the fact that beings wholly or partly spiritual (angels and men) contain "Within them every lower faculty / Of Sense" and have power to transform "corporeal to incorporeal" substance (V, 404–426). This exposition should prepare Adam and Eve to see the fallacy of Satan's later suggestion that they require divine food to advance in the scale of being.

Raphael also redefines hierarchy in the light of the common end and common substratum of all being: all things proceed from God and return to him if not depraved from good, and all things are of "one first matter . . . / Indu'd with various forms, various degrees / Of substance, and in things that live, of life" (V, 469–474). In this metaphysics the spiritual substance of angels is more highly refined but is not different in kind from man's substance, and angelic intuitive reason differs only in degree from man's discursive reason.[27] Furthermore, Raphael's statement that beings are "more refin'd, more spiritous and pure, / As nearer to him [God] plac't, or nearer tending" (V, 475–476) shows the

[27] For a review of traditional angelology, see Robert H. West, *Milton and the Angels* (Athens, Ga., 1955).

hierarchy of being depending not only upon rank at creation but also upon the dynamics of self-development. For illustration Raphael, like many other philosophers discussing hierarchy, uses a plant image. Aquinas, for example, declared, "So also is there order in the use of natural things. For the imperfect are for the use of the perfect: plants make use of the earth for their nourishment, animals make use of plants, and man makes use of both plants and animals."[28] But Raphael's application goes much beyond this. He traces the growth of the plant from root to odorous spirits in order to demonstrate that the transformation of corporeal into spiritual substance obtains in all orders of being; in order to show by analogy how body up to spirit works (for man is also a plant in a garden); and in order to suggest how man's proper sustenance, the plants of the Garden, will be utilized and transubstantiated by his higher faculties as he is gradually refined to angelic condition:

> So from the root
> Springs lighter the green stalk, from thence the leaves
> More aery, last the bright consummate flow'r
> Spirits odorous breathes: flow'rs and thir fruit
> Man's nourishment, by gradual scale sublim'd
> To vital spirits aspire, to animal,
> To intellectual, give both life and sense,
> Fancy and understanding, whence the Soul
> Reason receives, and reason is her being,
> Discursive or Intuitive; discourse
> Is oftest yours, the latter most is ours,
> Differing but in degree, of kind the same.
> Wonder not then, what God for you saw good
> If I refuse not, but convert, as you,
> To proper substance; time may come when men
> With Angels may participate, and find
> No inconvenient Diet, nor too light Fare:
> And from these corporal nutriments perhaps
> Your bodies may at last turn all to spirit,
> Improv'd by tract of time, and wing'd ascend
> Ethereal, as wee, or may at choice
> Here or in Heav'nly Paradises dwell.   (V, 479–500)

That this is not guesswork on Raphael's part is demonstrated to Adam and Eve by Raphael's own act of transubstantiating cor-

[28] Aquinas, *Summa Theologica*, Q. 96, A. 1, in *Basic Writings*, I, 918. For other parallels and some measure of Milton's divergence from them, see W. C. Curry, *Milton's Ontology, Cosmogony, and Physics*, pp. 156–177.

poral food to spiritual substance,[29] and also by Raphael's report of God's declaration about the gradual perfecting of man in Eden (and with him, all the earth),

> till by degrees of merit rais'd
> They open to themselves at length the way
> Up hither, under long obedience tri'd,
> And Earth be chang'd to Heav'n, and Heav'n to Earth,
> One Kingdom, Joy and Union without end.
> (VII, 157–160)

At this point Adam and Eve should better understand how they are expected to grow toward perfection in harmony with the very nature of things.

Adam again takes the initiative when he asks for a full account of the war in heaven. He seeks to pursue this topic, he says, because Raphael's brief allusion to fallen angels has raised in him "some doubt" regarding things "So unimaginable" as hate and evil in heaven (V, 554; VII, 54–55). The doubt is a temporary failure of imagination and comprehension, but Adam goes the right way to resolve it by asking his appointed teacher. As he well understands, Adam is asking here about matters "which human knowledge could not reach," for a revelation of the "secrets of another World" (VII, 75; V, 569); and the request is granted since the knowledge is for his good. The revelation shows Adam his enemy Satan, and also the Son in the role of conqueror of Satan. In addition, as Eve's dream provided a virtual experience of evil for Adam and Eve, so Raphael's epic and sometimes mock-epic tale provides a vicarious experience for them, as good stories will, which extends their comprehension of hitherto largely abstract moral concepts. From the story of Abdiel who upheld the cause of God even against his own companions, and of the faithful angels who fought without anxiety as if the whole issue depended upon each one's action, Adam understands much better than before what love of God, zeal, loyalty, and obedience are. Through Raphael's mimesis of the Satanic rhetoric, the Satanic manner of tempting the angels, the Satanic nature as re-

---

[29] Rajan overlooks the force of Raphael's demonstration when he conflates Raphael's promise of the gradual refinement of body into spirit in Eden with the commonplace Christian expectation of a spiritual body in heaven (*Seventeenth Century Reader*, p. 62), as does Broadbent also when he takes Raphael's "perhaps" as a basis for discounting the passage (*Some Graver Subject*, pp. 211–217).

vealed in action, Adam learns much more than he yet knows about temptation and sin. Also the story can help him form some conception of Death, which he has hitherto found incomprehensible—"whate'er Death is, / Some dreadful thing no doubt" (IV, 425–426). The increasing grossness of the fallen angels' substance after they sin shows him something of spiritual death, and their experience of pain and wounds—which Raphael informs him would be fatal to man—indicates something about physical death.

Adam's question about the creation of the world defines the next topic of discussion and it elicits additional "revealed" knowledge—the creation story from Genesis. Adam assures Raphael that he does not ask in order to explore God's secrets, but only to magnify his works; however, the form of Adam's question—"what cause / Mov'd the Creator in his holy Rest / Through all Eternity so late to build / In *Chaos*" (VII, 90–93) —shows Adam making a precarious beginning in theological speculation. Adam's question seems to assume that the creation somehow interrupted God's eternal rest, thus violating his immutability, and it intimates further that God's tardiness in undertaking the creation was somehow unworthy of his divinity. Such speculation as to God's activities before the creation of the world had long been taken as the very hallmark of curious, presumptuous inquiry into God's secret ways. Augustine described the posers of such questions as persons "who by a penal disease thirst for more than they can hold,"[30] and Calvin reprimanded them yet more sharply:

Indeed, that impious scoff ought not to move us: that it is a wonder how it did not enter God's mind sooner to found heaven and earth, but that he idly permitted an immeasurable time to pass away, since he could have made it very many millenniums earlier. . . . For it is neither lawful nor expedient for us to inquire why God delayed so long, because if the human mind strives to penetrate thus far, it will fail a hundred times on the way. And it would not even be useful for us to know what God himself, to test our moderation of faith, on purpose willed to be hidden. When a certain shameless fellow mockingly asked a pious old man what God had done before the creation of the

[30] Augustine, *Confessions*, in *Basic Writings*, ed. Whitney J. Oates, 2 vols. (New York, 1948), I, 202.

world, the latter aptly countered that he had been building hell for the curious.[31]

Origen and some others had been willing to speculate about such matters,[32] but Milton in the *Christian Doctrine* firmly aligns himself with the circumspect: "As to the actions of God before the foundation of the world, it would be the height of folly to inquire into them."[33]

Raphael's response teaches Adam the proper attitudes for seeking and receiving divine revelation. Raphael has commission from above to reveal so much of the creation story as Adam can comprehend, so much as will help him to glorify God and know his own happiness, and so much as he needs to inform his posterity. But Adam is to realize that "Knowledge is as food, and needs no less / Her Temperance over Appetite"; the temperance in question is defined as the foregoing of idle and presumptuous inquiry into God's hidden mysteries, "Things not reveal'd, which th'invisible King, / Only Omniscient, hath supprest in Night." This temperance observed, the way is open for Adam to seek further revelation and theological insight: "Anough is left besides to search and know" (VII, 122–127).

In describing the creation Raphael uses two great poetic metaphors to suggest to Adam the true nature of God's creative power —and man's. God (through the Son) is the cosmic geometer whose compass established the bounds, the just circumference of the world, marking it off from the boundless deep. And God is the vital male force impregnating the abyss of chaotic matter with all forms; causing in due season the "Embryon" earth to be born from the "Womb . . . / Of Waters," causing the great Mother Earth to be impregnated with all the seeds of life which, in her due course, "Op'ning her fertile Womb" she brings forth, gives birth to; and then blessing the creatures so that they reproduce after their kinds (VII, 230–498). The creation story culminates in God's charge to Adam to "Be fruitful, multiply, and fill the Earth" (VII, 531), and to keep the Garden, thus associating him closely as Image of God with God's continuous, prolific

[31] Calvin, *Institutes*, I.xiv, in *Library of Christian Classics*, XX, 160.

[32] See Origen, *De Principiis*, III.v.3, trans. F. Crombie, "Ante-Nicene Christian Library" (Edinburgh, 1869), X, 255–256; Aquinas, *Summa Theologica*, Q. 46, A. 1–3, in *Basic Writings*, I, 447–457.

[33] *CE*, XV, 3.

creativity in a constantly evolving universe. Adam should now better understand what the divine creativity is, and how he should share in it.

Adam then initiates a new subject of discourse, astronomy. As usual the angel graciously invites questions but does not embark upon a new subject until requested to do so. Adam's query grows directly out of the creation story. That story had been presented from the human perspective, as is obvious from the metaphors of procreation and birth, and accordingly the work of the fourth day (the creation of the sun and moon) was recounted in strictly geocentric terms. However the angelic hymn celebrating the creation had speculated about other inhabited worlds, implying other cosmic systems: "Stars / Numerous, and every Star perhaps a World / Of destin'd habitation" (VII, 620–622). The discrepancy evidently recalls to Adam the issues left unresolved in his earlier discussion with Eve about astronomy, and he seeks satisfaction of his "doubt" (VIII, 13). In this query Adam has not suddenly ventured upon forbidden knowledge as is sometimes supposed, and he is not now so near presumption as when he inquired about the creation. But as usual he proceeds by trial and error in his intellectual growth: he starts with certain faulty assumptions and formulations, and it is Raphael's province to teach him the proper spirit in which to approach natural science.

Adam repeats some of the Copernican objections to the geocentric theory—that the earth "better might with far less compass move" than the much larger, brighter, and nobler heavenly bodies (VIII, 30–38)—but he does not, as is often assumed, conclude that the earth does move. Rather he is distressed that the geocentric cosmos presents "Such disproportions" which seem a distortion in "wise and frugal" Nature (VIII, 26–27). And he implies a question as to whether there might not be some other uses for the heavenly bodies than "merely to officiate light / Round this opacous Earth" (VIII, 22–23).

Raphael begins immediately to clarify the issues in a tone that is not at all censorious, but "Benevolent and facile:"

> To ask or search I blame thee not, for Heav'n
> Is as the Book of God before thee set,
> Wherein to read his wond'rous Works, and learn
> His Seasons, Hours, or Days, or Months, or Yeers:
> This to attain, whether Heav'n move or Earth,
> Imports not, if thou reck'n right; the rest

From Man or Angel the great Architect
Did wisely to conceal, and not divulge
His secrets, to be scann'd by them who ought
Rather admire .... (VIII, 66–75)

The opening lines declare astronomical inquiry blameless in itself, including speculation about Ptolemaic and Copernican systems or any other, and the point is reinforced by Raphael's
bantering prediction that (unfallen) Adam will lead his sons in
Ptolemaic reasoning about cycles and epicycles and how to save
the appearances (VIII, 79–86). Such conjectures may provoke
God's laughter at man's quaint opinions, but there is nothing
forbidden about them: "he his Fabric of the Heav'ns / Hath
left to thir disputes" (VIII, 76–77). Raphael's next point,
"whether Heav'n move or Earth / Imports not" (VIII, 70–71)
defines the issue sharply for Adam who had not actually supposed that the heavens might move, and then affirms that Adam
need not resolve this issue in order to know that God's works are
indeed wonderful. In proof of this Raphael offers a critique of
Adam's complaint of disproportion in a geocentric universe: the
greatness and brightness of the other planets do not prove their
superiority to the fertile earth; the noble planets at any rate do
not serve the earth so much as man who is more noble still; and
a geocentric universe does not conduce to human pride for its
vast frame teaches man that he inhabits an edifice too large for
him, "Ordain'd for uses to his Lord best known" (VIII, 106).
Raphael's second proof is that another theory of planetary motion may explain many of the seeming disproportions. It is Raphael who suggests to Adam that the theory of a geocentric
cosmos may be the result of his limited human perspective: "But
this I urge, / Admitting Motion in the Heav'ns, to show / Invalid
that which thee to doubt it mov'd; / Not that I so affirm, though
so it seem / To thee who hast thy dwelling here on Earth" (VIII,
114–118). It is Raphael who invites Adam to consider much
more advanced scientific theories: that the sun might be a sta-
tionary center to the world, that the seemingly steadfast earth
might move "Insensibly three different Motions," fetching day
or night by her travels; that the earth might enlighten the moon
by day as the moon enlightens earth by night; that the spots on
the moon might be rain clouds to produce food for possible
moondwellers. Adam had thought of none of this, nor yet of Raphael's further speculations about other galaxies with inhabi-

tants—"other Suns perhaps / With thir attendant Moons . . . / Communicating Male and Female Light, / Which two great Sexes animate the World, / Stor'd in each Orb perhaps with some that live" (VIII, 122–152).

Since Raphael does not condemn Adam's speculations about astronomy, but rather advances them, why does he not resolve the geocentric / heliocentric issue for Adam? For one thing, to make the point that it is not his province as angelic instructor in metaphysics, theology, and ethics to resolve questions of natural science for man. Commentary on ancient and modern ideas of astronomy was traditional in the hexamera and in biblical exegesis of the Genesis creation story,[34] and Raphael, having just recounted for Adam his version of the creation, is now invited to give his observations on astronomy. As Grant McColley has shown, such commentary usually took the form of an open condemnation of heliocentrism, the moving earth, plural worlds, or all of these, as contradicting the Genesis account.[35] It was the defenders of the new science who argued that scripture did not intend to teach science and therefore that its supposedly "scientific" pronouncements were not to be taken literally. Galileo in a famous tract declared that in scripture "the intention of the Holy Ghost is to teach us how one goes to heaven, not how heaven goes,"[36] and he cited Augustine to similar effect:

> It is likewise commonly asked what we may believe about the form and shape of the heavens according to the Scriptures. . . . But with superior prudence our authors [the writers of scripture] have forborne to speak of this, as in no way furthering the student with respect to a blessed life—and, more important still, as taking up much of that time which should be spent in holy exercises.[37]

[34] Williams, *Common Expositor,* pp. 174–190; Howard Schultz, *Milton and Forbidden Knowledge* (New York, 1955), pp. 1–21; Robbins, *Hexaemeral Literature,* pp. 32, 41, 52, 63, 69; Kester Svendsen, *Milton and Science* (Cambridge, Mass., 1956), pp. 43–85.

[35] Grant McColley, *Paradise Lost,* pp. 92–97, 217–244; see especially Du Bartas, *Devine Weeks and Workes,* trans. Joshua Sylvester (1605), facsim. ed. Francis C. Haber (Gainesville, Fla., 1965), "The Fourth Day," pp. 118–121.

[36] Galileo, *Letter to Madame Christina of Lorraine . . . Concerning the Use of Biblical Quotations in Matters of Science* (1615), in *Discoveries and Opinions of Galileo,* ed. Stillman Drake (New York, 1957), p. 186.

[37] Augustine, *De Genesi ad Litteram,* II.9, cited by Galileo, *ibid.,* p. 184.

It would seem, then, that the usual interpretation of the Adam-Raphael discussion about astronomy does much less than justice to the angel's real liberalism. Unlike most biblical exegetes, he does not condemn the new theories: rather, it is he who spells them out. And his very refusal to "reveal" astronomy to Adam assumes, in the context of the contemporary argument about science and scripture, that scientific fact is not the concern of God's revelation to man. By so assuming he makes possible scientific inquiry for Adam and his progeny.

Another reason Raphael does not resolve the issue is that he is less concerned with Adam's store of scientific fact than with the attitudes Adam displays in scientific inquiry. Raphael presents his own dialogue on the two world systems as a model of such inquiry, from which Adam should learn not to conclude Nature defective and God's ways imperfect on the basis of his inadequate human understanding of the values and purposes operative in the cosmos, and not to assume that his earthbound cosmic theory of the moment—Ptolemaic or otherwise—is necessarily adequate to the whole. Then Raphael refers again, as he did in his introductory remarks on this question, to certain matters rightly hidden from men by God, whatever might be the truth of the geocentric/heliocentric issue:

> But whether thus these things, or whether not
> Whether the Sun predominant in Heav'n
> Rise on the Earth, or Earth rise on the Sun,
>
> . . . .
> Solicit not thy thoughts with matters hid,
> Leave them to God above, him serve and fear;
> Of other Creatures, as him pleases best,
> Wherever plac't, let him dispose: joy thou
> In what he gives to thee, this Paradise
> And thy fair *Eve*: Heav'n is for thee too high
> To know what passes there; be lowly wise:
> Think only what concerns thee and thy being;
> Dream not of other Worlds, what Creatures there
> Live, in what state, condition, or degree,
> Contented that thus far hath been reveal'd
> Not of Earth only but of highest Heav'n.
>   (VIII, 159–178)

It would seem that the "matters hid" referred to here are akin to those defined as such in the Creation sequence: the secret causes of things, God's reasons for disposing as he does in his cosmos—and specifically his plans for and ways toward other worlds and other beings. Adam may inquire about astronomy; but as for God's purposes and ways, he must be content with what is revealed. Later Satan will claim that the fruit brings power to "discern / Things in thir Causes" and "to trace the ways / Of highest Agents deem'd however wise" (IX, 681–683).[38] In conclusion Raphael directs Adam to his primary concerns and his primary joys, "thy being," "this Paradise / And thy fair Eve," identifying thereby the humanistic values that must not be displaced or violated by any scientific speculation or activity Adam may engage in: his own human condition, the human world, and human society.

Adam demonstrates his growth in understanding by applying the angelic precepts rigorously to his own situation: he will no longer interrupt "the sweet of Life" with "perplexing thoughts" and "anxious cares" about seeming disproportion in the cosmos, and about God's secret purposes (VIII, 182–187). His language alludes specifically to the analogy between his nature and his garden, "But apt the Mind or Fancy is to rove / Uncheckt, and of her roving is no end; / Till warn'd, or by experience taught, she learn . . . ." (VIII, 188–190). Having had his warning and his experience, Adam is prepared to prune away what is useless and obscure, mere "fume, / Or emptiness, or fond impertinence" (VIII, 194–195). Now he announces himself a committed humanist, and like Socrates[39] proposes to "descend" from specula-

---

[38] Andrew Willet, *Hexapla in Genesin* (London, 1608), p. 29, makes precisely the same interpretation of what "forbidden knowledge" is: "This tree of knowledge of good and evil may bee also mistically understood of that perfect and absolute knowledge, which God hath reserved to himselfe: the whiche they are forbidden to search after, but to content themselves with that gift and portion of knowledge, which God had alreadie aboundantly given unto them."

[39] See Xenophon, *Memorabilia*, I.i.11–16, trans. E. C. Marchant (Loeb, London, 1923), pp. 9–11:

[Socrates] did not even discuss that topic so favoured by other talkers, "the Nature of the Universe:" and avoided speculation on the so-called "Cosmos" of the Professors, how it works, and on the laws that govern the phenomena of the heavens: indeed he would argue that to trouble one's mind with such problems is sheer folly. In the first place, he would inquire, did these thinkers suppose that their knowledge of human affairs was so complete that they must seek these new fields for the exercise of their brains; or that it was their duty to neglect human affairs and consider only things divine? Moreover, he marvelled at their blindness in not seeing that men cannot solve these riddles; since even the most conceited talkers on these problems did

tion about the heavens (whether angelic warfare, or creation, or planets) and seek the "prime Wisdom," namely, "That which before us lies in daily life"—in Socratic terms, self-knowledge, ethics (VIII, 193–195). Accordingly, he proposes to tell the story of his own creation, and in it he emphasizes his rapid advancement in useful knowledge—of the animals and the Garden, of himself, and of Eve and their marital relationship.

Then Adam mentions the problem troubling him in this sphere of his primary concern, the "passion . . . / Commotion strange" stirred up in him by the experience of sex ("Transported touch"), and by the "charm of Beauty's powerful glance" (VIII, 529–533). Again he makes faulty assumptions. He supposes, as have many critics of the poem, that he should not be having these feelings and these difficulties and that, because he is having them, there must be some defect in human nature: either he has been made too weak, or Eve has been given "Too much of Ornament" in relation to her real inferiority in mind and inward faculties. He complains that in her presence he can hardly maintain, or even believe in, his own superior wisdom, knowledge, authority, and reason.

Raphael however does *not* assume that the "commotion strange" is an anomaly, that tension and difficulty are out of place in Eden; and he scores the theory that such feelings argue defects in the natures of Adam or Eve. His point is rather that Adam must learn to deal with the situation, to do his part as nature has done hers. He must not give way to such feelings so as to act under the influence of passion: "take heed lest Passion sway / Thy Judgment to do aught, which else free Will / Would not admit" (VIII, 635–637). Raphael recommends that Adam strengthen his proper self-esteem by contemplating how far superior his own qualities really are to the beauty, the outside loveliness, which so enchants him in Eve. He also urges Adam

---

not agree in their theories, but behaved to one another like madmen. . . . Do those who pry into heavenly phenomena imagine that, once they have discovered the laws by which these are produced, they will create at their will winds, waters, seasons, and such things. . . . His own conversation was ever of human things. The problems he discussed were, What is godly, what is ungodly; what is beauty, what is ugly; what is just, what is unjust; what is prudence, what is madness; what is courage, what is cowardice.

See also Irene Samuel, "Milton on Learning and Wisdom," *PMLA*, LXIV (1949) 708–723.

to apprehend and ascend the Neoplatonic ladder of love, disdaining subjection to the sense of touch which is "voutsaf't / To Cattle and each Beast," and loving Eve rather for her higher qualities—"attractive, human, rational." Such a love, he explains, "refines / The thoughts, and heart enlarges, hath his seat / In Reason, and is judicious, is the scale / By which to heav'nly Love thou may'st ascend" (VIII, 581–592).

Raphael began this speech "with contracted brow" and takes, it would seem, a harsh line on the pleasures of sex, but this is because Adam has unwittingly given the impression that his relationship to Eve is wholly based upon beauty and sex, and that his passion is indeed overwhelming. But of course Adam has found in Eve also the companion and helpmeet he desired from God, and has loved her dearly in these roles. Now, seeing that he has been misunderstood, Adam tries "half-abash't" to do better justice to himself. He indicates to Raphael that he does indeed value more highly than beauty or sex "those graceful acts, / Those thousand decencies that daily flow / From all her words and actions, mixt with Love" (VIII, 600–602); that these subject not; and that he was talking about "What inward thence I feel," not about any actual surrender to passion. To be sure this too facile assertion that he has himself firmly under control indicates that Adam does not realize the difficulties involved in the control of so strong a passion as he has admitted to, and therefore that he does not yet fully know himself. But his speech does show that he has understood Raphael's lesson: that he is not to complain of these feelings or motions in himself, but is to continue to control them as he has hitherto done—"yet still free / Approve the best, and follow what I approve" (VIII, 610–611).

But for all this, Adam, who in the first few hours of his life disputed so ably with his Creator, does not take Raphael's formulations on the subject of marital love without qualification. Raphael, to make his point about the folly of subjection by sex, has seemed virtually to identify human sexual love with animal copulation. But Adam's experience in his nuptial bower has been rather different, and it has been confirmed by the narrator's sublime testimony to the great human good of marital love in his epithalamium to Adam and Eve, "Hail Wedded Love." And so, though Adam accepts the scale Raphael defines—the same scale Milton urged in the divorce tracts—which regards companionship and social intercourse as higher and more specifically human joys than sexual intercourse, Adam qualifies. He enters his opinion that the relations of the "genial Bed" are "higher . . . by far" than animal copulation, and are worthy of "mysterious reverence" (VIII, 598–599). And his question about angelic love is part of this qualification. It is not, as is often assumed, an impudent question, or an evidence that Adam is avoiding his own problem, or an indication of his continuing pursuit of curious learning.[40] He has been urged by Raphael to ascend in the scale of love which, like the scale of Nature Raphael described at the beginning of the dialogue, will presumably culminate in Adam's elevation to something like the angelic condition, and Adam is concerned with the final state. He finds it hard to imagine on the basis of his own experience with the "genial bed," and his previous instruction about the nature of angels (who continue to require and to enjoy food), that the heavenly love can be so entirely Platonic, so entirely without expression through physical means as Raphael for the moment has seemed to imply. And so he asks, humbly enough but not without the consciousness that he is making a worthy argument: "Bear with me then, if lawful what I ask; / Love not the heav'nly Spirits, and how thir Love / Express they" (VIII, 614–616).

Raphael's answer has been as badly misunderstood as Adam's question. He does not blush like a Victorian schoolgirl because sex has been mentioned and hurry away after a mumbled answer.[41] He responds "with a smile that glow'd / Celestial rosy red, Love's proper hue" (VIII, 618)—and we are expected to remember that according to tradition those angels who most fully embody the quality of love, the Seraphim, are fiery red and flamelike.[42] Adam is not asking for a detailed account of angelic sexuality and the reader should not expect it. Rather, he asks for

[40] See Stein, *Answerable Style*, p. 100; West, *Milton and the Angels,* p. 173; Tillyard, *Studies in Milton* (London, 1951), pp. 12–13.

[41] Frye, *The Return to Eden*, pp. 61–62; John Peter, *A Critique of Paradise Lost* (New York, 1960), pp. 108–109.

[42] See for example, Dante, *Paradiso,* XXXI, 13–14 (Temple Classics, London, 1958): "They [the angels] had their faces all of living flame, and wings of gold." See also St. Teresa, *The Flaming Hart,* trans. M. T. [Toby Matthew?] (Antwerp, 1642), p. 419: "But in this Vision, Our Lord was pleased, that I should see the Angell. . . . His face was so inflamed, that he appeared to be of those most Superiour Angells, who seem to be, all in a fire; and he might well be of them, whome we call Seraphins."

confirmation of his intuition about the scale of love. To this Raphael's answer is fully adequate. Just as earlier Raphael admitted and demonstrated that angels enjoy food (their customary food being more highly refined and more delightful than human food) so here he admits to angelic sex—also more highly refined, more delightful, and more perfect than the human counterpart, since angelic embraces effect a total mixture, "Union of Pure with Pure / Desiring," without any obstacle of "membrane, joint, or limb" (VIII, 620–629). The angel's rosy smile is also evidence of his own love and friendship for Adam, and his gracious answer testifies to his pleasure in his pupil's right understanding of the scale of Nature and the scale of love, so that Adam is able to infer points omitted in the angelic account. We ought to recall here that at the outset of Adam's career in the Garden God was similarly delighted when Adam argued him down on the question of a mate.

It should now be evident that in his treatment of the prelapsarian state, Milton is not only, and not primarily, foreshadowing the Fall, but that he is undertaking to create, in quite unusual terms, the Life in Innocence. He is virtually unique in attempting this. Aquinas and a few Protestant exegetes had speculated about the possible development of Adam and Eve in the Garden but the matter remained wholly academic since in their view Paradise was lost so soon. Also, previous literary treatments of the Fall offered scant precedent for such an attempt.[43] Milton's vision of the prelapsarian life admits no dichotomy between the states of Innocence and Experience: they are not, as in Blake, "two contradictory states of the human soul." Rather, the Edenic portion of *Paradise Lost* displays the process whereby Adam and Eve grow in knowledge and acquire experience within the State of Innocence, and thereby become steadily more complex, more conscious of manifold challenges and difficulties, more aware of large responsibilities, and by this very process, more complete and more perfect. This imagination of the Life in Innocence is emphatically antiromantic, anti-Arcadian, anti-escapist, anti-

[43] Adam and an angel discourse in Grotius' *Adamus Exul,* but this is a purely formal exposition of hexameral material. In Serafino della Salandria's *Adamo Caduto* (1647), God responds to Adam's questions and instructs him about his nature and duties, but this is part of the creation scene and so gives no sense of continuing development. See Kirkconnell, *Celestial Cycle,* pp. 117–137, 292–302.

individualistic: it is an exaltation of humanism, maturity, civilization in happiest conjunction with vitality, change, growth. Such an imagination of the State of Innocence sets the Fall in the proper tragic perspective in the poem, as the event which blasted man's opportunity to develop—without suffering, violence, despair and death, though not in the least without tension and trial —the rich resources and large potentialities of the human spirit.

6

The Falls of Adam and Eve in
Paradise Lost

A. B. CHAMBERS

▼

In *Paradise Lost*, as in the Bible, the fall of Adam and Eve turns out, on examination, to be not one thing but two: separate violations of God's commandment in differing circumstances and at different times. In *Paradise Lost*, but not in the Book of Genesis, different explanations of the fall also are supplied. Deceived by Satan, Eve eats of the forbidden fruit in the mistaken belief that her action is right; unable to face separation from Eve, Adam "scrupl'd not to eat / Against his better knowledge, not deceiv'd" (IX, 997–998).[1] At this point Milton is not re-creating the biblical story but interpreting it, and the question that immediately arises is why he should interpret it in this particular way. The answer, for a modern reader, is simple. Milton merely accepts and employs St. Paul's explanation that "Adam was not deceived, but the woman being deceived was in the transgression" (I Tim. 2 : 14). For earlier readers, particularly those in Milton's "fit audience," the answer probably would have been complex. To begin with, the meaning of St. Paul's statement, far from being

[1] *Complete Poems and Major Prose*, ed. Merritt Y. Hughes (New York, 1957).

118

obvious, was vigorously disputed both before and during Milton's time. Deliberately and not at all inevitably, Milton chose one exegesis—Augustine's as it happens—from among the many ←— available to him. Perhaps he did so with deep conviction that his choice was unarguably correct, but other reasons may also have been at work. It is clear, at any rate, that Augustine's and Milton's understanding of the Pauline text was closely related to two other matters that should have been of considerable interest to anyone contemplating an epic on the fall of man. The first was a standard analysis of sin which distinguished between those sins committed because the rational faculty was deceived and those committed even though no deception occurred. The second was a widely accepted psychology of the temptation to sin, a psychology in which the rational faculty played a crucial role. These facts are worth establishing, and not merely because they allow one to see more precisely than before just why Milton interpreted the falls of Adam and Eve in the way he did; once understood, they have the further advantage of underscoring one of the important thematic patterns of the entire poem.

First of all, what did St. Paul mean when he said that Adam in some sense was undeceived? He meant, evidently, rather more or rather less than one might suppose. Three seventeenth-century divines, Andrew Willet, Edward Leigh, and John Mayer, conveniently summarize the principal possibilities.

Willet:
It is like [likely, i.e.] he was seduced by the same flattering and false perswasions, whereby the woman was first beguiled, beeing carried away with an ambitious desire, in knowledge, not to be equalized, but made like vnto God. . . . Neither doth that place of the Apostle contradict this opinion . . . for whether we expound it with Epiphanius and Caluin, that the Apostles meaning is, the woman was first deceiued, not the man: or with Mercurus, that the man was not deceiued, but entised by the woman: or with Hierome, that Adam was not deceiued by the serpent, but by the woman: or that Eua did not wittingly deceiue Adam, as the serpent beguiled Eua . . . by this text Adam is not wholly exempted from being deceiued.

Leigh:
Calvin [and] *Beza, say,* Adam *was not first deceived* . . . Chrysostom saith he was not properly, nor immediately deceived from the Serpent, but occasionally. . . . Ierome, and Drusius,

that he was not deceived by the Serpent, but by Eve. Theophylactus [that] the woman was seduced by cupidity, the man by the woman. He was not, at least, deceived by the serpent.

Mayer:

> But whether the man being tempted by her were deceived, as shee had beene, or by the womans flattery onely were allured to satisfie her desire, is a question, because *the man*, saith the Apostle, *was not deceived, but the woman.* For the one is *Augustine*: for the other, that he also was deceived, *Chrysost[om]*, *Ambros[e]*, *Prosper*, *Calvin*, and the author of this slender worke [i.e., Mayer himself.][2]

The curious thing about these surveys of opinion is, of course, the fact that all three suggest that Adam may have been deceived and that two of them conclude that indeed he was. This position was sometimes presented, moreover, as if it were the only possibility. Thomas Morton, for example, explains that St. Paul merely "meaneth that *Eua* was first, yea more easily and grossly deceiued." Thomas Jackson argues that the passage means no more than that Eve was "more deeply in the transgression than the man, because she seduced him to eat of the forbidden fruit, as the serpent had done her." John Gerhard's ingenious explanation is that "though wee should grant that Adam was not deceived by another; yet he was deceived by himselfe."[3]

The second curious thing about these surveys of opinion is that only one of them, Mayer's, mentions Augustine, and yet Augustine's interpretation was a popular one. It received support in the Middle Ages from Peter Lombard, Aquinas, Vincent of Beauvais, Nicolas of Lyra, and Hugh of St. Cher.[4] It was paraphrased and quoted, with or without acknowledgment, in six-

---

[2] Andrew Willet, *Hexapla in Genesin* (London, 1608), pp. 48–49; Edward Leigh, *Annotations upon all the New Testament* (London, 1650), p. 322, marginal note (I have translated the last two sentences from Latin); John Mayer, *The English Catechisme Explained* (5th ed.; London, 1635), p. 141. Cornelius à Lapide, *Commentaria in omnes Divi Pauli Epistolas* (Antwerp, 1635), p. 716, gives a comparable survey.

[3] Thomas Morton, *A Treatise of the Three-fold State of Man* (London, 1629), p. 23; Thomas Jackson, *A Treatise of the Primeval Estate of the first Man*, in *Works* (Oxford, 1844), IX, 56; John Gerhard, *A Golden Chaine of Divine Aphorismes*, trans. Winterton (Cambridge, 1632), pp. 109–110. See also Arthur Lake, *Sermons* (London, 1629), pp. 76–77, fourth pagination; Edward Leigh, *A System or Body of Divinity* (London, 1654), p. 304; and Thomas Browne, *Pseudodoxia epidemica*, I.i, in *Works*, ed. Sayle (Edinburgh, 1927), I, 121–126.

[4] Peter Lombard, *In omnes D. Pauli Apost. Epistolas collectanea* (Paris, 1538), f. 411v; Aquinas, *Summa theologica*, II–II, Q. 163, A. 4;

teenth- and seventeenth-century works by Zanchius, Musculus, Cooper, Mexia, Goulart, Cartwright, Ussher, and Diodati.[5] And since it was embraced by Milton too, it will be well to indicate Augustine's position at some length.

> We must believe that Adam transgressed the law of God, not because he was deceived into believing that the lie was true, but because in obedience to a social compulsion he yielded to Eve, as husband to wife, as the only man in the world to the only woman. It was not without reason that the Apostle wrote: "Adam was not deceived but the woman was deceived." He means, no doubt, that Eve accepted the serpent's word as true, whereas Adam refused to be separated from his partner even in a union of sin—not, of course, that he was, on that account, any less guilty, since he sinned knowingly and deliberately. . . . The distinction is here made between those who, like Adam, sin with full knowledge and those who are deceived because they do not know what they are doing is a sin. It is this distinction which gives meaning to the statement: "Adam was not deceived."[6]

Augustine is considerably more kind to Adam than Milton at this point in his poem could afford to be; Milton's Adam, instead of acting "in obedience to a social compulsion," is "fondly overcome with Female charm" (IX, 999). Kindness aside, the position in each instance is the same, as we can tell from the internal soliloquy in which Adam grieves for Eve's fall and resolves to accompany her in death:

> How art thou lost, how on a sudden lost,
> Defac't, deflow'r'd, and now to Death devote?
> Rather how hast thou yielded to transgress

Vincent of Beauvais, *Speculum naturale* (Strasbourg, ?1481), Bk. XXXI, cap. lxxii; Nicolas of Lyra, in *Biblia sacra cum Glossa interlineari, ordinaria, et Nicolai Lyrani Postilla* (Venice, 1588), VI, 119; Hugh of St. Cher, *Postilla* (Basel, 1502), *s.v.* I Tim. 2:14.

[5] Hieronymus Zanchius, *Tractationum theologicarum volumen* (n.p., 1597), p. 3; Wolfgang Musculus, *Common Places of Christian Religion* (London, 1563), f. 17r; Thomas Cooper, *A Briefe Exposition of . . . Chapters of the olde testament . . .* (London, 1573), p. 100; Pedro Mexia, *The Treasurie of Auncient and Moderne Times* (London, 1603), pp. 25–26; Simon Goulart, *A Learned Summary Upon . . . Bartas* (London, 1621), pp. 56–57, second pagination; T[homas] C[artwright], *A Treatise of Christian Religion* (London, 1616), pp. 52–53; James Ussher, *A Body of Divinitie* (2d ed.; London, 1647), pp. 134–135; John Diodati, *Pious and Learned Annotations* (4th ed.; London, 1664), *s.v.* I Tim. 2:14.

[6] *The City of God*, XIV.11, trans. Walsh and Monahan (New York, 1952), II, 378.

> The strict forbiddance, how to violate
> The sacred Fruit forbidd'n! some cursed fraud
> Of Enemy hath beguil'd thee, yet unknown,
> And mee with thee hath ruin'd, for with thee
> Certain my resolution is to Die:
> How can I live without thee, how forgo
> Thy sweet Converse and Love so dearly join'd,
> To live again in these wild Woods forlorn?
>   (IX, 900–910)

Neither Adam nor Milton proceeds to a moralization of this song. Adam, for obvious reasons, could not possibly know that his sin and Eve's were to be so repetitive as to be archetypal, that "the distinction is here made," as Augustine said, "between those who, like Adam, sin with full knowledge and those who are deceived." Milton knew but thought he did not need to mention the fact, for he also knew that Augustine's distinction had long since become standard in the moral theology of sin.

That this theology was enormously complex in detail is clear from even a glance at Jeremy Taylor's *Doctor dubitantum* or at Robert Sanderson's *De obligatione conscientiae*. It was simple, however, in essence. All discussions began by defining sin, along with St. John, as "the transgression of the law" (I John 3 : 4) and continued by attempting to describe and define the kinds of transgression that were possible. Milton's classification in the *De doctrina Christiana* illustrates one common method:

> Sin, as defined by the apostle, is . . . "the transgression of the law," I John iii. 4. . . . Sin is distinguished into THAT WHICH IS COMMON TO ALL MEN, and THE PERSONAL SIN OF EACH INDIVIDUAL.[7]

Milton's classification was standard because it dealt with the fundamental distinction between original sin and actual sin. Equally standard was a classification in terms of the internal faculties of the mind and soul. John Meredith, in *The Sinne of Blasphemie Against the Holy Ghost, Scholastically Examined*, provides a typical example:

> All, whatsoeuer Sinnes, proceed from a corruption in one of these principall faculties;
> Sometime, by default of the *Vertue Appetitiue*; when we fall into Sinnes through *Infirmity*, and notwithstanding all our resistance, wee canot fully auoyde them; but with Humiliation

---

[7] *De doctrina Christiana*, I.xi, in Columbia *Works*, XV, 179–181.

wee acknowledge them, and accuse our selues for the Commission.

Sometime, by default of the *Vertue Appetitiue*; when we fall sinnes through *error*, and commit euill, because we thinke it to be good; being deceiued by the vayle of a false opinion, which causeth in vs deniall of those sinnes.

Sometime by default of the *will*; when we commit sinnes of meere iniquity; knowing them, being able to resist them, and yet of purpose committing them.[8]

Sins of appetite or, to give them another name, sins of concupiscence result from what Mayer calls the "evil motions . . . in the minds" of men which the falls of Adam and Eve first introduced into the world.[9] They thus are identifiable as the symptoms of original sin and consequently ought not to be applicable to prelapsarian Adam and Eve, in whom there should have been, as Willet puts it, "no inordinate motion."[10] Some Miltonists, pointing to the perturbations of Eve's dream, her initial narcissism, Adam's confessed uxoriousness, and so on, nevertheless have thought that the sins of concupiscence are present even before the moment when the falls presumably occur. In fact, however, while Adam and Eve experienced "motions" and, because human, necessarily had to experience them, those motions were not "inordinate" until after the fruit was eaten. Milton, seizing upon the etymological meaning of "Eden" as a place of "pleasure" and depicting the garden as a *locus amoenus*, takes considerable pains to stress that the pleasure and delight of Adam and Eve included many "motions" of the appetite and flesh; among them, notoriously, was even voluptuous sexual experience.[11] The thematic importance of these delights is an emphasis

[8] (London, 1622), pp. 10–11. Cf. *Propositions and Principles of Diuinitie, propounded . . . by certaine students of . . . Beza* (Edinburgh, 1591), *passim*, but especially pp. 41 ff.; Thomas Goodwin, *Aggravation of Sinne: And Sinning Against Knowledge* (London, 1637), *passim*, but especially p. 49; Henry Hammond (?), *Sins of Weaknesse, of Wilfulnesse* (Oxford, 1645), pp. 18 ff.; H. R. McAdoo, *The Structure of Caroline Moral Theology* (London and New York, 1949).

[9] Mayer, *A Fovrefold Resolution* (London, 1609), p. 132.

[10] Willet, *Hexapla*, p. 46.

[11] On Eden as "pleasant," cf. James Sims, *The Bible in Milton's Epics* (Gainesville, Fla., 1962), pp. 22–23; on the topos of *locus amoenus*, see Ernst R. Curtius, *European Literature and the Latin Middle Ages*, trans. Trask (New York, 1953), pp. 195–200; on the lack of precedent for prelapsarian sexual experience, see Sister Mary Corcoran, *Milton's Paradise with Reference to the Hexameral Background* (Washington, 1945), pp. 76 ff.

upon the dissimilarity of prelapsarian pleasure and postlapsarian woe. To take only the strongest example, not until after the fall, are Adam and Eve afflicted by *tristitia post coitum*.[12] And these motions are not inordinate before the fall precisely because they are always ordered. Eve's "narcissism" is countered by her realization that "beauty is excell'd by manly grace / And wisdom, which alone is truly fair" (IV, 490–491); Adam's worry lest he be too uxorious is answered by his correct statement that not yet is he "therefore foil'd" by what he "inward" feels (VIII, 608). Finally, even were these motions reprehensible in some unspecified and undefinable sense, they could not constitute sin for Adam and Eve. First, from a literalistic point of view, the only sin Adam and Eve could commit was to eat of the forbidden fruit; nothing else had been prohibited. Second, no potentially evil motions, particularly if they occur in prelapsarian man, can constitute sin unless confirmed by the consent of the will. Evil, even into the mind of God, may come and go if "unapprov'd" (V, 117–118).

A sin of concupiscence or appetite could not have occurred, then, before the Fall. Could the sins of understanding and will? Depending on what authorities one reads, the answer is both yes and no. On the one hand, many discussions of prelapsarian existence state that man's reason and will were at that time not liable to error. Meredith's discussion of sin, quoted above, continues by pointing out that before the fall not only was the appetite "a prouident and faithfull Subiect" to the reason but also that the reason itself was then "prudent," though it now is "blind." John Wolleb, upon whom Milton is known to have depended for his own *De doctrina*, asserts that among the supernatural gifts bestowed upon prelapsarian Adam were clearness of understanding, liberty and rectitude of will, and conformity of the appetites.[13] Amandus Polanus, whose treatise of Christian doctrine probably influenced Wolleb's, maintains that in Adam "the soundnes of reason did shine foorth, both in the minde and also in the will."[14] Milton incorporates a part of this doctrine in the *De doctrina* when he argues that "Man being formed after

---

[12] See J. B. Broadbent, *Some Graver Subject* (London, 1960), p. 261.
[13] *The Abridgement of Christian Divinity,* trans. Ross (London, 1656), p. 69 (*Compendium theologiae Christianae* [Cambridge, 1642], pp. 43–44).
[14] *The Svbstanec* [*sic*] *of Christian Religion* (London, 1600), p. 62.

the image of God, it followed as a necessary consequence that he should be endued with natural wisdom, holiness, and righteousness."[15] He probably alludes to this doctrine again when Raphael says that Adam is "Perfet within" (VIII, 642). Polanus and Wolleb point out that only after the fall are the appetite, will, and reason corrupted. Again, Milton agrees. "Spiritual death," according to the *De doctrina*, "consists, first, of the loss . . . of that right reason which enabled man to discern the chief good. . . . and [second] in that slavish subjection to sin and the devil, which constitutes, as it were, the death of the will."[16] In *Paradise Lost*, the first consequence of the Fall is the degeneration of love into lust, the second is a darkening of the mind (IX, 1053–1054), and the third is a weakening of the will (IX, 1127). Wolleb could almost have used Michael's summary as his own:

> Since thy original lapse, true Liberty
> Is lost, which always with right Reason dwells
> Twinn'd, and from her hath no dividual being:
> Reason in man obscur'd, or not obey'd,
> Immediately inordinate desires
> And upstart Passions catch the Government
> From Reason, and to servitude reduce
> Man till then free.   (XII, 83–90)

On the other hand, Wolleb could not quite agree with Michael because Michael includes the detail that prelapsarian liberty can be lost through an obscurity of reason or through the refusal of the will to obey. Wolleb, moreover, took the position that the original rectitude of man's faculties was a supernatural gift, but Milton considers that rectitude to have been natural and therefore liable to change. J. B. Broadbent once surveyed the background underlying this distinction between natural and supernatural gifts.[17] He used that background to add qualified support for Millicent Bell's "fallacy" theory and to maintain that Raphael's injunction to Adam—"take heed lest Passion sway / Thy Judgment to do aught, which else free Will / Would not admit" (VIII, 635–637)—is "anachronistic" and therefore ap-

---

[15] *De doctrina*, I.vii, in *Works*, XV, 53. It is important to note, however, that Milton thought these endowments were "natural," not—as Wolleb has it—"supernatural."

[16] *De doctrina*, I.vii, in *Works*, XV, 207.

[17] Broadbent, *op. cit.*, pp. 193–199.

plicable "only to the fallen soul."[18] I think it can be shown, however, that Milton himself thought otherwise.

Milton was careful to mention in the *De doctrina* the "liability to fall with which man was created,"[19] and the considerable development of that liability in *Paradise Lost* explicitly turns upon the faculties of reason and will. Early in Book III, God states that man was created "just and right, Sufficient to have stood"—perfect as man ought, as Pope puts it[20]—but nevertheless "free to fall" (III, 98–99). Both conditions depend upon man's choices, however, and man, as God's foreknowledge perceives, will choose wrongly. God therefore states that "Reason also is choice" (III, 108), thereby echoing Milton's earlier statement in *Areopagitica* that "Reason is but choosing,"[21] and he prophesies that Adam and Eve will "trespass . . . in all Both what they judge and what they choose" (III, 122–123). God is establishing, well before we have even met Adam and Eve, that their falls will occur because of a blinded understanding ("what they judge") and a disobedient will ("what they choose"). The crucial importance of these faculties within prelapsarian man results from the even greater importance of them within God. God's infinite wisdom, as Milton explains in the *De doctrina*,[22] is coextensive with his omnipotent will, and what he wills, as God says in *Paradise Lost*, "is Fate" (VII, 173). Within God's image, however, reason and will are finite and therefore liable not only to change but to error. Adam is aware of that fact when he warns Eve that reason can "dictate false, and misinform the Will" (IX, 355); Raphael indicates his awareness when he cautions Adam against uxoriousness and urges him to "be not diffident of Wisdom" (VIII, 562–563); and Michael drives home the point when, in the speech already quoted, he says that Adam and Eve lost their freedom through an obscured reason and a disobedient will. The liability to fall with which Adam and Eve were created arises, then, from their existence as finite images of God; and it is identifiable with the possibility of sins of understanding and of will, those very evils, in short, which the moral theology of sin describes.

[18] See Millicent Bell, "The Fallacy of the Fall in *Paradise Lost*," *PMLA*, LXVIII (1953), 863–883.

[19] *De doctrina*, I.xi, in *Works*, XV, 181.

[20] *Essay on Man*, I, 70.

[21] *Works*, IV, 319.

[22] *De doctrina*, I.ii, in *Works*, XIV, 65.

While that theology classified sin under three fundamental categories, one of them, as we have seen, is not applicable to prelapsarian Adam and Eve. The other two, moreover, resolve into the same distinction already made by Augustine's reading of St. Paul. A sin of understanding or "knowledge" occurs, according to William Perkins' discussion, "when a man offends against his knowledge, doing euill when he knoweth it to be euill: and this is greater than a sinne of ignorance." Sins of ignorance, Perkins continues, either are "simple," those sins committed because of ignorance of things one could but does not happen to know, or are "affected," those sins committed because of ignorance of things one deliberately refuses to learn.[23] "Affected ignorance" is even worse than knowledgeable sin, but since Adam and Eve could scarcely be accused of refusing to learn—Adam, after all, is eager to learn as much as he can from Raphael—the possibilities actually are no more than two: to sin because deceived, as Augustine and Milton say Eve was, or to sin against one's knowledge, as Augustine and Milton say Adam did.

This moral theology, fundamental to most classifications of sin and thus significant in its own right, was also important because of its relationship to the traditional psychology of temptation. In its simplest form, this psychology states no more than that temptation leads to sin by means of a threefold process. William F. Foster's *The Means to Keepe Sinne from Reigning in our Mortall Body* contains this version of the formula:

> There are three degrees in sin; 1 Suggestion, offered by the Deuill. 2 Delight, administred by the flesh. 3 Consent, yeelded by our reason. . . . Suggestion begins sinne, Delight continues, Consent finisheth sinne.[24]

This process, however, was frequently presented in terms of an allegory of the fall. Foster, for example, continues with a statement that the serpent corresponds to suggestion, Eve to delight, and Adam to consent. Foster's avowed authority for these equations is Gregory, who once said that "the serpent tempted, in that the secret enemy silently suggests evil to man's heart. Eve was pleased, because the sense of flesh, at the voice of the serpent,

[23] *The Whole Treatise of the Cases of Conscience,* in *Works* (London, 1613), pp. 3–11. See also the references in notes 8–10 above.
[24] (London, 1629), p. 7. Cf. Perkins, *Works,* p. 10, and Robert Jenison, *The Height of Israels Heathenish Idolatrie* (London, 1621), pp. 13–14.

presently gives itself up to pleasure. And Adam . . . yielded consent . . . in that the spirit gives in from its uprightness."[25] Equally good authority could have been had from Augustine or from Aquinas' paraphrase of Augustine:

> In every sin we discover the same order as in the first temptation. For, according to Augustine, the temptation begins with concupiscence of sin by the sensuality, signified by the serpent; reaches to the lower reason by pleasure, signified by the woman; and extends to the higher reason by consent to the sin, signified by the man.[26]

Since the lower reason to which Aquinas refers is mankind's carnal reason, Aquinas and Gregory are closer in their interpretation of Eve than at first appears. Both have in mind, surely, the standard allegory of Adam as soul and Eve as body, an allegory as old as Philo Judaeus, but as new as Erasmus, Henry More, and even the sceptical Dr. Glanville: "The *Woman* in us, still prosecutes a deceit, like that begun in the *Garden*: and our *Understandings* are wedded to an *Eve*, as fatal as the *Mother* of our *miseries*."[27]

Whether this allegory is immediately relevant for *Paradise Lost* remains, of course, debatable. In my opinion, Milton's regular stress on Adam's wisdom and Eve's beauty almost inevitably must have had allegorical overtones for seventeenth-century readers. If so, Saurat's allegorical reading of *Paradise Lost* as a poem about the triumph of Passion over Reason nevertheless cannot be maintained.[28] Maurice Kelley was certainly correct in arguing that attempts to limit the first sin to one and only one particular sin necessarily oversimplify reality because, as Milton himself points out in the *De doctrina*, that first sin included within it every imaginable offense.[29] The reason it did, as

---

[25] *Morals on the Book of Job,* trans. anon. (Oxford, 1844), I, 215.

[26] Translated from Aquinas, *Summa theologica,* II–II, Q. 165, A. 2. See also Augustine, *De trinitate,* XII.12–13; Bonaventura, *Sententiarum libri IV* (Quaracchi, 1885), II, 496; Musculus, *Common Places,* f. 23r; Mexia, *The Treasurie,* p. 28 (quoting Leone Ebreo).

[27] See Philo's discussion of Genesis 3 in *De opificio mundi*; Erasmus, *Enchiridion militis Christiani* (London, 1905), pp. 43, 99; for Henry More, see Marjorie Nicolson, "Milton and the *Conjectura Cabbalistica,*" *PQ,* VI (1927), 1–18; Glanville, *The Vanity of Dogmatizing* (New York, 1931 [a facsimile of the London, 1661 edition]), p. 118.

[28] *Milton: Man and Thinker* (New York, 1925), pp. 149 ff.

[29] *This Great Argument* (Princeton, N.J., 1941), pp. 143–150. Milton's comment is in *De doctrina,* I.xi, in *Works,* XV, 181–183.

Rajan perceived, was that the "two faults" of Adam and Eve "—a defective understanding and a disobedient will—make up mortal sin, the compendium of every possible error."[30] One of the reasons Milton was able to present such a conclusion, however, was the psychology of temptation and its attendant allegory of Adam and Eve. This allegory and psychology must strongly have suggested to Milton's mind the probability of the biblical Eve's fall as the deceived reaction of mankind's flesh and carnal reason to a mental sophistication with which it is unprepared to deal. They must also have pointed toward the probability of Adam's fall as a knowledgeable assent of the mind to a temptation it self-consciously refuses to reject. They suggested, in short, that Adam was not deceived but that the woman was.

When Milton chose to have Eve's mind become progressively more dazzled by Satan's rhetorical sophistry and to have Adam fall, though "not deceiv'd But fondly overcome," his reasons, then, were relatively complex. He probably had in mind not only Augustine's explanation of St. Paul but also two other bodies of traditional materials which any reader interested in the poem might well have known. In making his choice, therefore, Milton achieved a very practical result. "In every sin," as Aquinas observed in a passage already quoted, "we find the same order as in the first temptation." It is equally true to observe that in the first temptation we find the same order as in every sin. By causing the falls of Adam and Eve to differ in the way they do, Milton was able to direct his reader's memory to an analysis of sin which was relevant to every man and to a psychology of temptation which was universally true. By depicting the falls in this way, he therefore could present not merely two dramatic and interesting variations on a theme but also a clear, though allusively made, statement that the first sin was a prototype and model for every subsequent sin. As a result, Milton was able to make a didactic statement in poetic terms, to indicate the universal relevance of his theme without resorting to moralization, to narrate his story in such a way as to convey at the same time that story's meaning.

He was also able to strengthen one of the poem's significant themes. Satan's fall results from his attempt to elevate himself above his proper position and to equal even the Most High. His

[30] B. Rajan, *Paradise Lost and the Seventeenth Century Reader* (London, 1947), p. 69.

rebellion against external order results, however, in his own de-basement and in the destruction of his internal order. His appe-tites and passions become irrational and uncontrollable: "For only in destroying I find ease" (IX, 129). And his reason be-comes so darkened that he tells lies even to himself: "Yet public reason just . . . compels me now / To do what else though damn'd I should abhor" (IV, 389–392). These events provide the pat-tern for the fall and degeneration of Adam and Eve. The true order of Paradise depends upon the "frisking . . . Beasts of th' Earth" (IV, 340–341) observing their subservience to mankind; on Eve, who was made for God in Adam (IV, 299), observing her subservience to her husband; and on Adam, the image of God, observing his subservience to his Maker. This order is threatened when Satan incarnates the snake, that normal symbol of the potential concupiscence within Adam and Eve and the archetype for those inordinate motions that have afflicted man ever since. That order is shattered when Eve, taking delight in the serpent's suggestion, obeys the lower creature, and when Adam willfully chooses to exalt his wife above himself as the "best of all God's Works" (IX, 896–897). The serpent has sug-gested, flesh has delighted, mind has consented, and the hierarchy of Paradise has been overturned. The internal hierarchy is im-mediately destroyed as well:

> For Understanding rul'd not, and the Will
> Heard not her lore, both in subjection now
> To sensual Appetite, who from beneath
> Usurping over sovran Reason claim'd
> Superior sway.   (IX, 1127–1131)

This inversion of true order, with all that it implies, could not have taken its present form in *Paradise Lost* were there not in the immediate background an analysis of sin, a psychology of temptation, as well as Augustine's understanding of St. Paul, all to insist that "Adam was not deceived, but the woman being deceived was in the transgression."

7

The Apocalypse within
Paradise Lost

MICHAEL FIXLER

▼

The purpose of what follows is to suggest that Milton based *Paradise Lost* on an elaborate systematic transformation of the Apocalypse or Revelation of St. John. This I did not set out to prove. Rather, when I first began the present study I had intended to argue that Milton conceived *Paradise Lost* as an act of worship, and that its sacramental character made it an early and significant instance of the deliberate substitution of literary for liturgical communion—in short, of the religion of art. Then, in the course of one part of the preliminary work, tracing how Milton had adapted choral liturgical materials from the Apocalypse, I came across evidence that seemed to indicate that not only the choral elements, but indeed *all* of Revelation was systematically involved in the very structure of *Paradise Lost*. Naturally, that quarry being much larger game, I took off after it, keeping in sight, however, the basic idea that the poem is what it is largely because it served Milton as the fulfillment of his self-dedication to serve God liturgically in his poetry.

The connection is important, for I do not find it possible even now fully to disengage the argument about the Apocalypse and *Paradise Lost* from the consideration that the poem functions as an act of worship. Nor is it possible to deal with either the source of Milton's poem or its sacramental function without being aware at every stage of a formidable problem; namely, the fact that the relationship of *Paradise Lost* to the Apocalypse is apparently cryptic. Hence almost as soon as the evidence is laid out it begins to warp under the pressure of an insistent question. Why should Milton have concealed the nature and extent of the relationship? Or if concealed is too strong a word, why should there be so little overt trace of an accomplishment so fundamental to the nature of the poem? The answers to that question must be far more speculative and inferential than the evidence I shall now be presenting in support of the argument that *Paradise Lost* is indeed based on Revelation. But I raise the matter of the explanation to indicate I am aware the relationship cannot be really satisfactorily established until reasons for its mystery have been found. Such reasons do exist, though at this stage I will not be directly concerned with them.

What I will try to do now is to suggest briefly something of the general nature of the imaginative appeal of the Apocalypse and then its relevance to liturgical forms, after which I shall attempt a straightforward comparison of it and *Paradise Lost*. Upon the success or failure of that, for the time being, my case will have to rest. The extent of the comparison will be limited more by the scope of this paper than by the extent of the evidence, and consequently the following argument should be considered incomplete.

I

Part of the difficulty many may have in imagining a priori that Milton could have used the Apocalypse on which to build his poem stems from the fact that although Revelation has been historically one of the most important works in the canon of Scripture, like Daniel and large parts of Ezekiel (to name only the better known prophetic texts dealing with visionary eschatology), its meaning involves the interpretation of a symbolic language alien and almost wholly opaque to most contemporary nonspecialists. There is a way, however of approaching Revelation nontechnically, and an impressive recent example of this approach is Frank Kermode's *The Sense of an Ending*, which begins a study of the relevance of the Apocalypse to the imagination of novelistic fictions by reducing the exegetical problems to a lucid, but by no means facile, simplicity. Kermode suggests that the Apocalypse is essentially a paradigmatic model of the basic form of the imaginative encounter with death. It is a type of all "fictions of the end." Since the end is immanent in our beginning, out of this implicit identity we have learned to devise fictions making the beginning and the end commensurable, as if death necessarily suggests rebirth. The central experience of living tends in the imagination to be seen as rounded off by symbolically equivalent terminals, like the Alpha and Omega of Apocalyptic recurrence. "Apocalypse," in short, "depends on a concord of imaginatively recorded past and imaginatively predicted future, achieved on behalf of us, who remain 'in the middest.' "[1]

Before modern historicism transformed our cultural sense of the past and of time generally, the devout and reflective Christian tended to see historical time in terms of this Apocalyptic pattern or as a kind of symmetrical resolution of Providence. His view was at heart typological in its basic assumption that history centered on the Incarnation of Christ, an event all of whose elements were anticipated by the earlier, almost rhythmic occurrence and recurrence of analogues (recorded in the Old Testament), acting as prophecies that would confirm the truth that Christ was their fulfillment. Furthermore, as a historical event, the Incarnation was to be followed by an eschatological repetition that would absorb the meaning of the central ministry of Jesus and the career of his Church, restoring all things to the condition of the beginning at Creation, but greatly enhanced. In effect the meaning of Christ as the central figure embraced a number of related paradoxes. As a historical personality he represented not only the marriage of the human and the divine, but also the symbolic union of the temporal with the timeless, and of the beginning with the end. Thus Tertullian wrote that Christ was called Alpha and Omega, the two letters which "the Lord assumes to Himself," because these symbols are "figures of the beginning and the end which concur in Himself: so that, just as Alpha rolls on till it reaches Omega, and again Omega rolls back till it reaches Alpha, in the same way He might show that in Himself is both the down-

---

[1] Frank Kermode, *The Sense of an Ending* (New York, 1967), p. 8.

ward course of the beginning on to the end, and the backward course of the end up to the beginning; so that every economy, ending in Him through whom it began . . . may have an end correspondent to its beginning."[2] From some imaginary, absolute perspective, time centered in Christ—as essentially in Milton's little poem, *On Time*, or in the perspectives of *At A Solemn Music* —is only an interval between the beginning of Creation and the Fall, and the ending or the beatific triumph of the Apocalypse. Milton's vibrant tone of triumph in these poems reflects his assurance of the personal, possibly immediate relevance of the promise that the end restores and perfects the beginning. Wide apart as the opposites are, they are one in Christ who might make their identity manifest soon.

By virtue of the fact that the Apocalypse rounded off the canon (in the Western churches) and thematically represented something like the direct antithesis of Genesis, the pattern of Alpha and Omega identifiable with Christ was also identifiable with the visible shape of his Word, the whole Bible. The point seems not to have been lost on Milton who spoke of rationalizing Scripture as if it were a process of balancing its parts, the obscure with the clear; the canon being "the just and adequate measure of truth, fitted and proportion'd to the diligent study, memory, and use of every faithfull man," with "every part consenting and making up the harmonious *Symmetry* of compleat instruction." Augustine had once called the whole world—its archetype, its secret proportions, and its full beauty—a poem the harmony of which would only be made manifest when all would be finally revealed at the end. And in Milton's time the Puritan and Platonist Peter Sterry took up the idea but wrote as if the archetype of that poem was already visible in the symmetrical design of Scripture, matching as it did the symmetry of Providence. "God's Poem" was the *"Original Patern in eternity,"* symmetrical and harmoniously conceived, the pattern of that "first supream Glory," to which as the heavenly worship at the end the saints would be restored. The design worked out its mysteries in Providence, which, said Sterry, from the "Most opposed Contrarieties, bindeth up all with an harmonious Order into an *exact Unity*, [and] which conveyeth things down by a gradual descent to the lowest

Depths, and deepest Darknesses; then bringing them up again to the highest point of all flourishing Felicities, opening the *beginning in the end*, espousing the end to the beginning." For Sterry the aesthetic proportions of God's Poem, the inner shape of the whole design, was apparently suggested by the concordance of symmetry in Scripture and of symmetry in Providence. *"What will you say,"* he wrote, *"when you shall see the Son of Man return there, where he was at first?"*[3]

Sterry's rhapsody on the design rather mildly reflected something else as well, the portentousness characteristic of those who looked upon such special knowledge as the privilege of the regenerate understanding, which alone was adequately suited to penetrate prophetic mysteries. Puritan preachers never tired of

[3] Milton, *Animadversions,* in *The Complete Prose Works* (henceforth referred to as *CPW*), ed. Don M. Wolfe (New Haven, 1953–), I, 700. Augustine, *The City of God,* XXII.xxx; *Of Music,* VI.xi. Cf. Thomas Campion's remark: "The world is made by Simmetry and proportion, and is in that respect compared to Musick, and Musick to Poetry" (*Observations in the Art of English Poesie,* repr. in *English Literary Criticism: The Renaissance,* ed. by O. B. Hardison, Jr., [New York, 1963], p. 233). Peter Sterry, *A Discourse . . . of the Will* (1675), repr. by V. De Sola Pinto, in *Peter Sterry, Platonist and Puritan* (Cambridge, 1934), pp. 164–165.
Sterry's Apocalyptic assumption is clear from the fact that in his paraphrase of the Gospel of John (6:62) quoted earlier, it is only said the Son of Man returns to heaven. Sterry altered the phrasing to assimilate to the verse the circular typological return of the Son of Man, who in the Apocalypse (3:14) describes himself to the visionary John as "the beginning of the creation of God." Cf. Nicholas of Cusa's meditation on Christ: "Thou dwellest within the wall of Paradise, and this wall is that coincidence where later is one with earlier, where the end is one with the beginning, where Alpha and Omega are the same." *The Vision of God,* trans. E. G. Salter (London, 1928), p. 49. And see also Griffith Williams expressing what C. A. Patrides (*Milton and the Christian Tradition* [Oxford, 1966], p. 129) calls a "conventional attitude." Christ "is the *First,* hee is the *Last* . . . The beginning of the *Law,* and the end of the *Gospell.*")
Concerning the relevance of Sterry's views to Milton's, it must be noted that William G. Madsen does not think it wise to stress affinities between them because Sterry was a Platonist and Milton was a Puritan typologist. ("Earth the Shadow of Heaven: Typological Symbolism in *Paradise Lost,*" *PMLA,* LXXV [1960], 521.) Madsen's study is a most perceptive introduction to Milton's use of typology, but I think the distinction he draws between Puritanism and Platonism on this point is too sharp. Surely the interesting thing about *Puritan* Neoplatonists (and this applies equally to Sir Henry Vane and Robert Greville, Lord Brooke, as well as to Sterry and Milton), is that they strained to reconcile Puritanism and Platonism— through typology.

saying that the Apocalypse was a mystery only the regenerate understanding could unlock. Milton explained that obscurity was dispelled by turning onto dark passages in one part of the canon the clear light from another part of the canon. But the purpose of obscurity itself was perhaps to intimate mysteries that could not be fully conceived, and to serve as a divine test of the regenerate understanding whereby the elect would distinguish themselves by some capacity for spiritual response not to be found in the darkness of unregenerate understanding. "It is only to those who perish that the Scriptures are obscure, especially in things necessary for salvation. Luke 6 : 10: "Unto you it is given to know the mysteries of the kingdom of God, but to others in parables; that seeing they might not see, and hearing they might not understand." Hence, though Milton wrote that the Apocalypse soared to a "Prophetic pitch in types, and Allegories," he also referred to it as "that mysterious book of Revelation which the great Evangelist was bid to eat, as it had been some eye-brightning electuary of knowledge, and foresight."[4]

I think the evidence will show that Milton did in fact digest the Apocalypse as "some eye-brightning electuary"; nor in his time was he singular in sustaining the full effect of the work. A sojourn in the devotional, homiletical, and exegetical literature of Puritanism is an experience of a country of the mind where certain mountain peaks dominate the landscape, and possibly the tallest of these is the Apocalypse. How impoverished the language of their religious invective would be without it, how unimaginable the quality and character of their enthusiasm! The Puritans, as others before them, and as fundamentalists after them, found in the work infinite resources to sustain the sense of the peculiar historical meaning of their election as saints; and at every stage in the evolution of their movement they had fresh recourse to the interpretation of the prophecies, as if these held the keys to the immediate meaning of shifting destinies. But what generally was it that was always there, the intrinsic thing that Revelation indubitably revealed, as if only to the regenerate un-

---

[4] *The Christian Doctrine*, I.xxx, in *The Prose Works of John Milton*, ed. J. A. St. John (London, 1848–1881), IV, 442, henceforth called the Bohn edition. *Animadversions* and *The Reason of Church Government*, *CPW*, I, 714, 803. On Puritan attitudes toward the interpretation of the Apocalypse, see my study, *Milton and the Kingdoms of God* (London and Evanston, 1964), *passim*.

derstanding, and that made the work so powerful and so self-renewing a force in the shaping of the Puritan imagination?

In a study written with great sensitivity to the creative processes involved in the kind of poetry-making that bases itself on sacred, almost inviolable materials, Austin Farrer provides the beginnings of an answer to such a question.[5] The meaning of the work, as he sees it, is inseparable from the way it grew in the mind of St. John—as "a rebirth of images"—out of a rich skein of traditional prophetic and liturgical materials. The result was a symbolic pattern of almost inexhaustible suggestibility whose poetic character and the power of its highly ordered, highly colored imagery probably had as much bearing in its subsequent influence as the fact that it bore the authority of Holy Writ. One particular aspect of Farrer's study, his emphasis on the work's liturgical origins, suggests the direction most likely to explain some large part of that influence. The materials and the sanctified numerical patterns varied, repeated, and transformed in the Apocalypse were by their very origins charged with Jewish liturgical associations that had been renewed in the typological identification of Jesus (as the Lamb) with the fulfillment of the Temple's worship, the Temple's calendar, and the Temple's sacerdotal symbolism. Revelation is thus a visionary poem built essentially around elements of ritual preserved within older versions of liturgical dramas of sacrifice and renewal. Even with all its complex symbolic patterning (or possibly because of it), it remains intrinsically a ritual calendar week modified to reflect the typological seasons and the revolving cycle of Providence. Thus like the liturgical materials on which it is based, Revelation simultaneously celebrates the enduring mythic combats and triumphs of agricultural and pastoral renewal, and the renewal or sanctification of the chosen people in their historical seasons.

II

A study of Apocalyptic interpretations suggests that men tended to find in it what they were looking for. Since historically

[5] *A Rebirth of Images: The Making of St. John's Apocalypse* (Boston, 1963). Inasmuch as I am not concerned with the problem of its authorship, I will continue, along with Farrer, to call the Johannine Apocalypse the Apocalypse of St. John.

most interpreting has been done by ecclesiastics, most interpretations tend to isolate in Revelation its auguries concerning the Mystical Body of Christ or the Invisible Church. From time to time, as happened during the Puritan Revolution, political fantasists also tended to find in it justification for revolutionary programs. Milton was prone to both these approaches in differing degrees at different times, but he was a poet before he was either an advocate of reformation or a political polemicist; and above all what he found in Revelation was poetry. In its apotheosis of the saints' worshipping with harp and song, he found divine evidence that poetry was the highest activity in beatitude. And in the very structure or form of St. John's visions, he found a divine sanction for a specific literary model that lent itself to the conception of his most ambitious poetic project. Thus, whenever Milton's imagination quickened to the thought of beatitude, it was in terms of choral worship around that throne of God on which sat the Apocalyptic Lamb, a worship in which he represented himself on several occasions as taking part in an individual felicity of poetic worship that would blend with the universal concord of the saints. And in several widely spaced intervals he recorded the fact that Revelation was a model, most amply in his description of it as "the majestick image of a high and stately Tragedy, shutting up and intermingling her solemn Scenes and Acts with a sevenfold *Chorus* of halleluja's and harping symphonies."[6]

It would be a matter for another discussion to consider how Milton endowed the Apocalyptic model itself with a spiritual potency related to his ideal image of visionary worship, as if in mortal life the imagination of that immortal beatitude was best

[6] The personal digression in *The Reason of Church Government, CPW,* I, 815. Cf. the reference in the *Commonplace Book* to Tertullian's commendation of Apocalyptic tragedies, *CPW,* I, 490, and the reference in the preface to *Samson Agonistes.* In the induction to the *Nativity Ode,* in *At A Solemn Music,* and in *Paradise Lost,* III, 410–415, Milton imagined himself joined with the angels in worship. In *Lycidas, Epitaphium Damonis,* and *Ad Patrem,* he described the celestial worship in terms of the consummation of spiritual bliss. In *Of Reformation* and *Animadversions (CPW,* I, 616, 706) the apocalyptic prayers show Milton anticipating an earthly consummation in which as a poet he would worship God much as he felt sure he would worship in the Kingdom of Glory, or in beatitude. Here and later I use apocalyptic as a general adjective and Apocalyptic to refer specifically to things pertaining to the Apocalypse.

framed in terms of the Scriptural work that so refulgently and
gloriously foreshadowed it. But in the worldly frame of things,
poetry was not beatific worship. Yet neither was the Apocalypse
a product of beatitude. Rather, as a prophetic work, its function
was inspirational and revelatory as if its visions told the saints
something about the relationship of mortal to immortal life and
of earthly to heavenly worship. In these terms Milton recurred
to its imagery repeatedly in his prose, once especially to emphasize the relationship of discipline to freedom and harmony, inasmuch as the image of perfect worship which the Apocalypse en-
shrined was a comprehensive analogue for the harmony of all
things in the worship of God on earth. Certainly, Milton wrote,

> discipline is not only the removall of disorder, but if any visible
> shape can be given to divine things, the very visible shape and
> image of vertue, whereby she is not only seene in the regular
> gestures and motions of her heavenly paces as she walkes, but
> also makes the harmony of her voice audible to mortall eares.
> Yea the Angels themselves, in whom no disorder is fear'd, as
> the Apostle that saw them in his rapture describes, are distin-
> guisht and quaterniond into their celestiall Princedomes, and
> Satrapies, according as God himselfe hath writ his imperiall
> decrees through the great provinces of heav'n. The state also of
> the blessed in Paradise, though never so perfect, is not therefore
> left without discipline, whose golden survaying reed marks out
> and measures every quarter and circuit of new Jerusalem. Yet
> it is not to be conceiv'd that those eternall effluences of sanctity
> and love in the glorified Saints should by this meanes be con-
> fin'd and cloy'd with repetition of that which is prescrib'd, but
> that our happinesse may orbe it selfe into a thousand vagancies
> of glory and delight, and with a kind of eccentricall equation be
> as it were an invariable Planet of joy and felicity.[7]

As a work whose place in Scripture made it a kind of symbolic
cornerstone of the divine structure, as a prophetic electuary of
foresight and knowledge, as the visionary source of the visionary
imagination of worship, and as itself a highly wrought symbolic
structure expressing the visible shape of free yet harmonic discipline, the Apocalypse was a literary model of extraordinary
authority for one who was both a Puritan and a poet.

How much so Milton evidently did not fully realize when in
1641 he first cited Revelation as a model. Partly he was to dis-

---

[7] *The Reason of Church-government, CPW*, I, 751–752.

cover its full possibilities by experimentation, but I would guess
that he came to recognize those possibilities more as he became
progressively less inclined to satisfy his need for public worship
in ecclesiastical services. Here again there is the subject for an
extended discussion. Suffice it now to say that biographical evidence and the bearing of many of his views in the *Christian Doctrine* suggest that Milton evolved out of Puritanism's more
extreme doctrines of worship a radical position justifying his
reliance on poetry as a formal surrogate for public devotion. In
the *Christian Doctrine*, ecclesiastical services—formal worship
on the Sabbath and almost every liturgical practice—were reduced to the rank of the *adiophora*, the things whose forms were
spiritually indifferent, a sacrament being, for example, any visible
sign of God's benefits and justice, and all worship being described
as essentially consisting of any form of thanksgiving or supplication. To offer worship or to dispense a sacrament was in the
power of every Christian, and hence on a negative basis alone
Paradise Lost might qualify as fulfilling these conditions.[8]

The poem, however, positively stands out as a sacramental act
of worship, like that work Milton had covenanted to produce in
The reason of Church-government, "by devout prayer to that
eternall Spirit who can enrich with all utterance and knowledge
and sends out his Seraphim with the hallow'd fire of his Altar
to touch and purify the lips." Thus when he claimed at the beginning of *Paradise Lost* to be pursuing "Things unattempted
yet in Prose or Rhyme," in at least one sense this was doubtless
true; for while neither his subject, nor epic treatment of it was
unique, probably no other poetic work he knew of was so thoroughly designed to justify God's ways in a sacramental literary
form comprehensively sustained throughout as an act of worship.
It was really an extemporary prayer. When within the poem
Adam and Eve worship God in what is their longest, most interesting devotional effusion, both form and style are free, in the
proper spirit of Milton's great faith in the superiority of extempo-

[8] I shall take up these matters in another study, or rather in an extension
of this study. See, however, the passage from John Toland's *Life,* in the
Early Lives of Milton, ed. by Helen Darbishire (London, 1965), p. 195.
See also the *Christian Doctrine,* I.xxiv, "Of Union and Fellowship with
Christ"; xxviii, "Of the External Sealing"; xxvi, "Of the Visible Church";
and II, iv, "Of External Worship." On Puritan worship generally and its
tendencies, see Horton Davies, *The Worship of the English Puritans* (London, 1948).

rary prayer: "Unmeditated, such prompt eloquence / Flow'd from thir lips, in Prose or numerous Verse." (V, 149–150). It may be straining a point to call *Paradise Lost* in its entirety a similar but more elaborate extemporary expression of devotional service, but its congruence with the Apocalypse, if proven, should make it more likely that Milton did in fact so conceive it. In any event the poem's structure is manifestly a suite of parts, a number of which formally begin as invocations of the kind Milton speci-fied as religious supplications and which correspond in nature to the invocations to the divine Light and the Holy Spirit opening the great apocalyptic prose prayers in *Of Reformation* and *Animadversions*; the style whereof, Milton said of the latter, "as a hymne in prose, frequent both in the Prophets and in humane authors . . . was greater than for ordinary prayer."[9]

Generally speaking, in a number of obvious and not so obvious ways, the poem reflects a variety of liturgical inspirations, some of which are associated with the Psalter, and some with the Apoc-alypse. The comprehensive liturgical relationship of *Paradise Lost* to the Apocalypse as a whole I shall discuss later. Of the more conventional liturgical forms in the poem, the most note-worthy are Adam and Eve's great prayer of degrees in Book V (153–208), and the angelic choruses which both echo the Psalter and obviously reflect their provenance in Revelation. It is no coincidence that the Psalter and the Apocalypse tend to provide a kind of dual complementary inspiration. Puritan interest in the Psalter was often powerfully enhanced by the disposition to in-terpret many of the psalms in apocalyptic terms. For Milton the provocation was twofold. At times he did tend to read the Psalter apocalyptically, and while it was "in esteem with him above all poetry," the Psalms were hymns, or the models for hymns, such as the one that had been the particular inspiration of the visionary transport in *At A Solemn Music*, where in the rapt imagination of beatitude he described the moment when men and angels might be restored to the full harmony of common worship, as once they had sounded together before the Fall, "in perfect diapason."[10]

---

[9] See Milton's "Covenant" with his reader, in *The Reason of Church-government, CPW*, I, 820–821; and his defense of the style of his prayer in *An Apology, CPW*, I, 930.

[10] There is an apocalyptic interpretation by Milton of Psalm 149, which he linked with Revelation 17 and 18 (as well as Genesis 10 : 10), in *Eikonoklastes, CPW*, III, 598; and cf. his translations of Psalms 80–88,

The angelic choruses in *Paradise Lost* are not always so ec-
statically conceived since partly they function in the manner of
Greek choruses providing specific dramatic commentary. More
particularly, however, they mark with climactic devotion crucial
phases in the unfolding of the scheme of Providence. Milton's
express interest in their literary possibilities can be traced backward through the primitive dramatic drafts of Adam Unparadiz'd
to his opinion that the Apocalypse was a tragic model with its
sevenfold chorus of halleluiahs. In *Paradise Lost* at least one
section, the Creation of the world in Book VII, represented as a
hexameron with seven choruses, preserves something of that
original idea. Rounding out the week is a Gloria that precedes
Creation, as the Word of God goes forth, and a concluding chorus
transmuting elements of Psalm 145 and the Song of Moses from
Exodus, the latter as it had already been transformed in Revelation 15 : 3, 4. In between there are matin and evening choruses
on the first and second days, with a great choral acclamation on
the evening of the sixth day (the beginning of the Old Testament
Sabbath), based on Psalm 24 : 7: "Lift up your head, O ye
gates; and be ye lifted up, ye everlasting doors; and the King of
Glory shall come in."

Clearly, then, *Paradise Lost* in general and in its parts manifests a devotional character with liturgical affinities to elements
of worship that may be said to be both practical and visionary. In
this last respect it shared, and as a poem exceeded, a disposition
in Puritanism itself to treat practical worship under the aspect
of a visionary ideal. Puritan worship generally consisted of services that might be divided under three rubrics: evangelical services of exhortation and edification, choral services of praise or
supplication, and communion services centering around the
Lord's Supper and signifying the sealing of the elect in God's
mercies. In their flight from the idolatry of the Eucharist, the
Puritans tended to insist strongly on the purely symbolic character of the Lord's Supper, to the point, in fact, where it began
to lose its specific emotional power as a communion service re-
enforcing the sense of saintly solidarity. On the other hand this

---

which, considering their tone and the period in which they were made,
suggest a degree of apocalyptic animus. The anonymous "Life of Milton,"
in *The Student's Milton*, ed. F. A. Patterson (New York, 1957), p. xxi,
records Milton's preeminent preference for the Psalter as poetry.

is precisely what the choral services tended to compensate for,[11] as Milton's *At A Solemn Music* shows; and inasmuch as the choral services were representations of that truly spiritual communion the saints would experience worshipping around the Lamb, the visionary influence of the Apocalypse tended to exalt that particular element of the congregational service at the expense of the Lord's Supper.

Some of this development is reflected in the way *Paradise Lost* functions devotionally, its high moments being the choral passages, the evangelical edification sustaining and unifying the whole work, and its sacramental character being generally symbolic and diffused, as if communication had for Milton replaced communion. A sacrament for Milton was a visible seal of great significance, but any man might offer it, and in any form representing God's mercies to the elect. The references in *Paradise Lost* to something like the Lord's Supper, direct and oblique, suggest that Milton inclined to turn away from emphasizing the communion service in any other form than a symbolic one. To partake of food, even with an angel, was not communion. When Adam and Raphael sit down to eat together, the prosiness is so outrageous that the passage has been a safe mark for every critic who wants to catch Milton with his tact down. I would rather read "No fear lest dinner cool," and "So down they sat, / And

---

[11] There is no specific study of the relationship of the visionary ideal to Puritanism's practical worship, but both Davies, *The Worship of the English Puritans,* and Geoffrey Nuttall, *The Holy Spirit in Puritan Faith and Experience* (Oxford, 1946) are helpful. My division of Puritan worship into three practical rubrics follows no established analysis but is based on a study of Puritan orders of worship. On choral singing as a type of the worship in heaven, cf. George Wither's description of congregational singing and music as calling to mind "the worshippers of the Lambe." In truth, he wrote, "I am perswaded that in the Quires and Musicke, vsed in the Christian Churches there be great Mysteries; and that they have in them, as proper representations of somewhat in that triumphant assembly to which we all aspire" (*A Preparation to the Psalter* [London, 1619], p. 85).

Milton's early association of choral singing with a heavenly archetype is suggested by his entry in the Commonplace Book referring to the tradition that antiphonal singing was introduced into the liturgy by Ignotius, third bishop of Antioch. Annotating this entry Ruth Mohl points out that Ignotius was said to have been inspired to introduce choral singing by a vision of the archetypal angelic worship of the Trinity (*CPW*, I, 383). See also generally Leo Spitzer, *Classical and Christian Ideas of World Harmony* (Baltimore, 1963), particularly his discussions of the Ambrosian hymn.

to thir viands fell" (V, 396, 433–434) as deliberately calculated to inhibit any symbolic, and therefore sacramental, resonance in the action. Another more obviously careful reference to communion, with the intention this time to suggest something like the Lord's Supper, nicely illustrates both Milton's disinclination to regard the Lord's Supper as practically of more moment than its symbolic essence and his readiness to exploit the symbolic overtones of the Supper when it was useful to him.

The passage occurs after the Son is proclaimed in Heaven with God's offer of bliss or woe to those angels who "confesse him Lord" or deny him. "All seem'd well pleas'd, but were not all." In the festivities that follow there is a heavenly banquet whereat the angels eat and drink "and with refection sweet / Are fill'd before th'all bounteous King." Thus it is in the 1667 edition. Revising the poem for the second edition, however, Milton wrote, "and in communion sweet / Quaff immortality and joy," (V, 637–638), taking out the deliberately neutral "refection," substituting for it "communion," and emphasizing the spiritual blessings of the sacrament. Evidently he realized he could subtly instill a quiet awareness of what was to happen—the fall and the damnation of the rebellious angels. In the words of St. Paul which he had quoted on the Lord's Supper in the *Christian Doctrine*, "He that eateth and drinketh unworthily, eateth and drinketh damnation to himself."[12]

With these implications the passage points not only to the fall of the angels but also to the fall of Adam and Eve, who, in Christian terms applicable to the abuse of the Lord's Supper, eat their way to their own destruction. Upon this basis the Fall may be reconsidered, with the full support of its most characteristic and persistent imagery, as a feast of destruction, and Nature's involvement as a Thyestean banquet upon her own children. But the key in which Milton elaborated these images had been struck in Revelation, and the correspondence in position of source to development tends to confirm the general hypothesis that Milton

[12] *PL*, V, 635–636; *CD*, I, xxviii; Bohn edition, IV, 420. The text is I Cor. 11:29. J. B. Broadbent, *Some Graver Subject* (London, 1960), p. 221, noting the change in wording from refection to communion, seems to relate as analogues Adam's dinner with Raphael and the heavenly communion. But there is no sacramental suggestion at all about Adam's dinner. The implication would point to the contrast of the dinner and the banquet as communion.

drew upon the Apocalypse of St. John for his whole design. Therefore that pattern of transformation will now be taken up before we return to the Fall in its proper place in the sequence of development.

III

Revelation has long been recognized as one of the sources for particular elements and allusions in *Paradise Lost*.[13] But the obscurity of the work, its notorious association with the wilder reaches of Puritan enthusiasm, and the apparent absence of any coherent evidence in Milton's work to indicate a sustained and artistically meaningful interest in it on his part have tended to discourage a really close examination of what the work may have meant to him and how, on the basis of that significance, he may have drawn upon it poetically. But truly, it is as if hearing we do not hear and seeing we do not see how powerful those images were that climactically mark the *Nativity Ode, At A Solemn Music, Lycidas, Epitaphium Damonis*, some of the more interesting prose passages, and more peripherally *Comus* and *Ad Patrem*. I believe Milton studied Revelation with great care as a poet as well as a Christian; that he abandoned the interpretation of its prophecies for the understanding of its symbolic scheme, finding then that it had a clear structure and a penetrable intention; and that as he matured his plans for *Paradise Lost* it dawned

[13] Merritt Hughes' edition of *Paradise Lost* in *The Complete Poems And Major Prose* (New York, 1957), the text I am using for the poetry, fairly bristles with notes on the references and allusions to Revelation, while James Holly Hanford in "The Youth of Milton," in *Studies in Shakespeare, Milton and Donne*, ed. by E. S. McCartney (New York, 1925), long ago remarked on Milton's extraordinary interest in the Apocalypse and its crucial significance, particularly in *Lycidas*. With respect to *Paradise Lost*, any familiarity with Scripture would lead to the ready identification of the sources for Hell's lake of fire and the War in Heaven, if not to the less obvious borrowings. But no one, to my knowledge, has suggested there is a structural, or even any kind of sustained relationship between Revelation and *Paradise Lost*. Allan H. Gilbert, in his work *On The Composition of Paradise Lost* (Chapel Hill, N.C., 1947), pp. 118–119, n. 13, recognized the resemblance of Books V and VI to Revelation 12, but then went on to conclude that Milton could not have been following St. John since the order of materials differed. Apparently what threw Gilbert off was the fact that Milton distinguished between the eschatological sense of Revelation and the inverted use to which the material was put in *Paradise Lost*.

upon him, possibly as a real sense of a divine inspiration, that what he wanted to do in his poem St. John had done in his, renewing a visionary tradition in "a rebirth of images."

Milton himself, probably inadvertently, misled his readers when in *The Reason of Church Government* he referred to the Apocalypse, on the authority of the Swiss Reformer David Pareus, as a work whose sevenfold dramatic structure was clearly separated by choral intermissions. What Pareus actually wrote is that Revelation is a "PROPHETICAL DRAMA REVEALED IN SEVEN VISIONS," which he outlined in terms of their "APPARITIONS AND PERSONS." These main visions were subdivided into "certain visionall Acts, which ever and anon . . . are renewed with Chores of singers both for dramaticall decencie, as also for a sound pleasantness and delectation."[14] In the preface to *Samson Agonistes*, presumably written after he had composed *Paradise Lost*, Milton did not again attribute to Pareus a description of the work as having a "sevenfold *Chorus* of halleluja's," but simply said that Pareus called Revelation a tragedy with "Acts distinguisht each by a Chorus of Heavenly Harpings and Song between," which indeed is what Pareus said of the *acts within* the visions. Apparently in 1641 Milton had not yet read Pareus carefully. By 1671 he evidently had. The seven visions are really the important things, and neither in Revelation nor in *Paradise Lost* do the choruses consistently separate the larger visional segments. But the division of the Apocalypse into seven visions is easy to recognize. Pareus was not the first to do so, and the seven-visional structure remains a basic segmentation for the work, as, for example, in Farrer's study, or in the Westminster Study edition of the Authorized Version. Seven is, in fact, the most consistent, although not the only, numerical element of visionary organization within the Apocalypse.

Milton apparently did not know at first what to do with the Apocalyptic model he cited along with other possible dramatic prototypes. His early drafts of Adam Unparadiz'd suggest that his classical training led him to the five-act structure, but as the fourth draft shows, this did not allow adequate opportunity for

---

[14] *A Commentary Upon The Divine Revelation of the Apostle and Evangelist Iohn,* trans. by Elias Arnold (Amsterdam, 1644), pp. 30 and 475. Pareus provides a table divided into seven parts, and the entire organization of his book is meshed in with his analysis of the sevenfold structure of the Apocalypse.

three main elements he was to include in *Paradise Lost*: the representation of Hell, the War in Heaven, and the Creation of the world. Of these only the War in Heaven and Creation figure in the fourth draft, huddled up in choral narration. When Milton made his decision to write in epic form he again took up Revelation, finding within its framework a suggestive flexibility allowing for the mixture of visional, dramatic, narrative, and choral elements. All these harmonized most readily with the technical possibilities of the epic form. Moreover, Revelation to a high degree had already organized within its structure the very materials Milton had planned for his drama on the Fall.

To understand the relation between *Paradise Lost* and Revelation one must bear in mind that Milton's materials were essentially hexameral, dealing with the week of Creation, whereas the Apocalypse was eschatological, with a sequence of visions concerned with the "week" that takes the historical Creation into the timelessness of the millennium. Hence Milton, in adapting the Apocalyptic sequence, transposed and inverted where necessary the content of each vision, a technique he described in his *Art of Logic* as "crypsis or concealment." Logical method, he wrote, is "a dianoetic [reasoned, deductive] disposition of various homogeneous axioms arranged one before another according to the clarity of their nature. . . . But when the auditor is to be allured with pleasure or some stronger impulse by an orator or poet—for they commonly make that their chief concern—*a crypsis of method will usually be employed*; some homogeneous axioms will be rejected, as the lights of definitions, partitions, and transitions. Certain heterogeneous axioms will be taken up, as digressions from the fact and lingerings on the fact. *And especially the order of things will be inverted.*"[15] *Ars est celare artem!* The business of art is to conceal art.

My assumption that Milton used this technique I do not take

[15] *The Works of John Milton,* ed. by F. A. Patterson (New York, 1931–1940), XI, 297–299, 471, 483–485. The italics are mine. Cryptic technique did not invariably imply esotericism. The meaning of crypsis belongs to the general distinction between logic and rhetoric. Logic being demonstrative and rhetoric persuasive, the latter, so to speak, resorts to techniques for teasing the reader out of thought. Bacon distinguished cryptic method (among others) as a standard technique, preferring however a broader rhetorical classification of *Exoteric* and *Acroamatic,* or "enigmatical method." See *The Advancement Of Learning,* VI.ii, in *Works,* ed. by James Spedding (New York, 1869), IX, 124–127. Milton's definition of the principle was, of course, Ramist, as is the entire treatise.

as a license for cabbalistic or impressionistic matching of elements. It means that I think Milton might have found a suggestion of authority in Revelation for the belief that St. John himself practiced crypsis; and more broadly my assumption is founded on the supposition that Milton was powerfully drawn to the structural possibilities that scriptural typology afforded his inventiveness as a poet. Only one must recognize that typology allowed not merely the random association and enlargement of figures, but the possibilities of systematic reduplications and inversions as well. In a related art, the kind of patterns such imitation and inversion may produce would have been aesthetically familiar to Milton; and these patterns are, in fact, epitomized in a brief passage called by one musical authority "the most accurate as well as the most vivid description ever given of the essentials of a fugue."[16] The lines were suggested by the account in Genesis of Jubal, "the father of all such as handle the harp and organ," and in them Milton, himself an organist, describes a seventeenth-century mode and performer with exact, virtuoso terms: "his volant touch / Instinct through all proportions low

What appealed to Milton in Ramism, I think, is that it really tended to reduce logic to rhetoric, instead of the opposite tendency perceptible in Bacon's treatment, which would have made rhetoric more an art of demonstration and less an art of persuasion. While Milton's crypsis is essentially an allowance made to the special needs of rhetoric within a logical handbook, he also treats crypsis logically as a technique of disposition related to the enthymeme, where something implied is left unsaid. Moreover, there is a certain relevant suggestiveness in a particular kind of cryptic syllogism, the *sorites,* which he describes as a sequence of propositions that returns upon itself "until the consequent of the last proposition is concluded of the antecedent of the first." The illustration for this is striking, it being the circular sequence of Pauline propositions on predestination, ending with "Therefore whom he did foreknow them he glorified" (pp. 467–469). His illustration is, in effect, a compressed representation of the symbolic pattern of the mystery of election, where end and beginning are concordant, glorification being the ultimate revelation of the primordial election of the saints. Finally, while crypsis is, strictly speaking, a technical principle, it nevertheless has affinities with the whole traditional attitude toward scriptural obscurity as presenting the "constituents of a divine cryptogram designed to conceal ineffable truths from all but the blessed few." Israel Baroway, "The Bible as Poetry in the English Renaissance," *JEGP,* XXXIII (1930), 450. Pareus plainly describes Revelation as cryptic in this sense, the visions being mysterious "that indeed prophane men might always set lightly by things so obscure: but the godly even by the obscurity thereof be more stirred up to the searching out of divine mysteries" (*A Commentary,* p. 9).

[16] D. F. Tovey, "Fugue," *Encyclopedia Britannica,* 11th ed.

and high / Fled and pursu'd transverse the resonant fugue."
(*Paradise Lost*, XI, 561–563). Almost all the terms in this passage are physically and technically complementary, describing
the simultaneous or sequential reproduction in the manner of an
early fugue of a leading part by a duplicate, or proportioned, or
inverted rendition of it. The rule or canon for the duplication was
often indicated in the leading part by some enigmatic form. That
Milton had in mind here a proportioned inversion as possibly the
most attractive characteristic of this kind of fugue is indicated
by the word "transverse," for which the O.E.D. lists a number of
mid-seventeenth-century meanings, almost all varying the sense
of inversional transformation.

Elements of this technique are familiar to every reader of the
poem who has been impressed by Milton's thorough architectonic
disposition of parallelisms and inversions affecting almost all the
constituents of the work. A close look reveals that generally there
is a dominant element and an imitative one in the balancing of
these constituents, and usually these can be easily distinguished.
But when the dominant pattern is outside the poem, recognition
is complex and depends upon the reader's readiness to respond
to the shape of the cryptic archetype. This is, of course, a technique we are more familiar with in the way it had been used by
James Joyce in the composition of *Ulysses*. I do not think that
Milton, any more than Joyce, expected the reader to be fully
aware of what he was doing. At any rate, he did not have at hand
a class of professional critics, as Joyce did, to interrogate him
immediately as to his intention. In consequence, with the general
cultural relegation of the Apocalypse to the back of the shelf, its
relationship to *Paradise Lost* has become almost completely
obscured.

What ought not to be obscured at this point, however, is that
the Apocalypse would not have appealed to Milton simply by
virtue of its architectonic possibilities. The whole orchestration
of the prophecy, so to speak, is around the theme of worship and
apostasy, in which all mankind and all the angelic hosts are involved. Part of the strategy throughout Pareus' commentary is
not merely to emphasize the dramatic structure as an analytical
tool but to use the dramatic frame of reference to remind the
reader that in understanding Revelation he is turned into a spectator of a ritual drama and even a participating worshipper him-

self. Thus he writes, explaining one passage, "Whereas therefore the heavenly Herauld doth stir up in *generall* all the servants of God to praise him, and in *speciall,* all his hearers, he sheweth, that not only God is to be celebrated by the heavenly inhabitants apart, but with joynt wishes and voyces of all Gods servants together, as wel of Angels, as men, as wel of the Saints triumphant in heaven, as of the militant on earth, that is, by the universal consent or accord of the whole Catholick Church. . . . No one therefore of Gods servants is to be silent."[17] This is an effect that, in the light of my preceding argument, I would imagine Milton might have desired his own work to be able to inspire.

In the following section, however, I shall turn from Milton's devotional intention to what appears to be his method of construction—the reduplication and inversion of a design he found in the Apocalypse. My examination, of necessity, will be incomplete, for to describe in any degree of comprehensiveness the extent of adaptation would be an extraordinarily complex matter. On a primary level it is not difficult to recognize that the seven Apocalyptic visions sequentially bear a vaguely suggestive resemblance to the seven major phases of development immediately evident in *Paradise Lost* if we think of the poem in episodic blocks. Considerably simplified, the visions in the Apocalypse may be summarized in the following terms:

1. The admonitions to the seven churches of Asia representing the spectrum of purity and impurity in worship. (Chapters 1, 2, 3. This and the following divisions are those of Pareus.)
2. The vision in heaven of the judgments of God and of the offering of the Lamb that was slain to redeem the faithful and the Church. (Chapters 4, 5, 6, 7.)
3. The affliction of Creation and of the Kingdom of the World by divine permission so that the wicked might be separated from the faithful. (Chapters 8, 9, 10, 11.)
4. The war in heaven that follows when the dragon is alarmed by the birth to the Church of a redeemer, and the victory over the dragon. (Chapters 12, 13, 14.)
5. A seven-phased vision of the destruction of the sinful earth. (Chapters 15, 16.)
6. The fall of Babylon, balanced by the triumph or Marriage Supper of the Lamb and his bride, followed by a feast of the destruction of the wicked. (Chapters 17, 18, 19.)
7. The vision of the end of things and of the New Jerusalem. (Chapters 20, 21, 22.)

[17] *A Commentary,* p. 479.

As may readily be recognized, the movement of the Apocalypse represents a stage-by-stage transformation of the impure Church of the World (the Visible Church) into the purified Church of the heavenly hereafter (the Invisible Church or the Mystical Body of Christ). In terms of the prophetic application to the Reformation, Pareus saw it also in something like this fashion. The movement is not, however, plainly temporal or linear. It both spirals in cyclical fashion and weaves back and forth across itself on its own axis in the fourth vision, as well as in minor patterns within particular visions. Their inner principles are beyond my competence to describe, although in some sense the laws of progression seem to be a reflection of psychological alternations within a movement toward a climax.

Paradise Lost is more coherently rational in its structure and development, but it is also plainly and most naturally divisible (even without any reference to the Apocalypse) into seven main sections or episodes which I shall henceforth refer to as visions. Each begins with a human voice addressed in supplication to a divine personification or to an angel, beseeching inspiration or enlightenment, grace or sustenance. These seven visions may be summarized as follows:

1. The vision of Hell (Books I and II), beginning with Milton's invocation to the Heavenly Muse.
2. The vision of Heaven, God's judgment, and the Son's intercession for Man who is to Fall (Book III), beginning with Milton's invocation to Holy Light.
3. The vision of Eden, which by divine permission Satan may approach to afflict and possibly destroy (Book IV and Book V to line 562), beginning with Milton's apostrophic evocation of the warning angel in the Apocalypse.
4. The account of the War in Heaven (Book V, line 563 through the end of Book VI), beginning with Adam's supplication to Raphael for enlightenment.
5. The account of Creation, including the creation of Adam and Eve (Books VII and VIII, which in the first edition of 1667 were one book), beginning with Milton's invocation to Urania.
6. The Fall of Man and the feast of destruction (Books IX and X), beginning with an oblique address to Urania and the reader.
7. The recovery of grace and the vision of the future, including the New Jerusalem (Books XI and XII, which in the first edition were one book), beginning with Adam and Eve supplicating God for grace.

Even on the schematic level of these classifications there appears to be a sufficiently interesting resemblance between the Apocalypse and *Paradise Lost* to warrant closer study.[18] The resemblances become more suggestive as one moves from the overall schematic picture to episodic arrangements and details, but the actual relationships are then seen to be quite intricate and unevenly sustained. In some instances there are almost dazzling identities; in others one surrenders to intuition (not too uncritically), and senses the presence of large metaphorical patterns transmuted from Apocalyptic correspondences by subtle and sometimes identifiable keys or signatures. Frequently there are very regular numerical transpositions of themes, as in the eleventh and twelfth books of *Paradise Lost*. But most unmistakable is the resemblance to Revelation of what sculptors call "the big shape," the blocky internal structure which makes anything distinctly recognizable, even at a distance. Hence I shall stay mainly, though not altogether, with the bigger elements, except for an experimentally closer look at the visions of Eden and of the Fall. For one thing, I have not yet quite grasped what

---

[18] At least one other major Renaissance epic poet, the French Huguenot, Agrippa D'Aubigné, appears to have adapted the sevenfold Apocalyptic pattern and its episodic materials in his work, *Les Tragiques*. According to Richard Regosin, the epic, published in 1616 but written more than a half-century earlier, incorporates a great number of Apocalyptic themes ("D'Aubigné's *Les Tragiques*: A Protestant Apocalypse," *PMLA*, LXXXI [1966], 363–368). Actually the relationship of D'Aubigné's work to Revelation is closer than Regosin seems to recognize, for not only are there cryptic episodic adaptations but D'Aubigné's seven books appear to correspond thematically with the seven parts of Revelation. (Regosin seems unaware of the generally recognized fact that Revelation has seven parts.) D'Aubigné's character and career are suggestive in our context, for he had apparently been inspired in his work by an apocalyptic view of the French Civil Wars in which he had played a significant role as a soldier and a polemicist. Internationally he had a heroic reputation, and both his poems and his temperament have induced French critics to liken him to Milton. On the basis of Milton's reference to his readings in contemporary French literature in *Ad Patrem*, a safe guess would be that he had read D'Aubigné; and if he had read *Les Tragiques*, it is inconceivable that he would not have recognized what the Huguenot was doing artistically with Revelation. In any event the idea of the Apocalypse as a cryptic epic model had occurred to at least one other major Protestant poet in the Renaissance. Equally pertinent may be the use to which Spenser put the Apocalypse after he had learned to handle its structural symbolism by translating Jan van der Noot's *Theatre for Worldlings*. See J. W. Bennet, *The Evolution of the Faerie Queene* (Chicago, 1942), pp. 109–123.

Milton did in some of the more elusive transformations, which may perhaps not be Apocalyptic transformations at all, but something else. (Behind each verse of the Apocalypse there is an intricate skein of scriptural concordances.) For another thing, I want as much as possible to keep the discussion here in the perspective that I feel alone explains *why* the relationship exists, namely Milton's aim to write a poem that would be a unique, coherent adaptation of Scripture to an act of literary worship. Finally, the full discussion of the structure would require a broader survey, in which I could do justice, as I cannot here, to the many who, like Arthur Barker and John Shawcross, have thoughtfully disengaged the possibilities of manifold, interpenetrating structural designs. I do not simply discount these possibilities, but neither can I here attempt to reconcile them with what I see.[19]

What I propose now is to consider the Apocalypse and the poem in parallel terms, relying in the first instance on the relationships that emerge through simple correspondences, then on those that emerge by assuming Milton's use of the principle of crypsis, finally by assuming that certain relationships are due to fuguelike

[19] Barker, "Structural Pattern in *Paradise Lost*," *PQ*, XXVIII (1949), 16–30; Shawcross, "The Son In His Ascendance: A Reading of *Paradise Lost*," *MLQ*, XXVII (1966), 388–401; and "The Balanced Structure of *Paradise Lost*," *SP*, LXII (1965), 696–718. Here it is also relevant to note James Whaler's penetrating study of the prosodic patterns in *Paradise Lost*, in which he suggests that Milton's prosody was based upon an inner play upon the symbolic significance of the number seven and its permutations (*Counterpoint and Symbol* [Copenhagen, 1956]). In addition, since I completed this essay, Maren-Sophie Røstvig's study of Milton, *The Hidden Sense* (Oslo, 1963), has become available to me, and her direction and methods prompt me to notify the reader that I am not engaged in the exercise of numerological interpretation. Primarily my study is concerned with the underlying structure of *Paradise Lost* and Milton's ways of transforming images and thematic materials. The validity of numerological studies seems to me to rest on the credibility of the artistic motivation for their alleged use. One understands why Milton might have used symbolic numerical patterns in his prosody, as Whaler argues, since prosody, like music, consists of numerically disposed patterns; and if one arrangement had for Milton symbolic implications, presumably it also had a prior and more important aesthetic function as a rhythmic pattern of sounds, stresses, and meanings. That Milton practiced other forms of cryptic numerology has not as yet been demonstrated. See the criticism of Miss Røstvig's work by Douglas Bush, in "Calculus Racked Him," and by Ernest Sirluck, in "Recent Studies," both in *Studies in English Literature*, VI (1966), pp. 1–6, 190–191. Miss Røstvig's reply appears in the same publication, Vol. VII (1967), pp. 191–194.

transversions. By correspondence we would find approximately similar elements in approximately the same place. By crypsis we would find antithetical or inverted elements, but still on parallel planes. By transversion we would find the matching of corresponding or inverted elements in patterns conformable to the following arrangement: the first vision of *Paradise Lost* with the seventh of the Apocalypse; the second of the poem with the sixth of St. John; and so on, with the fourth vision providing only internal transversion, the beginning of the one being associated with the end of the other.[20] In using these techniques, it may be that in some instances I shall strain resemblances, or that in others my identifications should be considerably more qualified. But if by applying these methods the basic congruence of the two structural patterns can be established, the more problematic questions of detail can be cleared up later. I am probably wrong in a lot of things here, but not, I think, in finding seven parts in the Apocalypse and seven in *Paradise Lost*. In the light of Milton's in-

[20] Using these three principles simultaneously may seem like hedging all bets. Actually they are reducible to the musical analogue of the fugue itself and of counterpoint which permit the concurrent playing of one melodic line in several patterns. Another way of looking at it is that the three principles reflect the kind of relationship implied by Alpha and Omega (as discussed earlier), where Alpha, as the past, is revealed, but Omega, as the end, is cryptic or only prophetically adumbrated, and hence not to be fully revealed. The concordance between the two, however, involves a sort of free play of clear-obscure relationships in the manner of variations that both elaborate and conceal an original theme. This kind of ingenuity may be Baroque and Byzantine, but it does not equal the fantastic techniques defended by Juan Euebio Nieremberg, a Jesuit writing in 1645:

> Plotinus called the world the Poetry of God. I add that this Poem is like a labyrinth, which is read in every direction, and gives intimations of, and points to its Author. Among the poetical devices of antiquity were [many] celebrated. . . . But above all the Panegyric addressed to the Emperor Constantine is most cunning and incomparable and was celebrated by St. Jerome, Fulgentius and Bede. . . . All this Panegyric consists of seventeen most artfully contrived labyrinths, where one verse joins and is knitted together with another in different manners, and the praises of Caesar are celebrated in all parts, by the beginning, the middles and the ends of the lines, and crosswise, from the first letter of the first line to the last letter of the last line, and then by combining crosswise the remaining letters of the lines between the first and the last, the second letter of the second line, the third of the third, etc., so as to form a thousand other sentiments in praise of Caesar. So do I imagine the world to be a Panegyric of God. *Oculta Filosofia*, chap. xi, cited by Mario Praz, in *Studies in Seventeenth Century Imagery* (London, 1939), p. 16.

terest in Revelation, the relevance it would have to his ambition to create a work which would be an act of worship, and his citations of it as a literary model, every relationship between the parts of these two works ought somehow to be rationally explicable lest we burden probability with the strain of incredible coincidences.

IV

In the first and last chapters of Revelation, the divine voice announces it is Alpha and Omega, the beginning and the end. The first of its main visions is set in the context of immediate historical time, an age of persecution and apostasy, where to the threat of violence are added the temptations of the false worship of the synagogues of Satan. The voice bids the faithful in the seven churches to be comforted, warns the wicked and backsliders, and chides the lukewarm. The visions that follow seem intended to purify the righteous and separate them from the wicked. Their keynote is the necessity for zeal. The last vision presents the absolute separation of the blessed and the damned, with Satan cast onto the lake of fire, into the bottomless pit. Being eschatological, the overall movement of the Apocalypse is from experience in historical reality, to the ending and transcendence of time. Conversely, being essentially hexameral, the overall movement of *Paradise Lost* begins with a vision of Hell (which is the first absolute separation of evil from good) and moves forward to an ultimate historical perspective wherein the Church of Christ is like the seven churches of Asia in Revelation's first vision, neither fully perfected nor fully faithless, having to learn good through evil. In a tremendous prophetic foreshortening there is an evocation of the final New Jerusalem, with the saints forever separated from the damned. We have Alpha and Omega, the beginning and the end.

The first visions have some certain affinities, some dubious ones. It is a fallen angel, not the Son of Man, who in the first vision of *Paradise Lost* affirms the essential Apocalyptic idea that God is Alpha and Omega: "he be sure / In highth or depth, still first and last will Reign" (II, 323–324). And there is a correlative of this identification in Milton's statement of his theme in the invocation, concerning

the Fruit
Of that Forbidden Tree, whose mortal taste
Brought Death into the World, and all our woe,
With loss of *Eden*, till one greater Man
Restore us.

The fruit of the tree is death, but paradoxically it brings a redeemer, called in Revelation 1 : 5, "the first-begotten of Death,"
or as Milton phrased it, he who "should taste death for every
man."[21] In the prophecy after the Fall, in Book X, he is called the
woman's seed, and the last words of the last speech of the poem
are Eve's affirmation of faith: "By me the Promis'd Seed shall all
restore." In the Apocalypse the promise of the fruit of the tree of
life (to nullify the curse of the Fall) is made only twice, in the
first and last visions (Rev. 2 : 7, 22 : 2), that fruit being Christ
who is Alpha and Omega. The mystery of "the doom appli'd /
Though in mysterious terms" (X, 172–173) to the serpent at the
Fall, in the Son's words, the woman's "Seed shall bruise thy
head," is partially fulfilled in the dramatic triumph that serves
as the climax of *Paradise Regained*, where Satan's fall from the
pinnacle of the Temple, beneath the heel of Jesus, is immediately
followed by the angelic banquet prepared for him with "Fruits
fetcht from the tree of life" (IV, 589).

More problematic is the next sequence of relationships. At the
beginning of the Apocalypse, the Son of Man exhorts, comforts,
and warns his seven churches; and at the end he is said to be at
the door that opens toward salvation and through which, in a
broader sense, history passes into eternity. Similarly, in Hell
Satan exhorts and comforts his followers, but as often seems to
take counsel. His journey to the gates of Hell at one end of time
seems to be associated with the Son of Man at the other end, at
Salvation's door, of whom St. John says, near the beginning of
his vision, that it is He, Christ, who holds the "keys of hell and
death." It is also just possible to detect in the pageant of Milton's
fallen gods the dim outlines of the seven churches. The procession begins with "First *Moloch*, horrid King" (I, 392), and
concludes with "*Belial* came last . . ." (I, 490). The intervening
gods seem casually but surely grouped as principals and auxil-
iaries with Chemos, Tammuz, Dagon, and Rimmon leading their

[21] *Christian Doctrine*, I.xiv, Bohn ed., IV, 285–286.

trains. An Egyptian contingent is separately grouped as *"Osiris, Isis, Orus,* and their train."* The affinity is worth pursuing if only because a similar segmentation is more emphatically presented in the symmetrically balanced seventh vision, where the first prophetic vision shown to Adam is that of Abel's murder, slain because his worship was more acceptable, and this happens to match the first of the processional gods, *"Moloch* homicide."* Moreover, Moloch, Milton tells us, had his temple built by Solomon "right against the Temple of God," although more usually he was worshipped in Ammon. Now one of Ammon's cities was later called Philadelphia and may have been identified by Milton with the Philadelphia in Revelation, whose church most purely held to the faith though it was persecuted by the synagogue of Satan and "those who call themselves Jews." We shall never know for sure whether Milton could have been intrigued by such connections, but there is little doubt that the first vision of *Paradise Lost* transversely borrows most of its setting from elements of Revelation's seventh vision which provides Hell itself, Satan's bottomless pit, the lake of fire, as well as the suggestion in the vision of the descending New Jerusalem for Pandemonium raised from the depths of Hell. The actual view of Heaven and its towers seen by Satan at the end of Book II, where also from Heaven's great chain he sees the earth suspended, seems derived from Revelation's seventh vision (20 : 1, 2 and 21 : 21), describing an angel come down from Heaven with a great chain to bind Satan, and where also the image of the heavenly city coming down to earth is described. This relationship, like so many others, would be a unified perspective of two views, one seen by correspondence, and the other imposed upon it as an inverted mirror image.

The second vision of the Apocalypse presents God asking who is worthy to open the seven-sealed book of judgment that must be opened. None dares until the Lamb who was slain for the sins of men takes the book, whereupon a two-part chorus sings the Lamb's worthiness for having redeemed men to God. One by one the first six seals, signifying days of wrath and judgment, are opened by the Lamb, until at the opening of the seventh seal the vision ends and there is silence in heaven. In Milton's second vision God in heaven foresees Man's Fall, pronounces judgment, but offers salvation if some other heavenly being will intercede on Man's behalf and pay "the rigid satisfaction." Whereupon "silence was in Heav'n" (III, 218); none dares, until the Son offers himself, for which the Father praises the Son and the angelic chorus follows with a hymn to both the Father and the Son. Nevertheless the train of damnation has begun as Satan wings his way upward through similitudes and proleptic images.

Here the identification of details is tempting but uncertain. The first four opened seals of the Apocalypse reveal the four horsemen mounted on white, red, black, and pale horses: the first horseman is identifiable by the whiteness of his horse, his crown and bow, as Christ; the one on the black horse and the other two, by their nature and mission, are demonic agents of wrath and destruction. The white horseman is associated by Milton, I take it, with the Son's promise that he will lead Hell captive and the angelic chorus' praise of the regal Son's flaming chariot wheels in the days of his triumph (III, 255, 393–396). The other three horsemen would then come immediately thereafter: in the person of Satan himself (the red dragon), as his black transformation into a vulture, and as his pale disguise in the form of a stripling cherub whom Uriel calls a "Fair Angel" (III, 694).

Milton's transformation of the fifth and sixth seals are less uncertain, the fifth seal in Revelation being John's glimpse of the souls under the altar, whom Milton in the *Christian Doctrine* explicitly identified as "the souls of those who were not yet born,"[22] and who, by reversing Revelation's account of the martyrs for the true faith, become the unborn false witnesses of God, or precisely those whom Milton placed in the Paradise of Fools. In the sixth seal a great convulsion or earthquake disintegrates the world, and antithetically in *Paradise Lost* Uriel describes the contraction or resolution of chaos into order. Between the sixth and seventh seal, an angel descends from heaven to earth to seal and protect the children of God, the 144,000 of the tribes of Israel; and by prolepsis in *Paradise Lost*, the stairway which Satan sees between Heaven and earth becomes Jacob's ladder and then a passage whereby God's angels descend to bless and "to visit oft those happy Tribes" (III, 532). Transversely, Satan, in his ascent to the Sun, finds there the symbolic stones and metals which in the sixth structural vision deck the Scarlet Woman of Babylon; and his first sight of Uriel is described with Milton himself identifying

[22] *Ibid.*, p. 281.

him in what seems to be a signature as "The same whom *John* saw also in the Sun" (III, 623), that is to say, in the transverse Apocalyptic vision.

The third Apocalyptic vision begins with the silence of the seventh seal, after which seven angels sound seven trumpets before the throne of God, each signifying God's will that Creation be afflicted. With each of the first four trumpets, a third of some part of Creation withers: the first destroying greenery; the second turning the sea into flaming blood; the third, by the fall of the star Wormwood, embittering sweet inland waters; the fourth shadowing the sun and darkening the stars. At the fifth, a star again falls into a bottomless pit, releasing smoky locusts of destruction. With the sixth trumpet, four angelic horsemen in "the great river Euphrates" are loosed. Then, between the sixth and seventh seals, a mighty angel with a rainbow over his head appears, prophesying the coming of the seventh angel, who will blow the last trumpet. This mighty but particularly enigmatic angel bids St. John swallow the bittersweet book of visions, which he does before he goes on to measure the Temple of God. There he sees two olive trees and two candlesticks, or witnesses, "standing before the God of the earth," and who will be persecuted, overcome, and slain by the beast who comes out of the bottomless pit. After John sees the witnesses, the seventh trumpet sounds, whereupon a vision of the second coming of Christ ensues, with a chorus of worship, and the Temple of God opening in heaven.

Whereas Revelation's third vision begins with a profound silence, Milton's begins with the loudest cry in *Paradise Lost*, transposing almost verbatim in a dramatic signature the cry of the angel of woes in the corresponding vision, Revelation 8 : 13.

> O for that warning voice, which he who saw
> Th'*Apocalypse*, heard cry in Heav'n aloud,
> Then when the Dragon, put to second rout,
> Came furious down to be reveng'd on men,
> *Woe to the inhabitants on Earth!*

Antithetically, however, at precisely the point where Milton's third vision ends, and Adam asks Raphael to relate the War in Heaven, Milton has Adam confirm the keynote of sacred silence, suggesting the inapprehensibility of what is beyond the language of accommodation. Adam's words to Raphael illustrate as well how Milton rationalized his cryptic materials:

> though what thou tell'st
> Hath past in Heav'n, some doubt within me move,
> But more desire to hear, if thou consent,
> The full relation, which must needs be strange,
> Worthy of Sacred silence to be heard.   (V, 553–557)

A few lines earlier Raphael had come to the point of his mission, which was to warn Adam and Eve of the bliss or woe consequent to obedience or disobedience of God. To this Adam had replied that the sound of angelic revelation or instruction was more delightful to his ear than the sounds of angelic worship.

The warning voice that begins as a loud cry of what is to come not only inverts the corresponding silence at the beginning of Revelation's third vision, it is also based on three other coordinate Apocalyptic passages whose relationship to one another Milton must have found intriguing. At the very end of the transverse fifth Apocalyptic vision, St. John hears a voice cry out, "It is *done*," as the seventh angel pours out the seventh and last vial of wrath and woe upon the world. Now that seventh angel corresponds to his counterpart, the seventh angel in the transverse (balancing) third vision, who stands crying out with a loud voice and to whom another voice bids St. John approach and ask for the bittersweet book of prophecy which he must swallow. This is that same book which Milton referred to in *The Reason of Church-government* to justify the intensity of his zeal: "Yea that mysterious book of Revelation which the great Evangelist was bid to eat, as it had been some eye-brightning electuary of knowledge and foresight, though it were sweet in his mouth and in the learning, it was bitter in the belly, bitter in the denouncing." Milton's identification of himself with that action was now complete, and what his cry in the poem announces is the anticipation of woe at the flight of Satan downward toward the sweet beauty of Eden. The actual Apocalyptic warning voice his words echo is that of the angel of woes who cries out in "a loud voice, Woe, woe, woe, to the inhabiters of earth," at the fall of the great star Wormwood from heaven, a fall which embitters the sweet waters and fountains of the earth (Rev. 8 : 10–13).

Bliss and woe are the tonal motifs of the whole vision in *Paradise Lost*, transposing the bittersweetness of the visionary book St. John swallows. Thus the vision of Paradise begins with a warning, while immediately thereafter Satan takes up the theme, recalling his former bliss and his present woe. The bittersweetness is reenforced on every plane of suggestion: more bitter than sweet in Satan's mingled memories and his delight at the perspectives of Eden; more sweet than bitter as the motif shades the paradisial tranquillity of Adam and Eve. As in Revelation's third vision, *Paradise Lost* has six phases wherein Satan's presence overshadows Eden and in which are transposed the six felicity-destroying trumpets of Revelation. Satan's execration of the sun whose light diminishes the stars recalls the fourth trumpet wherein the sun was smitten and the stars diminished. The shaded fresh greenery of Eden, seen as Satan approaches, recalls the withered greenery of the first trumpet. The sea transformed to blood and the ships destroyed at the second trumpet, apparently suggested the similitude of the gentle winds cheering the ships at sea, "Beyond the *Cape of Hope* . . . / . . . from the spicy shore / Of *Araby* the blest" (IV, 159–163). In the fifth trumpet sequence, the smoky locusts, whose sexually suggestive stinging tails destroy sinners, possibly evoke the Apocryphal similitude Milton introduced, contrasting Satan with the sexual fiend Asmodeus, whom Tobias in the Book of Tobit exorcised with fishy smoke (IV, 168–171). The four horsemen of "the great river Euphrates" at the sixth trumpet were apparently transposed into Satan's four manifestations as he leaps into Eden and wanders within it: first as himself; then by similitudes being seen as a thief, a wolf, and finally a cormorant. Confirmation of this identification would seem to be in the city Satan spies, Telassar, the city of Eden, near "a River large" (IV, 214, 223). As Merritt Hughes notes, on a contemporary map Telassar is put near the Euphrates. This paradisial river, representing the sweet inland waters of Eden, contrasts with the waters embittered in the third trumpet sequence by the falling star Wormwood.

Where I suspect Milton most thoroughly transformed his materials are those places where his poetic powers for some reason worked at their greatest ease and in their most impressively allusive or complex depths. Here technical principles are only a stick to scratch the surface with; to penetrate we must rely on intuition. This is true when we consider what Milton seems to have done with the mighty angel of the interlude *after* the sixth trumpet. St. John sees him "come down from heaven, clothed with a cloud: and a rainbow was upon his head, and his face was as it were the sun, and his feet as pillars of fire" (Rev. 10 : 1). The rainbow is the arc of the covenant, first seen on earth after the Flood, and which in that connection Milton later figured as "A dewy cloud, and in the Cloud a Bow / Conspicuous with three listeu colors gay, / Betok'ning peace from God, and Cov'nant new" (XI, 865–867). Its archetype is what Milton evokes near the beginning of the first full view of Eden, at a point which corresponds to the *beginning* of the six phases that parallel the six trumpet sequences. Higher than the walls of Paradise,

> a circling row
> Of goodliest Trees loaden with fairest Fruit,
> Blossoms and Fruits at once of golden hue
> Appear'd, with gay enamell'd colors mixt:
> On which the Sun more glad impress'd his beams
> Than in fair Evening Cloud, or humid Bow,
> When God hath show'r'd the earth; so lovely seem'd
> That Lantskip.   (IV, 146–153)

This is the mighty angel's nimbus, caught up by Milton's imagination and transformed. The rest of him is found *after* the six trumpet-paralleling phases and before Satan's first glimpse of the two witnesses, at the point where, in Revelation, John swallows the bittersweet book and is told to measure the Temple of God on earth and them that worship therein. Here, in measuring Eden, or the Temple of God on earth, Milton disposes of the angel's other attributes, in every touch transforming the image of holy wrath into paradisial gentleness, withal shadowing every line with anticipated pathos.

The angel, who seems to be the fiercely militant archangel Michael, is introduced in Revelation straddling the sea and earth, roaring like a lion, thundering that the mystery must not be revealed by the visionary, but that with the seventh angel yet to appear God's purpose will be accomplished. What I take to be Milton's corresponding passage more than any other in *Paradise Lost* recalls the powerfully mysterious serenity of the flower section in *Lycidas*, beginning "Return Alpheus, the dread voice is past / That shrunk thy streams," and culminating in the vision of the archangel Michael guarding the sea and shore. There it immediately precedes the apotheosis of Lycidas in the Marriage Supper of the Lamb. The same haunting serenity tonally dominates the passage in *Paradise Lost* which stunningly inverts Revelation's final vision of the last sight of fallen creation before the seventh trumpet makes "the Kingdoms of the World become the Kingdoms of Christ." Instead of mounting wrath and destruction, we move through the freshness of the new Creation to catch the first sight of Adam and Eve, whose fall will make the world the Kingdom of Satan. Unfortunately, the passage, lines 246 through 288, is too long to quote here. Its earthly flowers transpose the rainbow colors of heaven, its gentleness transposes the wrath and terror of the angelic vision, its cool recesses and crystal waters invert the fiery pillars of the angelic feet. The roaring of the angel's voice becomes "The Bird's thir choir apply; airs, vernal airs, / Breathing the smell of field and grove, attune / The trembling leaves . . . (ll. 264–266). The vision is clouded by the evocation of Proserpin, gathered by gloomy Dis. The burning face of the angel is muted to bountiful Amalthea's "Florid Son, / Young Bacchus," until finally, undelighted by the delight of all this Temple of God he too has measured, Satan sees at last the two worshippers, Adam and Eve, "Godlike erect . . . in their looks Divine."

In Revelation John sees the two witnesses "standing before the God of the Earth" in the vision of the earthly Temple of God. When the seventh trumpet restores the world to Christ, a chorus in Heaven sings a Thanksgiving and in the heavenly temple there appears the ark of the testament, or the Law of God. Correspondingly, in *Paradise Lost*, Adam and Eve worship God in the Temple on earth with a great hymn of Thanksgiving, allusively involving all Nature in God's worship as well (V, 153–208). This hymn, beginning "These are thy glorious works, Parent of good, / Almighty, thine this universal frame," also draws upon the Apocalyptic chorus that begins the transverse fifth vision: "Great and marvellous are thy works, Lord God Almighty," and which asks, "Who shall not fear thee, O Lord, and glorify thy name? . . . For all nations shall come and worship before thee." (Rev. 15 : 3, 4) After this hymn again "the temple of the tabernacle of the testimony in heaven" is opened and a purification ensues. In *Paradise Lost* it is after Adam's corresponding prayer is completed that Heaven, so to speak, is opened and God bids Raphael to go instruct Adam in the divine law, to know how he may prosper. Raphael turns this into a doctrine of perfectibility in understanding, a sublimation by ascent to the spirituality of celestial creatures, if Adam and Eve obey the highest law (the heavenly ark of the testament), which is obedience to the will of God.

By transversion, the fifth vision of Revelation, with its sustained destructive wrath, is implicit in the threat of woe for disobedience which runs through the whole of Milton's third vision, but there seem to be particular transformations as well. The Son of Man, who in Revelation promises to come as a thief, may have suggested the image of Satan leaping like a thief over the wall of Eden; while the lying spirits that come out of the mouth of the dragon as frogs, deluding their victims by their miraculous powers, resemble Satan's transformation into a toad whispering sinful dreams to Eve, and his apparition in her dream as an angel who offers her the forbidden apple and soars with her into the air.

Central in both the Apocalypse and *Paradise Lost* is the fourth vision of the War in Heaven. As Pareus observed, it "is exhibited to Iohn, touching the woman in travaile, and the dragon standing to devour her childe and persecuting her, and of the two *Beasts* warring against the Saintes: as also of the Lambe overcoming them, and of the Angels preaching at the last harvest and vintage."[23] The woman is the Church, and the child she begets is the Son of Man who inspires the rebellion of a third of the host of heaven. The first beast rises out of the sea and is "as it were wounded to death; and his deadly wound was healed." The second beast "made fire come down from heaven." Both are aspects of the dragon whose rebellion is alternately described in terms of violence and idolatry. When the Lamb who is to destroy the dragon appears with a multitude of the elect, a voice in heaven is heard "as the voice of many waters." Before the Lamb conquers, there is a new song in Heaven "and no man could learn that song" but the one hundred and forty-four thousand.

The fourth vision of *Paradise Lost* begins with Raphael's account, "High matter thou injoinst me, O prime of men" (V, 563), and quickly moves to God's proclamation of his Son: "This day I have begot whom I declare My only Son." The situation unmistakably parallels the woman in travail, begetting the redeemer and provoking the dragon. Satan "fraught / With envy . . . / . . . resolv'd / With all his legions to dislodge, and leave / Un-

23 *A Commentary*, p. 252.

worshipt, unobey'd the Throne supreme" (V, 661–670). In two stages of the battle, the rebel hosts lose and gain advantage: the first time when Satan is wounded and his wound quickly heals, the second when the rebels bring fire out of Heaven's earth (instead of "down from heaven") in the form of gunpowder and artillery. Before the Son leaves the presence of God to conclude the battle, he reaffirms the underlying essence of the rebellion and victory, which is mixture and separation, the mingling of the impure and pure, promising that, in the final fulfillment of God's will, he will lead

> thy Saints unmixt, and from th'impure
> Far separate, circling thy holy Mount
> Unfeigned *Halleluiahs* to thee sing,
> Hymns of high praise. . . .   (VI, 742–745)

This eschatological hymn presumably will be the new song none can learn except those who accompany the Lamb at the end. Finally, when the Son goes forth, "his fierce Chariot roll'd, as with the sound / Of torrent Floods, or of a numerous Host" (the multitude and the voice of many waters), and he drives the rebellious angels "Into the wasteful Deep" (VI, 829–830, 862). The same vision that in Revelation is preceded by lightning, voices, thunders, and great hail nears its end in *Paradise Lost* with the Son routing his enemies to the accompaniment of earthquakes, lightnings, thunders, voices—"terrors and . . . furies"—and great hail—"on either side tempestuous fell / His arrows" (VI, 859, 844–845).

In the fifth vision, the alignment of *Paradise Lost* inverts the seven vials of wrath poured out to destroy the world as Milton transformed them into the seven days of Creation with their oddly balanced choruses. As I have earlier indicated, he incorporated into the Sabbath hymn at the end of Book VII the elements of the Song of Moses, which in Revelation begins this vision. Apparently he also returned to the transverse third vision of the Apocalypse where the destruction and the creation of the world were associated in the great and mysterious oath of the mighty angel who swore "by him that liveth for ever and ever, who created heaven, and the things that therein are, and the earth, and the things that therein are, and the sea, and the things which are therein, that there should be time no longer" (Rev. 10 : 6). For the second half of Milton's vision of Creation, Book VIII, the suggestions derive mainly from the same transverse vision. Here the themes of creation and procreation, both physical and evangelical, are mingled as Adam relates his awakening and Eve's creation from his own substance. We are reminded that the two witnesses were seen by John as candlesticks, an image which combines the suggestion of worship and enlightenment that make up evangelical edification. Adam is created instinct with the desire to worship and is a living temple of God. His reason, in a contemporary phrase, is the candle of the Lord within him, but needs to be sustained by Raphael's instruction and admonition. Eve's instinct is also to worship, but her light is Adam's to sustain.

Quite appropriately the sixth vision in *Paradise Lost* betrays a most vital relationship to its counterpart in the Apocalypse, since climactically, as the vision of the Fall, it bears a special congruence with what is its exact antithesis, the image of redemption in the triumphal marriage of the Lamb to his bride. Despite the antithesis, the configurations are essentially similar. In pattern and reduplication both visions present a fall, a feast of rejoicing, and a feast of death. The Apocalyptic vision's three parts are more clearly articulated as the fall of the Whore of Babylon, the Marriage Supper of the Lamb, and its closely related images of Christ going forth to judge the wicked whose carrion will be fed to the fowls of prey. The sixth vision of *Paradise Lost* inverts the fall of wickedness into the Fall of innocence, the feast of life into the feast of death, and less obviously anticipates once more, through the concluding notes of human contrition and the angelic *felix culpa* hymn, the redemptive feast of life. Among other related elements we find that the personified Word of God who goes forth to judge mankind in wrath at the end of Revelation's sixth vision, appears in *Paradise Lost* as the Son who "from wrath more cool / Came the mild Judge and Intercessor both / To sentence Man." To Adam and Eve he is "the voice of God . . . / Now walking in the Garden, by soft winds / Brought to thir ears" (X, 95–99). In another structural resemblance we note that in the midst of Revelation's feast of life John hears "the voice of a great multitude and as the voice of many waters" sing a Halleluiah chorus. At the same point in the reversed design of the sixth vision in *Paradise Lost*, in the midst of the feast of death God pronounces judgment, at which "the heav'nly Audience loud / Sang *Halleluiah*, as the sound of Seas, /

Through Multitude that Sung: Just are thy ways . . ." (X, 641–643). Finally, in bracketing the vision at the end, St. John sees the angel in the sun who bids the fowls to the feast of death. This is the same angel Uriel whom, as "Regent of the Sun," Milton evokes near the beginning of his vision to account for Satan's approach by night.

Coming to the elements of the three main groups, the most obvious identification is the fall of Babylon, "the woman drunken with the blood of saints" and decked out in gold ornaments. Babylon is both a woman and a city, "the hold of every foul spirit." It is notable, therefore, that when Satan finds Eve alone, her beauty and freshness in Eden spontaneously become the foil for an image of a filthy, noisome city.

> Much hee the Place admir'd, the Person more.
> As one who long in populous City pent,
> Where Houses thick and Sewers annoy the Air,
> Forth issuing on a Summer's Morn to breathe
> Among the pleasant Villages and Farms
> Adjoin'd. . . .   (IX, 444–449)

The image of the city transforms Eve into a country maid at whose sight and expected loss of innocence Satan *delights*, though regretting he cannot have her in fornication. Then as a "ship by skilful Steersman wrought" he tacks about to catch her eye, seduces her by flattery and fraud, and returns to Hell triumphant, having enlarged his empire. In Revelation, *after* the city falls, the kings, merchants of vanity, and shipmasters of the earth stand off at sea and *mourn* for her with whom they have committed fornication. Eve first, and then Adam, in eating the apple become drunk as with wine, fornicate in earnest, but arise "destitute and bare / Of all thir virtue; silent, and in face / Confounded . . ." (IX, 1062–1064). Or, as Adam says, "naked thus, of Honor void, / Of Innocence, of Faith, of Purity, / Our wonted Ornaments now soil'd and stain'd . . ." (IX, 1074–1076). The bride in Revelation is "clean and white: for the fine linen is the righteousness of saints." Upon this passage Pareus comments: "It is the solemne and most joyful copulation of the bride and bridegroom." The bride, or the Church, though "destitute, naked and uncovered" of herself, is clothed in virtue by her bridegroom.[24]

---

[24] *Ibid.,* pp. 480, 482.

The Fall, then, is in a sense a marriage supper, but a grim one, a feast of universal death. "At that tasted Fruit / The Sun, as from *Thyestean* Banquet turn'd / His course intended" (X, 687–689). With this image an oblique light is cast backward at the vision's invocation, where Milton renounced the courtly heroic poem symbolized in part by the "marshall'd Feast / Serv'd up in Hall with Sewers, and Seneschals," a feast reminiscent of the complex Eucharistic parody, replete with courtly trappings, that Satan offers Jesus in the banquet scene in *Paradise Regained*. In the same imagistic pattern, the bitter ashen apples of Hell are part of the feast of death, as are also the sustained images of Sin and Death seen from above and below as they are loosed to feed on life.

I take it that the key to the whole complex pattern of these images is derived from the vision in Revelation of the angel of the sun, Uriel, bidding the ravening fowls to "the great supper of God," the battlefield carrion of sinners. But it is not Uriel, the watchful protector of Eden, who bids the feast begin in *Paradise Lost*; rather it is his successful adversary Satan who sends Sin and Death to feed on life. Revelation's image is transformed by Milton into a marvelous proleptic similitude of Death, who from the gates of Hell

> snuff'd the smell
> Of mortal change on Earth. As when a flock
> Of ravenous Fowl, though many a League remote,
> Against the day of Battle, to a Field,
> Where Armies lie encampt, come Flying, lur'd
> With scent of living Carcasses design'd
> For death. . . .   (X, 272–278)

Not content with leaving this major transformational pattern altogether unrecognized, Milton introduced a revelatory signature pointing toward the transverse second Apocalyptic vision with an explicit imagistic reversal, as

> in Paradise the hellish pair
> Too soon arriv'd, *Sin* there in power before,
> Once actual, now in body, and to dwell
> Habitual habitant; behind her *Death*,
> Close following pace for pace, not mounted yet
> On his pale Horse: . . .(X, 585–590)

As Merritt Hughes notes, the source is Revelation 6 : 8; but there Death rides his pale horse "and Hell *followed* with him."

Substituting Sin for Hell and dismounting Death, Milton inverts the order of their appearance, all entirely according to the principle by which eschatological images are reversed when they are put into the setting of the beginning of history.

The balancing and the inversion of materials has ultimately, therefore, a kind of cosmic justification as the expression of the typological rhythms and the overall symmetry of God's Providence. Moreover, just as Revelation's visions tend to balance one another, as if they reflected a balance in the downward and upward curves of historical experience, so too we find Milton's visions balancing one another across the middle fourth. The best example is in the relationships of the sixth and second visions. The whole of the second vision (Book III) soars elementally upward from the very outset, its motifs being fire and air, with Milton himself rising in the invocation to Holy Light, while parallel movements develop in the flight of Satan from the depths to the Sun and in the vision of the heavens. The doom of Man foretold in heaven is an eddy in the motion, not a descent; for the Son's offer leads to an even higher pitch, culminating in the angelic hymn. In contrast, the sixth vision is heavy, its momentum downward. The invocation is apologetical, almost gloomy, a sort of *de profundis*, with the poet hesitating, the meter stammering, fearful, lest "an age too late, or cold / Climate, or Years damp my intended wing / Deprest . . ." (IX, 44–46). The "answerable style" invoked here is specifically one appropriate to the tragic notes and the elemental heaviness of water and earth, contrasting with the serene confidence of the invocation to the second vision, where the poet's mind on "bolder wing, / Escap't the *Stygian* Pool . . . / . . . up to reascend" (III, 13–20). Throughout the first half of this sixth vision the downward movement is intensified by recurrent evocations of cold damp Satanic mists, unctuous vapors, and exhalations: while in the second half the momentum is involved with cold, dry images of ashes, earth, and dust. The two patterns come together at the end of the sixth vision and the immediate beginning of the seventh, when Adam and Eve, prostrate upon the ground, water the ground with tears, whereupon, etherialized again, their prayers rise as incense to the altar of God.

The second and sixth visions of the Apocalypse similarly balance antithetically and elementally. At the beginning of the second vision a voice says to St. John, "Come *up* hither . . . And immediately," he writes, "I was in the Spirit: and behold a throne set in heaven," which establishes the ethereal, spiritual tonality of the vision, inasmuch as spiritual fire is the highest of the elements, or the quintessence, the fifth essence. The sixth vision begins with another voice saying: "Come hither . . . I will show thee the judgment of the great whore that sitteth upon many waters," and she was called "Mother of Harlots and Abominations of the Earth." Nevertheless, even as earth and water, Babylon burns, and the vision is dominated by imagery of smoke, dust, the gross and fiery desolation of luxury being consumed.

The seventh vision compresses a great deal of material Milton might have originally considered for his earlier epic plans apparently directed toward some representation of God's providential dealings with his Church. This is what most of the last vision is about, with the Church basically conceived in its simplest terms; first as the place where God is worshipped, and then in terms of its Old Testament types. The first and seventh visions of the Apocalypse seem to have provided Milton with the elements of his scheme: the first with its seven earthly, imperfect churches, inextricably mingled with the dross of the world; and the last with its vision of the perfect New Jerusalem descending, which has "no temple therein: for the Lord God Almighty and the Lamb are the temple of it" (Rev. 21 : 22). The last vision of Milton's poem is on this basis a kind of homiletic consolation. Adam's grief on learning that they must leave Eden is partly an uninstructed confusion of Eden with God's Temple, where he "could frequent / With worship, place by place" (XI, 317–318), and build altars on the spots God had made himself manifest. Michael first explains that God is everywhere, then through the visions and prophecies shows him the Old Testament types of the Church and their New Testament successor. But notwithstanding the extension of God's Grace, external worship is invariably perverted, and finally Adam learns that the true Church has no temple except for the Paradise within. The concluding historical act at the Second Coming is simply the translation into actuality of the visionary correspondence between the Paradise within and the ultimate beatitude, the Marriage Supper of the Lamb.

In the Apocalypse the last vision begins with an angel descending from Heaven to bind Satan for a specific historical period, during which time the saints in their first resurrection will live and reign with Christ. Satan being loosed, another period of battle ensues, lasting until the final conflagration. Then John beholds the New Jerusalem, "a new heaven and a new earth," where the dwelling place "of God is with men" (Rev. 21 : 3), and where all impurity is banished. From a high mountain to which he is taken, John sees seven visions and hears seven prophecies concerning the New Jerusalem with its river and tree of life to heal and sustain the faithful. After blessings, warnings, and promises concerning the sanctified inviolability of all the visions, the book ends. The seventh vision of *Paradise Lost* begins with the prayers of Adam and Eve being found acceptable through the intercession of the Son, and renewed life is promised Man. But the judgment of God must go forth, as it does with a trumpet blast, which as it begins the first postlapsarian period I take to be identified with the first trumpet blast blown in Revelation's third vision, the one that brought in hail and fire, the seasonal extremes, and withered the greenery of a third of creation.[25] God's decision is that Adam and Eve are to be driven from Eden lest they taste of the tree of life, something they are not to do until, as in the last vision of Revelation, the New Jerusalem descends. Nevertheless, as Revelation promises in its last vision, the tears of the now righteous Adam and Eve are to receive divine consolation.[26]

The rest of the vision concerns the knowledge of God's true

[25] This identification and a small number of others that seem possible and are not presented here, are anomalies. I have experimented with complicating the structural scheme to accommodate them in systems of inner and transverse symmetries, using as a further base in two symmetrical arrangements the three first visions and the last three visions. Possibly these may work. For the time being, I prefer, however, to think that there is in fact a great deal that is anomalous and irregular in the poem since I cannot imagine Milton slavishly binding himself to any pattern. On occasions in the early prose he recorded his preference for the freedom of what he called "Asiatic exuberance." He once wrote to his tutor that at times even verse constrained him with its "cramped style straitened by fixed feet and syllables" (*CPW*, I, 311). And in his first poetic manifesto, *At A Vacation Exercise,* he referred easily to the tension between the spontaneous associative play in his mind and the forms to which he submitted that play without apparently enslaving it. Moreover, his prosody seems visibly the proof of his instinctive tact in introducing irregularities and anomalies that bring him often to the edge of free verse. It seems preferable therefore to assume that Milton could and did adapt elements of Revelation outside the strict limits of the design I have been suggesting.

[26] *Paradise Lost,* XI, 108–113; XII, 645; Rev. 21:4.

worship manifest through the vicissitudes of the historical Church. Whereas Adam originally aspired to understand God's purpose in setting the ways of the stars and heavens, Michael now teaches him the only knowledge necessary for salvation, the pattern of God's just ways with men on earth. Like John, Adam is shown by an angel on a mountain, the Temple of God, that is to say the Church on earth. The visions and prophecies, what he sees and hears, are each seven in number; and the visions, at any rate, appear to be thematically related to the opening Apocalyptic admonitions to the seven churches of Asia. Adam's first vision, the murder of Abel, suggests the lack of brotherly love among the Ephesians. The sight of the Lazar-house filled with sickness and disease recalls the tribulations and poverty of the church of Smyrna. When Adam sees the seduction of the Sons of God by fair atheists, we are reminded of the sin of the Thyatirians who had allowed "that woman Jezebel" to seduce the faithful to idolatry and fornication. The panorama of armies, conquerors, and wars derives, I think, from the single image of the sword threatening the iniquities of the church of Pergamos. Adam's cheering vision of faithful Noah preserved from the general destruction of the flood would be related to the praise of the few in Sardis who were not defiled and who would be preserved. Then the postdeluvian period seems related to the lukewarm Laodiceans who will yet again be spewed out of God's mouth. Finally the vision of the rainbow of the covenant, "this last sight" (XI, 872), betokening the concord of Man and God, would be appropriately related to the church which had never denied God, that of Philadelphia, a city whose name means brotherly love or true communion.

Milton's whole sequence in Book XI seems to parallel the sequence in the procession of fallen angels in Book I, but mainly by way of their mutual relationship to Revelation's sequence of admonitions to the seven churches. The first three elements of Book XI, for example, evoking homicide, bodily sickness and wantonness, have affinities with Moloch, obscene Chemos, and erotic Thammuz. The sword of Pergamos and the vision of wars are both fourth, as is in the whole poem's seven part structure, the War in Heaven, and, in the next sequence in Book XII, the militant ministry of Jesus, of which the epitome is concentrated in the main action of *Paradise Regained*. It almost seems as if the fourth phase, reflecting the central aspect of history, is the archetype of redemptive struggle and choice, for if we look back to the transverse first vision, the fourth of Milton's fallen gods is Dagon, whose contest with God Samson takes on in *Samson Agonistes*. What Milton notes of Dagon in the procession is a militant detail, namely, that when Jehova's ark was captive among the Philistines it nevertheless smashed Dagon "Where he fell flat, and shamed his Worshippers" (I, 461).[27] The last three sequences in Book XI are far less distinct, seeming to be deliberately intermingled, but in evoking purification by water, brutishness, and general dissoluteness, they suggest a remote parallel to Rimmon, the Egyptian gods, and Belial. And just as Philadelphia was the true communion, the men of Belial (as the phrase is used in Hebrew) signify all those who are joined together in a communion of lewdness and little understanding.

The visionary sequence ends with Book XI, and Book XII takes up the history of the Church in prophetic terms, as something heard, not seen. After the first prophecy, which goes from the Tower of Babel to the calling of Abraham, the Church is more recognizable in the familiar terms of the communion of the chosen seed and later of the Christian elect. From Abraham to Moses and Joshua a second prophetic phase is manifest; and the period from Joshua to Jesus, who are type and antitype, is

[27] Cf. William Madsen, "Earth the Shadow of Heaven," p. 525, and J. H. Adamson, "The War in Heaven: Milton's Version of the *Merkabah*," *JEGP*, LVII (1958), 690–703, both of whom regard the War in Heaven as typologically central in the scheme of Providence. Raphael's account of the war, says Madsen, is not an allegory, "nor primarily a metaphorical description of what happened a long time ago in heaven. It is a shadow of things to come, and more particularly it is a shadow of this last age of the world and of the Second Coming of Christ." Adamson, who takes the war back to the source which Revelation itself transformed, Ezekiel, interprets the war in the light of the belief that the Son's victory foreshadows the New Creation of the Last Day. Being central in *Paradise Lost*, the war therefore points backward and forward to the Alpha and Omega of the poem itself. On the essentially "completed" eschatological nature of the whole typological scheme of Providence which rendered it almost inevitable that the historical ministry of Christ should become a central episode linking backward and foreward to the War in Heaven and Armageddon, see Erich Auerbach, "Figura," in *Scenes From The Drama of European Literature*, trans. Ralph Manheim (New York, 1959), pp. 11–76; and Amos N. Wilder, "Myth and Symbol in the New Testament," in *Symbols and Values*, 13th Symposium of the Conference on Science, Philosophy and Religion, ed. L. Bryson *et al.*, (New York, 1954), p .128.

the third. The life and ministry of Jesus is a whole phase unto itself (again the central fourth), and it is followed in turn by the career of the Visible Church after the time of Christ, and a parallel prophecy of the Invisible Church guided by the Holy Spirit. Finally the Church of the Last Days and the Last Judgment are described, out of which will come the new heavens and the new earth transcending history. The sequences are compressed history, and as such lack the dramatic interest of the earlier actions; but the stimulation of that dramatic interest, however aesthetically preferable, was only collaterally Milton's concern. Rather, the whole poem ought to be seen as a movement into and away from the time when Man must learn good through evil. In the beginning it was not so. Nor would it be so in the end. The panoramic history of the Church is not quite a guided tour for entertainment. It is, instead, the apocalyptic vision of the inseparably mixed condition in which God's worship takes place, until at last the Paradise within and without must become one.

V

A summary blueprint is of lesser interest than the actual experience of looking at the impressive exterior of a magnificent building and wandering within its halls and rooms. Yet if the exact function for which the building was really designed is to come under scrutiny, even a simplified blueprint may be of some use. It seems to me that the reconstruction of the system by which Milton transformed the Apocalypse begins to offer something like such a blueprint for *Paradise Lost*, one that corroborates what we may have from time to time suspected, that the building, now serving as a kind of literary museum, was originally conceived as a church, designed, that is, for a unique act of public or liturgical worship. Moreover, the blueprint confirms the existence of that highly intricate systematic inner structure whose presence has been always felt, I believe, but hitherto in its true form has been concealed from our sight. This is, I realize, to advance a very large and possibly extraordinary claim, but I do not know how else we may account for the striking correspondence between the Apocalypse and Milton's poem.

It is possible that as my hypothesis evolved out of the initial shocks of recognition I may have sought out and strained the resemblances I have presented, forcing, to some extent, the evidence. Whether this is so is a matter others must determine by close study of the materials, and particularly by considering the validity of my assumption that what Milton meant by crypsis is what he did in the poem. It would also be necessary to test the soundness of my assumption that an analogy such as the technique of the fugue gave Milton the hint as to how he might transpose eschatological materials into a poem dealing with the beginning of the world. But then why not, when we remember Milton's delight in "The hidden soul of harmony?"[28] I think Milton used these techniques. Nonetheless, I do not myself believe that every resemblance or affinity I have suggested has equal weight and plausibility, and I have tried to distinguish in a general way the relative degree of certainty I could feel about the correspondences, inversions, and transversions. Since I do not propose to stop here, the materials will be checked again. Where it may prove necessary I shall make the limitations of the evidence more exact, and where it is possible I hope to be able to enlarge the extent of the evidence.

Obviously a critical factor in determining the plausibility of this whole argument is the question as to how important Milton considered models and precedents to be and whether the function of a model was simply to serve as a sanctioned point of departure for a poet's work, a means enabling him to satisfy traditional expectations and organize his experience and view of things in terms of normative forms. I would guess Milton had a far more complex attitude toward literary genres and the way to use them than that. I think he tended to use specifically meaningful structural patterns imposed into genres, and that the patterns generally had for him a high degree of symbolic or religious significance, not always calculated to appear overtly. This, for example, is true in *Paradise Regained* with its inner development structured on the identification of Jesus as Prophet, Priest, and King, and in a different way it has been recently shown to be true of *Lycidas*.[29] In *Paradise Lost* a working structural pattern would

[28] *L'Allegro*, 1. 144.
[29] See *Milton and the Kingdoms of God*, chap. vi; Barbara K. Lewalski, *Milton's Brief Epic* (Providence, 1966), chaps. v and xiii; and J. A. Wittreich, Jr., "Milton's 'Destin'd Urn': The Art of *Lycidas*," *PMLA*,

have been an even more imperious necessity, and because I think Milton was that kind of a poet, the pattern would have had to have, at least in his own cognizance, a symbolic significance. There is no doubt about the symbolic significance of the Apocalyptic design, and when we find its elements suggesting the disposition or ordering of all the main events and episodes in *Paradise Lost*, to say nothing of the larger metaphoric patterns, we should consider the real possibility that we have the actual inner design, indeed the model for the poem.

If the Apocalypse as the model should stand confirmed, we would be confronted with something in Milton's poem that is different from what we have generally assumed to be its familiar shape and which would bring into question the meaning or authenticity of Milton's epic intention. For example, the poem appears to begin *in medias res*, transposing a natural narrative sequence in epic fashion; but in the grand apocalyptic design, the poem may be said to begin where psychologically it really began for Milton, with a vision of the congruence between reality and Hell. Reality is perpetually the history of the seven churches of Asia: neither hot nor cold; some pure, some wicked; some offering brotherly love, others perverting communion and fellowship. Whether as an archetype in Revelation or as the image of historical reality, the vision of the seven churches is the counterpart of Milton's vision of Hell; for in terms of apocalyptic psychology, Hell is the present which generates the insatiable dream of its visionary antithesis, Heaven. The movement from Hell to Heaven in *Paradise Lost* is not epic but apocalyptic, and made concrete as the movement from idolatrous reality to the visionary perspective of perfected worship. Finally, what follows Hell and Heaven (which ultimately are polarized states of mind) in *Paradise Lost* is the intervening experience of understanding how reality first became marred and confused, and how out of that confusion once more good and evil will be separated, with the good preserved and the evil finally destroyed.

The questions that naturally follow from these propositions are two: why would Milton choose to leave his design obscure; and what are we to make of the apparent epic structure of *Para-*

LXXXIV (1969), 60–70. Wittreich demonstrates that the rhyme scheme of *Lycidas* and its stanzaic organization is based on an intricate pattern inscribing the Neoplatonic circle of perfection and the Apocalyptic pattern of Alpha and Omega.

dise Lost? Finding valid answers to these questions would, I think, ultimately take us into the matters of Milton's working convictions about how the processes of poetry are generated, how they effect others, and precisely who those others are or should be. More immediately it is worth considering a practical aspect of the problem Milton faced. A very long poem by a blind man, meditated over many years and presumably worked at with frequent and protracted interruptions, would have required a well-wrought schematic design shaped on an outline at once simple and yet capable of extensive complication in detail. The work would not "be obtain'd by the invocation of Dame Memory," but she would certainly have had a careful hand in its execution. Such a scheme would in part be a mnemonic structure, a memory theatre; and if that memory theatre had an intrinsic symbolic signficance, all the better.[30] But from a functional point of view the scheme is a working apparatus whose external traces need not be evident in the finished product.

As to the relationship of that structure or design to Milton's epic intention and the poem's epic structure, again a preliminary consideration is that the two obviously dovetail and interpenetrate to such a remarkable extent (as in the image of the golden chain at the end of Vision I, derived simultaneously from Homer and the Apocalypse), that the manner of the blending would seem to be one of the most crucial secrets of Milton's imaginative techniques. In such dovetailing and blending the scriptural form would have a peculiar virtue, as deriving from the quickening power of the Word of God, and so would dominate, as idea to substance, the epic structure. Beneath the epic vestments there is a sacramental postulant.

I am suggesting that the poem is somehow other than it seems,

[30] *Reason of Church-government, CPW,* I. See Frances Yates, *The Art of Memory* (London, 1966) for a most suggestive study of Renaissance mnemonic systems based on imaginary memory theatres. Some systems were structurally sevenfold, but all were organized on the principle that, to remember encyclopedic quantities of learning, symbolic associations were to be imagined for particular things in relationship to parts of a coherent meaningful structure. Seven was a commonplace basis because of the seven heavens, the seven ages of the world, and so forth. Comenius, for example, found a "septenary gradation" in the whole Scale of Nature because he, like Augustine, like Macrobius, like Philo, and countless others, saw a cosmic significance in the number seven. On Comenius' septenary scale embracing all things, see C. A. Patrides, *Milton and the Christian Tradition,* pp. 62–63.

for in the recognition of its depth, its appearance is altered and we begin to see unities hitherto unimagined and half-concealed, and hear throughout new harmonies and new resonances, with nuances of meaning yet undefined. Milton himself best described the effect I have in mind in a passage that perhaps is the finest in *Paradise Lost* and which, appropriately enough, suggests the harmonic subtlety and beauty of a concert of worship involving others whether or not they are aware of having been drawn into the fullness of the design. The figure is that of the heavenly dance celebrating the day on which the Son was proclaimed as the only begotten of God, and in which the already-falling angels move, involved, reconciled, and resolved in a pattern not fully understood, nor quite inapprehensible.

> That day, as other solemn days, they spent
> In song and dance about the sacred Hill,
> Mystical dance, which yonder starry Sphere
> Of Planets and of fixt in all her Wheels
> Resembles nearest, mazes intricate,
> Eccentric, intervolv'd, yet regular
> Then most, when most irregular they seem:
> And in thir motions harmony Divine
> So smooths her charming tones, that God's own ear
> Listens delighted.   (V, 618–627)

Index

▼

Adam: in the Garden, 91–117 *passim*; as hero, 18, 19; language of, 29–30; sin of, 118–130 *passim*; temptation of, 10; visions of, 159–160, 172

Angels, 103, 112, 115

Apocalypse (of St. John), structural relation to *PL*, 131–178 *passim*

Aquinas, St. Thomas, 98n., 128

Areopagitica, 94, 96

Argument (of *PL*), 9, 19, 20, 26

Astronomy, 101, 108, 109

Augustine, St.: on knowledge and wisdom, 3, 9, 13; on sin, 98n., 119, 121, 127, 128; on vision of the divine, 61, 63, 64, 65; mentioned, 106, 134

Bacon, Francis, 80n.

Bede, Ven., 78

Beelzebub, 41–42

Burke, Kenneth, 39–40

Calvin, John, 79, 106

Christian Doctrine (Milton), 66, 107, 122, 124–125

Comus, 83

Correspondence (structural principle), 154

Criticism of *PL*, v–x, xi–xii

Crypsis (structural principle), 147, 154

D'Aubigné, Agrippa, 152n.

Decorum, 15–17, 18, 27, 35

Dialogue in Heaven, 28–29, 157–158

Dryden, John, 20–21

Enlightenment, 36, 40

Epic tradition, 18, 19, 23, 26–27, 32

Eve: in the Garden, 91–117 *passim*; sin of, 118–130 *passim*; temptation of, 10; mentioned, 18, 52–53, 68–69

Fall, the, 166–168. *See also* Sin

Farrer, Austin, 137

Form, discovery as, 1–14. *See also* Structure and structural principles

Foster, William T., 127

Garden (of Eden), portrayal of, 88–94

179